W9-BZY-090

Praise for *Resilience*

"*Resilience* is a truly comprehensive guidebook that shows you that you have everything inside you to skillfully meet all of life's challenges, great or small, with a wise, kind heart. In her clear, well-researched style, filled with user-friendly exercises and practices, Linda Graham reveals how we can train our brains, our bodies, and our hearts to access our intuitive wisdom not only to get through the tough times but to grow and become more conscious in the process. A real gem!"

— **James Baraz,** coauthor of *Awakening Joy: 10 Steps to Happiness* and cofounding teacher of Spirit Rock Meditation Center

"This is a wonderfully comprehensive, hugely informative, engagingly written book. Linda Graham's voice — personal, knowledgeable, confident, and inspiring — kept me reading as if it were a novel."

— **Sylvia Boorstein,** author of *Happiness Is an Inside Job*

"What I especially love about this book is the kindly and 'You can do this!' way Linda Graham speaks to us readers. She shows us that rich resources of resilience are inside us and that we can easily learn to tap them using her exercises. Beautifully combining mindfulness and neuroscience, Linda has crafted what we always wanted: a guide for sane, serene living."

— **David Richo, PhD,** author of *How to Be an Adult in Relationships*

"Linda Graham's pioneering expertise on cultivating resilience has transformed countless lives. Now, in *Resilience*, she has compiled a clearly sequenced set of best practices that can guide us in finding freedom in the midst of life's greatest challenges. Highly recommended!"

— **Tara Brach,** author of *Radical Acceptance* and *True Refuge*

"If you want the practical know-how to strengthen your ability to uncover resilience in any situation, I recommend diving into *Resilience*! Take your time with this, soak in Linda Graham's practical strategies and wisdom, and make it a part of your life!"

— **Elisha Goldstein,** creator of *A Course in Mindful Living*

"Though we cannot control what happens to us, we can learn to respond in a healthier, more adaptive way. Perhaps more than any other book I've encountered, *Resilience* offers us the necessary tools to respond effectively to life's challenges and strengthen the vital skill of resilience. With a treasure trove of practical exercises, this gem of a book provides us with a step-by-step guide to bouncing back from life's struggles and creating lasting change. Writing with both expertise and immense compassion, Linda Graham has given the field and her readers an immense gift with this book."

— **Jonah Paquette, PsyD,** author of *Real Happiness* and *The Happiness Toolbox*

"In this powerful book, Linda Graham shares remarkable insights, practical tools, and essential skills to learn how to navigate life's challenges. She draws on a wealth of research, personal wisdom, and heartfelt compassion from her work as a psychotherapist to show how we can all develop this much-needed quality of resilience. I can think of no better guide for this important work."

— **Mark Coleman,** meditation teacher and author of
Make Peace with Your Mind and *Awake in the Wild*

"Even though we want life to be comfortable and pleasurable — and even though we often expect it to be so — life is often difficult, disappointing, and painful. (Darn it!) When things don't go our way, we need specific skills and strategies to regain our balance and to keep ourselves from spiraling downward. This book is an essential reference and guide to developing those skills in ourselves and also in our kids (for parents) and clients (for coaches and therapists)."

— **Christine Carter, PhD,** author of *Raising Happiness* and *The Sweet Spot*

"What can we do when overwhelmed by life's challenges? This clear, comprehensive guide offers practical answers. It's chock-full of proven practices from spiritual, psychotherapeutic, and scientific traditions that anyone can use to respond effectively to the challenges of modern life. Linda Graham's years of experience and deep understanding as a psychotherapist and teacher shine through as she offers effective, easy-to-use tools to not only survive but flourish during difficult times."

— **Ronald D. Siegel, PsyD,** assistant professor of psychology at
Harvard Medical School and author of *The Mindfulness Solution*

"This book draws from a wide variety of empirically proven programs to offer a smorgasbord of ways to cope with life's difficulties. With over ten dozen practices and exercises, this book has what you need when things get tough, all in one convenient place. Look no further for the help you need to cope."

— **Kristin Neff, PhD,** author of *Self-Compassion*,
coauthor of *The Mindful Self-Compassion Workbook*,
and associate professor of educational psychology at the University of Texas at Austin

"Resilience is a powerful concept because it refers to our underlying capacity to meet challenging times with grace and skill. It's pure denial to say, 'Don't worry, nothing bad will ever happen.' We need skills for coming back from hard times, and that's what this book is all about. So many of us today struggle to find emotional balance and to heal the web of our human connections in the face of increasing anxiety and disorder. This book, with its astonishingly wide range of resources, could not have come at a better time. Linda Graham is the ideal guide to cultivating resilience, a calm, wise voice speaking from the interface of science and compassion. This book has so many valuable tools!"

— **Ann Weiser Cornell, PhD,** CEO of Focusing Resources and author of *The Power of Focusing*

"In this generous book, Linda Graham offers a cornucopia of practices — 133 in all — to help people bounce back from hardship and cultivate emotional strength. She clearly understands the difference between a wobble and a wallop and has organized the practices to sensitively address diverse needs. Highly recommended for anyone going through a tough time and for those who care about them."

— **Christopher Germer, PhD,** author of *The Mindful Path to Self-Compassion*, codeveloper of Mindful Self-Compassion training, and lecturer at Harvard Medical School

"I offer a deep bow of gratitude to Linda Graham for her book *Resilience*, which provides us with an array of simple yet powerful experiential tools for growing and strengthening inner resilience — our innate ability to skillfully recognize, respond to, and bounce back from whatever life throws at us. Our ability to experience joy, love, and well-being depends on our possessing a robust foundation of resilient responses to the stressors we encounter throughout life. Linda offers us such a guidebook for life, one we should all have in our hands, one I now look forward to passing on to all my friends, students, and clients."

— **Richard Miller, PhD,** author of *The iRest Program for Healing PTSD*

"What a treasure trove of useful and powerful practices to help us thrive! Linda Graham's wise and practical approach to strengthening resilience guides us to recovery and renewed joy. Well organized and simple to learn, *Resilience* offers a remarkably powerful selection of tools for creating and enhancing our ability to navigate life stresses — from minor inconveniences to major tragedies."

— **Ashley Davis Bush, LICSW,** author of *Simple Self-Care for Therapists* and *The Little Book of Inner Peace*

"Linda Graham's warmth and compassion shine through in this wonderful and informative guide to strengthening resilience. She seamlessly weaves neuroscience into creative, easy-to-follow exercises designed to enhance emotional intelligence, neuroplasticity, social engagement, gratitude, and compassionate self-awareness. Clinicians and clients alike will greatly benefit from tools that include guided imagery, somatic resourcing, mindful meditations, journaling, and reconnecting with nature. I highly recommend this uplifting and inspiring guide! It's a beautiful contribution to the self-help genre and the mental health field."

— **Lisa Ferentz,** trauma therapy specialist and author of *Finding Your Ruby Slippers*

"Most of us think of resilience as something either we have or we don't. But in *Resilience*, Linda Graham uses the latest research to create an evidence-based brain-training program that can build and protect anyone's well-being and resilience — for the rest of their life. In this empowering book, Linda walks you step-by-step through exercises that gradually rewire your brain and transform your sense of well-being. Practical and hopeful, this is a book that can change your life."

— **Laura Markham, PhD,** author of *Peaceful Parent, Happy Kids*

"In this engaging and empowering book, Linda Graham teaches us how to respond to life's inevitable challenges with strength, calm, and grace. Highly recommended."

— **Tim Desmond,** author of *Self-Compassion in Psychotherapy* and *The Self-Compassion Skills Workbook*

"With *Resilience*, Linda Graham has surpassed herself. *Bouncing Back*, Linda's first book, was superb, and this one is even better. It is self-help with the potential to really help. It also manages to be a page-turner for those of us who feel an urgency to better understand and navigate the human condition. Integrating the latest findings of contemporary psychology and neuroscience while drawing on the wisdom traditions of the East, *Resilience* offers the reader practical guidance, illumination, and inspiration. Perhaps what I most appreciate among the book's many virtues is its utterly convincing optimism about our capacity as human beings to confront suffering and, in the process, change ourselves for the better."

— **David Wallin, PhD,** author of *Attachment in Psychotherapy*

"A powerful and practical path for empowering your brain, body, and spirit to bounce back from any challenges in your past, present, or future."

— **Chris Willard,** author of *Mindfulness for Teen Anxiety* and coauthor of *Mindfulness for Teen Depression*

"Most of us face the challenges that life brings our way by just trying our best to get through. But what would our lives be like if we could not merely survive in the face of adversity but actually thrive? In this amazing synthesis of cutting-edge science, practical wisdom, and compassionate guidance, master teacher Linda Graham shows us how to do just that. Join her on a comprehensive journey of personal transformation that will rewire your brain, restore your well-being, and revitalize your life. No doubt you will be all the better for it."

— **Ronald J. Frederick, PhD,** author of *Living Like You Mean It*

"Linda Graham combines her wealth of knowledge of ancient practices and neuroscience with years of clinical work to create a masterful guide to building flexibility and stability — qualities essential to resilience. *Resilience* offers a rich array of practices for navigating both the ordinary and extraordinary challenges of being human. Linda's wisdom in crafting a pathway to resilience is woven into every page. I encourage you to take the journey with her."

— **Deb Dana,** author of *The Polyvagal Theory in Therapy*

"Linda Graham has created a beautifully organized book with an array of over 130 carefully constructed exercises to change the way our brains operate. Reading the book will help — but practicing the exercises is what will really set this book apart from the rest."

— **James Bennett-Levy,** professor of mental health and psychological well-being at the University of Sydney

"*Resilience* is an excellent addition to the growing field of resilience principles and practices. Linda Graham has written an extremely practical, grounded book that will serve both practitioners and laypeople alike. I highly recommended it as one of the most thorough books on the subject."

— **Daniel Ellenberg, PhD,** Rewire Leadership Institute

"In *Resilience*, Linda Graham walks us skillfully to the edges of our struggles, where resilience is patiently waiting if only we know the path. This book shows us the way, as Linda brilliantly offers practical tips and creative ideas to rewire our brains for inner calm and wise action. I will come back to this resource over and over again for my personal life and work projects."

— **Michelle Gale,** author of *Mindful Parenting in a Messy World*

"We all want and need to be resilient; the question is, How do we become more so? Linda Graham's *Resilience* guides us with wisdom, kindness, and gentleness through a rich and detailed process that is sure to enhance not only our resilience but also our vitality and well-being. Make sure to take advantage of this remarkable theoretical and practical resource!"

— **Anat Baniel,** founder of Anat Baniel Method® NeuroMovement® and author of *Move into Life: NeuroMovement for Lifelong Vitality* and *Kids beyond Limits*

"With humor and intelligence, Linda Graham masterfully weaves together neuroscience, psychology, and contemplative teachings to create a wise and immensely practical set of tools for everyday people to meet adversity with wisdom and compassion."

— **Susan Kaiser Greenland,** author of *Mindful Games* and *The Mindful Child*

RESILIENCE

RESILIENCE

Powerful Practices for Bouncing Back
from Disappointment, Difficulty,
and Even Disaster

LINDA GRAHAM, MFT

New World Library
Novato, California

New World Library
14 Pamaron Way
Novato, California 94949

Copyright © 2018 by Linda Graham

All rights reserved. This book may not be reproduced in whole or in part, stored in a retrieval system, or transmitted in any form or by any means — electronic, mechanical, or other — without written permission from the publisher, except by a reviewer, who may quote brief passages in a review.

The material in this book is intended for education. It is not meant to take the place of diagnosis and treatment by a qualified medical practitioner or therapist. No expressed or implied guarantee of the effects of the use of the recommendations can be given or liability taken.

Text design by Tona Pearce Myers

Library of Congress Cataloging-in-Publication data is available.
Names: Graham, Linda, [date]–author.
Title: Resilience : powerful practices for bouncing back from disappointment, difficulty, and even disaster / Linda Graham, MFT.
Description: Novato, California : New World Library, [2019] | Includes bibliographical references and index.
Identifiers: LCCN 2018022778 (print) | LCCN 2018033117 (ebook) | ISBN 9781608685370 (ebook) | ISBN 9781608685363 (alk. paper)
Subjects: LCSH: Resilience (Personality trait) | Self-acceptance. | Self-consciousness (Awareness) | Neuropsychology.
Classification: LCC BF698.35.R47 (ebook) | LCC BF698.35.R47 G734 2019 (print) | DDC 158.1—dc23
LC record available at https://lccn.loc.gov/2018022778

First printing, September 2018
ISBN 978-1-60868-536-3
Ebook ISBN 978-1-60868-537-0

Printed in Canada on 100% postconsumer-waste recycled paper

New World Library is proud to be a Gold Certified Environmentally Responsible Publisher. Publisher certification awarded by Green Press Initiative.
www.greenpressinitiative.org

10   9   8   7   6   5   4   3   2   1

This book is dedicated to practice — because dedicated practice
is what recovers and strengthens our resilience.

Contents

Introduction

It's one thing to misplace your house keys and your wallet two minutes before you have to rush out the door to catch the 6:15 AM bus for work. You do your best to breathe slowly and deeply, stay calm, and try to think if maybe you were wearing something else with pockets before the early morning mad dash. We all experience these hiccups in life — spilling the entire dish of lasagna on the way to serve six guests in the dining room, shredding the wrong client file at work, leaving a laptop on a plane, discovering mold in the bathroom walls, learning that the car needs a new transmission or the washing machine has gone on the fritz — and these hiccups can create quite a startle in the nervous system. These kinds of things tax our coping capacities on a fairly regular basis. Our capacity to cope with these inevitable ups and downs is then further tested when we layer on our own critical messages: "You stupid klutz!" or "I knew it; I knew it. I can't ever get anything right."

But usually we can right ourselves again. We put on our big-girl or big-boy pants, face the distress of the moment, and deal.

Occasionally we are called on to deal with greater troubles and adversities, not just hiccups but earthquakes that overwhelm our capacities to cope, at least temporarily. They include troubles like infertility or infidelity, a diagnosis of lung cancer, losing a job several years out from retirement, a daughter arrested for selling pot, or a son wounded in combat overseas. When these bigger bumps happen, we have to dig deeper into our inner reserves of resilience and our memories of times when we've successfully coped before, while also drawing on external resources such as family and friends. Here, too, finding our way back to our center, our inner equilibrium and ability to cope, can be more difficult if we are told we are — or perceive ourselves as — less than capable, less than skillful, less than good enough, or unworthy of help.

And then there are times when too damn many disasters happen all at once: we

1

lose a child in a car accident or cause the death of a child in a car accident at the same time that an aging parent has a stroke and a freak thunderstorm causes flood damage to half the house. When catastrophes like these strike, we are vulnerable to losing our resilience altogether, temporarily or even for a long time. We may dissolve into a trauma response, finding that our world no longer makes sense or no longer exists, and we have to scramble to find any lessons or meaning at all in what we're going through. If we have experienced too many unresolved traumas in the past, we can be especially susceptible to falling apart and not being able to recover. When our reserves are already depleted, we can begin to feel like we're just barely afloat and about to go under.

How in the world do we bounce back from traumas like these? By strengthening our resilience.

Resilience — the capacity to bend with the wind, go with the flow, bounce back from adversity — has been pondered, studied, and taught in tribes and societies, in philosophical and spiritual traditions, and through literature and academies for eons. It is essential to the survival and thriving of human beings and human societies. We now also know that it is one of the behavioral outcomes of a mature, well-functioning prefrontal cortex in the brain. Whether we're facing a series of small annoyances or an utter disaster, resilience is teachable, learnable, and recoverable.

In this book we'll look at how to cope resiliently no matter what life may throw at us, no matter what level of disruption to our resilience we're facing. We'll begin at the beginning and look at how we develop the capacity for resilience in the first place — or don't — and then what tools and techniques we can reliably use to build or recover our resilience so that it is ready to help us cope with whatever challenges or catastrophes might come along next — to cope with anything, anything at all.

> *Let me not pray to be sheltered from dangers, but to be fearless in facing them.*
> *Let me not beg for the stilling of my pain, but the heart to conquer it.*
> — RABINDRANATH TAGORE, *Fruit-Gathering*

Resilience guides you step by step through a process of cultivating more well-being in your life by strengthening your resilience so that you can respond skillfully to *any* upset or catastrophe that would derail that well-being. You can see yourself as more competent in coping with the disappointments and difficulties that are inevitable in life and trust more deeply that you can bounce back from disasters or even forestall them.

You'll also become more knowledgeable about how the brain works, how *your* brain works, and how you can work with your brain to create new habits of responding more flexibly (flexibility is the core of resilience). We'll explore safe, efficient, and effective tools and techniques that can even rewire long-established patterns of responding when they're no longer working well for you. Most important, you will not only learn practices that will help you bounce back from any adversity, but you will also learn to see yourself as someone who *can* learn, who *can* cope, who *can* strengthen your resilience and well-being. And that not only builds up further resilience, but it makes life more satisfying and fulfilling in every way.

What You Will Find in This Book

Because resilience is truly recoverable, I have designed this guide to resilience specifically as a brain-training program to help you strengthen your capacities to bounce back. You will find over 130 experiential exercises that will train you — and your brain — to steady or right yourself no matter what is happening around you, to respond skillfully to the most common and the most challenging external stressors, and to help you work through any negative internal messages you may be believing about your ability to cope with those stressors.

These practices tap the brain's phenomenal ability to adapt. They are organized by the five different kinds of intelligence that are foundational to resilience: somatic, emotional, relational within ourselves, relational with others, and reflective. You will learn to strengthen each of these five intelligences through three key processes of brain change — what I call new conditioning, reconditioning, and deconditioning — that will reliably increase your ability to respond with flexibility to stress and trauma. You can apply these processes to any level of disruption to your resilience, from barely a wobble to serious sorrows and struggles to a potentially traumatizing "too much." Practiced regularly, they will build your resilience, strength, and wisdom, enhancing your well-being for the long haul.

How to Use This Book

These tools are presented in a deliberate sequence, one building on another, which is a process very similar to the way your brain develops these skills in the first place. I encourage you to work through the book from beginning to end and not skip around too much until you've gone through the book at least once. You can use *Resilience* like a self-guiding workshop.

Chapter 1 explains how resilience developed in your brain (or did not), how to choose the experiences that will strengthen your brain's response flexibility now, and five conditions that accelerate your brain's learning and rewiring.

Chapters 2–7 contain most of the book's exercises. Within each chapter, the exercises progress from simple to complex and address increasing levels of disruption to your resilience. The introduction to each chapter explains how these exercises work, what outcomes you can expect, and why you might want to use them to strengthen the specific kind of intelligence the chapter deals with. You may choose to download selected exercises from my website, www.lindagraham-mft.net, to play back whenever and wherever you wish.

Please approach these exercises with a sense of curiosity and experimentation. If an exercise works for you, continue practicing it. If something doesn't work for you, let it go and try something else.

A large body of research has shown that the brain learns best through the repetition of experiences, little and often: small, incremental changes repeated many times. Through practicing any of these exercises for just ten to twenty minutes a day, you'll experience immediate shifts in how you respond to stressors. Over weeks and months of consistent practice, you can create permanent changes in your brain — and thus in your behavior. As you encounter new stresses, small or large, you will start to notice these long-term changes in how you can think and respond.

Chapter 8 suggests lifestyle choices you can make to keep your brain functioning optimally, protecting your resilience for the rest of your life.

Where Does This Program Come From?

I have been a licensed psychotherapist in private practice for over twenty-five years, helping clients meet their personal challenges and catastrophes with greater skill and resilience. For at least twenty of those years, I have also been focused on integrating cutting-edge research discoveries in Western behavioral sciences with advances in modern neuroscience, attachment theory, interpersonal neurobiology, positive psychology, resilience training, trauma therapy, and post-traumatic growth. In that same period I have also studied and taught practices from Eastern contemplative traditions, focusing on mindfulness and self-compassion practices, which are recognized as two of the most powerful agents of brain change known to science.

My first book, *Bouncing Back: Rewiring Your Brain for Maximum Resilience and Well-Being* (2013), offered a tool set I had created by integrating research data and perspectives from all of the above paradigms. *Bouncing Back* won several national awards and broke new ground in the teaching of resilience. Since the book was published, I have continued teaching the neuroscience of resilience to thousands of mental health professionals and seekers of personal growth and self-transformation, in clinical trainings and workshops throughout the United States, Europe, Australia, and the Middle East. And I have collaborated closely with mentors and colleagues, sharing our most effective practices in an interactive network of learning.

Now, with this guidebook, I supplement the teachings in *Bouncing Back* with new understanding gleaned from those trainings and experiences, as well as dozens of new tools and resources to help you recover the resilience, vitality, and well-being that are your birthright. Through the practices described here, you can increase your response flexibility to make the wise choices that allow you to cope with anything, anything at all.

I am no longer afraid of storms, for I am learning how to sail my ship.
— LOUISA MAY ALCOTT, *Little Women*

Let's begin.

CHAPTER ONE

The Basics of Strengthening Resilience

How We Learn to Bounce Back

All the world is full of suffering. It is also full of overcoming.
— **HELEN KELLER**

Life is full of challenge. We can't avoid that. No matter how hard we try, how earnestly we seek, or how good we become, life throws us curveballs and pulls the rug out from under each and every one of us from time to time. No one is immune from that reality of the human condition. Bumps and bruises, even occasional catastrophes and crises, are so inevitable in human experience that we don't have to take bad things happening to good people so personally.

We can't change the fact that shit happens. What we *can* change is how we respond, and that's what this book is all about.

> *Mishaps are like knives, that either cut us or serve us, as we grasp them by the blade or the handle.*
>
> — JAMES RUSSELL LOWELL, *Literary Essays*

When something challenging or even devastating happens, we have the power — the flexibility — to choose how we respond. It takes practice, and it takes awareness, but that power always lies within us. This chapter gives you a clear map of how you can train your brain to respond to life's challenges in ways that are increasingly skillful and effective. You'll also gain an understanding of how the changes that occur in your brain pathways make the brain itself more resilient.

When Shit Happens: Developing Response Flexibility

When faced with external problems and pressures — car accidents, catastrophic illness, divorce, the loss of a child — or when we are called on to help others face sudden and disastrous shifts in their lives, we can hardly be blamed for seeking to fix the problem by changing the circumstances and conditions "out there." Even when we are tormented by internal messages about how badly we are coping — "I could have thought of that before. Dumb, dumb, dumb!" — we often still focus on fixing the external problem "out there" in order to make ourselves feel better "inside."

Of course, it's important to develop the life skills, resources, and wisdom to create changes in those external circumstances when we can, and to learn to cope well, again and again and again, when we can't. That's part of what resilience is all about. It's all good work, all necessary, all helpful. But every bit as important as focusing on what's "out there" is how we perceive and respond to what's "inside"— to any external stressors, to any internal messages about those stressors, to any internal messages about how well or poorly we're coping, and even to any implicit memories of danger from the past that are triggered by the current event and may feel very real right now. Our capacities for perception and response are among the most important factors determining or predicting our ability to be resilient and regain our balance going forward.

> *In trying to sort out what accounts for a person's ability to cope with stress, it is useful to distinguish three different kinds of resources. The first is the external support available, and especially the network of social supports. The second bulwark against stress includes a person's psychological resources, such as intelligence, education, and relevant personality factors. The third type of resource refers to the coping strategies that a person uses to confront the stress. Of these three factors, the third one is both the most important factor in determining what effects stress will have and the most flexible resource, the one most under our personal control.*
> — MIHALY CSIKSZENTMIHALYI, *Flow: The Psychology of Optimal Experience*

Thus the motto of this book is: "How you respond to the issue...*is* the issue." (Deep bows to my colleague Frankie Perez at the Momentous Institute in Dallas, Texas, for that phrase.)

Shift Happens, Too

Whatever shit might be happening, the key to coping with the situation is how we shift our perception (our attitude) and our response (behavior). It may seem that there's no end to external stressors, or to negative internal messages about how we're coping with them. That's why creating a shift in perception (attitude) and in our responses to those stressors and those messages (behaviors) may be the most effective choice we can make to strengthen our resilience.

You can experience this power of shifting your attitude and behavior by refocusing your attention from what just happened to how you are coping with what just happened.

Darn! I dropped the plate! It's shattered in a dozen pieces. Double darn — that was the special plate my aunt gave me when I graduated. Sigh. I'll call my aunt to tell her. We'll commiserate. Maybe we can shop for another special plate next week — it will be a good excuse for a visit.

Three thousand bucks for a new transmission! That's a lot of money. And... at least it's something fixable. The car will still run for another five years, and...we'll take one less week of vacation this year, and...in the very long run this is just a big bump on a pickle.

The doc wants to run more tests. Not such good news. This is really, really hard. Well, better to know, better to get the information I need to deal with this head on.

The big lesson of this practice is that if we can shift our attitude and behavior in these circumstances, we can shift them in *any* circumstances. Knowing this *is* the big shift.

Between a stimulus and response there is a space. In that space is our power to choose our response. In our response lies our growth and our freedom. The last of human freedoms is to choose one's attitude in any given set of circumstances.
— attributed to VIKTOR FRANKL

This shift is how we move from "poor me" to an empowered, active "I." It's a shift from a fixed mindset to a growth mindset, a way of keeping the mind open to learning. We can change any internal messages we may be hearing about how we are coping (or not) or have coped (or not) in the past. Strengthening resilience includes coming to see ourselves as people who *can* be resilient, are *competent* at coping, and are competent at *learning* how to cope.

Neuroplasticity

All of the capacities that develop and strengthen your resilience — inner calm in the midst of the storms, seeing options clearly, shifting perspectives and responding flexibly, choosing to choose wise actions, persevering in the face of doubt and discouragement — all of these capacities are innate in your own being because they are evolutionarily innate in your own brain.

All your life, your brain has the flexibility to create new patterns of response to life events because of its *neuroplasticity*. A mature adult brain is physically stable, but its functioning is fluid and malleable, not inert or fixed. Your brain can grow new neurons, connect those neurons in new circuits, embed new learning in new neural networks of memory and habit, and rewire those networks whenever it needs to.

The adult brain's ability to continue to develop and change its functioning — lifelong — is without question the most exciting discovery of modern neuroscience. Neuroplasticity in the adult human brain was accepted as scientific truth only about thirty years ago, with the development of imaging technology that allowed neuroscientists to see these changes actually happening in the prefrontal cortex, the brain's center of executive functioning, as well as elsewhere in the brain. Neuroplasticity is the engine of all learning, at every point in the human life span.

Neuroplasticity means that *all* of the capacities of resilience you need are learnable and recoverable. Even if you didn't fully develop your capacities for resilience in early life — maybe because of a lack of healthy role models, less-than-secure early attachment, or the experience of too many adversities or traumas before your brain had developed the necessary circuitry to cope — you can develop them now. That's right. The human brain can always learn new patterns of coping, install those patterns in new neural circuitry, and even rewire the old circuitry when old patterns no longer serve a constructive purpose. The neural networks underlying your coping strategies and behaviors can be shaped and modified by your own choices, by self-directed neuroplasticity. You can learn, change, and grow now because your brain can learn, change, and grow always.

Nurturing Response Flexibility in the Brain

Self-directed neuroplasticity requires the engagement of the prefrontal cortex, the center of executive functioning in the brain. It's the structure we rely on most for our planning, decision-making, analyses, and judgments. The prefrontal cortex also performs many other functions essential to our resilience: it regulates functions of the body and the nervous system, manages a broad range of emotions, and quells the fear response of the amygdala. (That quelling is essential for resilience!) The prefrontal cortex allows us to attune to the felt sense of our experience and that of others, to empathize with the meaning of our experience and that of others, and to become aware of the self as it evolves through time. It is the seat of our inner moral compass. And it is the structure of response flexibility — our capacity to shift gears, perspectives, attitudes, and behaviors.

All of these capacities, especially the capacity to shift gears smoothly, mature as your prefrontal cortex matures. All of the brain's growth, development, learning, unlearning, and rewiring is dependent on experience. Experience is how the brain learns, unlearns, and relearns anything, ever. That's obvious in our initial development: learning to walk, talk, read, play baseball, and bake cookies.

We now know that experience is the catalyst of the brain's neuroplasticity and learning for our entire lives. At any time, we can choose the experiences that direct the brain's learning toward better functioning. Resilience can be strengthened — or diminished — at any time by experience.

As noted by Richard J. Davidson, founder and director of the Center for Investigating Healthy Minds, University of Wisconsin, Madison: "The brain is shaped by experience. And based upon everything we know about the brain in neuroscience, change is not only possible, but is actually the rule rather than the exception. It's really just a question of which influences we're going to choose for the brain. And because we have a choice about what experiences we want to use to shape our brain, we have a responsibility to choose the experiences that will shape the brain toward the wise and the wholesome."

How Response Flexibility Can Get Derailed

Let's look at four sets of experiences that can affect the development of the brain's response flexibility and can explain why we sometimes experience difficulties in being resilient and coping.

1. EARLY ENTRAINMENT AND ATTACHMENT CONDITIONING

Because our earliest experiences kindle the development and maturation of the brain's prefrontal cortex, we get a head start in developing response flexibility when the people closest to us growing up — parents, other family members, peers, teachers, coaches, and other important adults — have and demonstrate this capacity themselves. We learn from these role models by observing what helps them cope and what doesn't — keeping calm and carrying on or stomping out the door in tight-lipped anger.

We have this capacity to observe and replicate responses because our brains are *entrained* to function in precisely the same way that other brains around us are functioning, especially when we are very young. This *entrainment* in our early attachment relationships (other brains doing our learning for us) is the neurobiological underpinning of conditioning our behavior: it is nature's way of being efficient. Your brain learns to regulate its own nervous system as a result of that nervous system being regulated by people around you. It learns to manage and express a wide range of emotions by having those emotions perceived and validated by people around you. And it learns to attune to its own experiences by people around you attuning to your experiences.

Much of this conditioned learning happens by three years of age, before there is even any conscious awareness of its happening. The brain encodes this procedural learning into implicit memory (out of awareness). This, too, is part of the brain's extraordinary efficiency.

The brain learns most of its processes for regulating itself, responding and relating to others in this way, from others before we begin to make our own choices and learn on our own. Research has shown that secure attachment and early entrainment to other healthy brains and well-regulated nervous systems are the best buffers we have against later stress and trauma.

As we grow older, we *do* begin to make our own choices and learn on our own. The prefrontal cortex matures, and we learn less through entrainment (though that process can continue throughout life) and more from our own expanding capacities of self-awareness, self-reflection, and self-acceptance. These capacities support an increasing ability to select the experiences we want to use that can develop all of our brain's capacities, and all of those experiences create changes in our brain's neural circuitry and thus in our behaviors.

2. If Response Flexibility Didn't Fully Mature

Alas, if our earliest attachment relationships didn't provide that skillful entrainment and shaping of the brain's development or the role modeling of resilience — if we experienced too much neglect or indifference, criticism or rejection, or mixed messages and unpredictability — our brain will struggle to develop the capacities it needs to be resilient: regulating our stress responses and powerful emotions of anger, fear, sadness; learning how to trust ourselves and trust others; learning how to make sense of what's really happening and what to do about it; learning how to shift gears; learning how to learn.

The growth of the neural circuitry needed to support resilience can bog down in defensiveness and rigidity or fail to gel and remain chaotic — states that my colleague Bonnie Badenoch calls "neural cement" or "neural swamp." Instead we develop habits of coping that are not very skillful — either not flexible enough or stable enough. (Please note: This is entirely normal in human experience.)

3. Adverse Childhood Experiences and Trauma

Too many adverse childhood experiences, such as abuse, addiction, or violence in the home or community, can make it difficult for a growing child to learn to cope at all because those experiences compromise the organic development of the brain. For a child who grows up with an alcoholic parent and a bullying older brother and another parent in denial about the behaviors of either, the trauma in the home can overwhelm and even traumatize the growing brain. Such disruption can prevent the brain from developing properly, which impairs its capacities for learning to cope. Thinking and memory can be impaired, and the ability to regulate emotions and relate to others can be very compromised. A young person may learn to cope by *dissociating*: "checking out," not being present. In this state, a person's sense of aliveness, of hope for the future, and sense of self can disappear, too.

4. Acute Trauma

At any time, the impact of acute trauma — such as catastrophic illness, the death of a loved one, the loss of a home in a natural disaster — can knock the functioning of the prefrontal cortex offline, at least temporarily. Without the more comprehensive options offered by the higher brain, we find ourselves resorting to the more limited re-activity of the survival-oriented lower brain and the automatic patterns already conditioned in our neural circuitry. Researchers have found that 75 percent of all Americans experience at least one traumatizing event in their lifetime, so most of us can expect a real challenge to our resilience at some point in our lives. Researchers have also found, as stated so eloquently by Peter Levine, developer of Somatic Experiencing trauma therapy, that "trauma is a fact of life. It doesn't have to be a life sentence."

Here's the good news. Even if your capacity for response flexibility didn't fully mature as you were growing up or seems derailed now by some disruptive life event, you can still make the choices *now* that will help you fully develop and recover your capacities of resilience.

Let's explore processes of brain change you can learn now to do precisely that.

Conditioning, and Three Ways to Change Your Conditioning

These processes of brain change are all amply validated by the discoveries of modern neuroscience. All of them are simplified here for ease of understanding and application.

1. Conditioning

The brain learns from experience. You'll be able to say that in your sleep by the time you finish reading this chapter. Any experience, any experience at all, positive or negative, causes neurons in the brain to fire: that is, to exchange information through electrical and chemical signals. Repeating the experience causes the brain to repeat the neural firings, thus repeating patterns of response, whether positive or negative. This is known as *conditioning*. The well-known axiom in modern neuroscience is from the Canadian neuroscientist Donald Hebb: "Neurons that fire together wire together."

Picture rain falling down a hillside. At first it trickles down the hillside more or less at random, but eventually the flow of water carves grooves and ruts, and then bigger gullies, into the hillside. Once those have formed, the water travels down the hillside *only* in those grooves and gullies. In the same way, our brain develops pathways and patterns of response that, unless we intervene, cause us to automatically respond to a stressor in the same way that we have responded before. Conditioning is what encodes all of our early learning about coping.

The brain does this kind of learning and encoding all the time, on its own, when we're not directing it to do something else. When we're not guiding the installing of new patterns of coping in the brain, or rewiring old patterns, the brain continues to do its own learning and automatically encodes responses in its neural circuitry. We don't have to teach the brain how to learn, and we can't stop it from learning. We can, however, guide that learning when we wish to rewire what the brain has already learned.

The brain comes equipped with many patterns that have become hardwired over the course of human evolution. The *fight-flight-freeze-fold* responses are the automatic survival responses of our nervous system that cause us to recoil from a spider, jump out of the way of a speeding car, or collapse in helplessness without any conscious processing at all. *Negativity bias* is the tendency (again, an unconscious one) to store memories of negative events more readily than memories of positive events. This trait, which alerts us quickly to danger, has been essential for human survival, but it is not always supportive of individual well-being. Our brain unconsciously filters our perceptions of other people into "like me" and "not like me," based on gender, race, language, and culture. This tendency to automatically perceive *us* versus *them* is another trait that is important for survival but potentially problematic in daily living.

We can intentionally create new habits of response to these automatic reactions.

In the next several chapters we'll explore ways to rewire habits or rules of response learned from our family or culture of origin that are no longer serving us, such as withdrawing in passive anger rather than telling someone directly we need them to be kinder, or dismissing someone and their potential because they don't fit our preconceptions of "good" or "capable."

Any time we want to lay down new wiring or rewire old previously conditioned patterns of coping, we can use the three processes of brain change described below.

2. New Conditioning

New conditioning is my term for the process of deliberately and intentionally choosing to engage in a new activity or experience that will shift the functioning and habits of the brain in a particular direction. Any time you begin a gratitude practice, deepen your listening skills, work on strengthening the focus of your attention, cultivate more self-compassion or self-acceptance, and repeat the practice over time, you are using new conditioning to create new learning, new circuitry, and new habits of response to life events, even potentially or previously traumatizing ones. You are creating new wiring in the brain, new memories, and new ways of being that can become long-lasting positive habits.

New conditioning does not *undo* old conditioning. When you're stressed or tired, your brain will default to its old patterns. It's easier and more efficient for the brain to do what it already knows how to do. But with enough repetition, you can create a choice point in the brain's functioning, and with the next process, *reconditioning*, you actually can rewire the old circuits.

3. Reconditioning

The technical name for reconditioning is *memory deconsolidation-reconsolidation*. In recent years, new scanning technology has allowed neuroscientists to see this process actually at work in the brain, but it has been the basis of trauma therapy for decades.

You begin the process of reconditioning by deliberately, carefully, and skillfully bringing to your conscious awareness a memory of a previous experience that derailed your resilience, your reactions to that experience, and the way you think and feel about yourself *now* because of that derailing. By focusing on this experience, you activate or "light up" the entire neural network that holds the memory of the experience: visual images, body sensations, emotions, locations in your body where you feel those emotions, thoughts you had about yourself at the time, and thoughts you have about yourself now. This activating of the neural network is the key to rewiring it.

For instance, if you're still haunted by the memory of the time that you failed to show up for an important meeting and then lied to people about why you didn't make the meeting, and you're now hesitant to attend any more of those meetings because you're afraid of what people will think of you, and your hesitancy is getting in the way of advancing in your job, you start addressing the issue by bringing to mind every detail that you can remember of that original event, including how that makes you feel and think about yourself now.

You can learn to use this reconditioning process by yourself. However, it's crucially important to avoid becoming overwhelmed or retraumatized by the old memory. For this reason, it's important to work with only a small part of the memory at a time, so that your brain feels safe enough to do the learning and rewiring. (The exercises in chapters 2–7 provide many opportunities to learn the process.)

Once the negative memory has been activated and is available for rewiring, you deliberately juxtapose it in your awareness with a stronger, more positive, more resilience-based memory or even an imaginary event, holding both the original negative and the new positive experiences in your awareness at the same time (or alternating between the two). The juxtaposition causes the original neural network to fall apart (deconsolidate) and rewire again (reconsolidate) a fraction of a second later. That's the process that neuroscientists can now see with brain imaging technology. When the new positive memory or experience is stronger than the previous negative one, it will "trump" and rewire the negative memory.

For example, you can rewire the memory of failing to show up for the meeting and then lying about that by imagining a different ending to that scenario, even if that scenario couldn't have happened in real life. You might imagine that you met with two key people from that meeting a few days later and explained to them why you didn't come to the meeting, even if your reasons were pretty lame; you imagine apologizing for your lapse in good judgment and even more for lying, and offering ways to make amends. You imagine these two people being understanding and forgiving (even if that could never happen in real life), and then imagine yourself showing up for the next meeting.

This mechanism doesn't change what originally happened — it can't — but it does change your *relationship* to what happened. It doesn't rewrite history, but it does rewire the brain. You don't forget the old memory, but it no longer has the same charge or power to throw you off track. People who use this process of reconditioning to rewire a previously negative memory often say, "Huh! What was I so upset about?"

MODES OF PROCESSING

Both new conditioning and reconditioning rely on a focused mode of processing in the brain. We deliberately focus the attention of the brain on a particular task, a particular exercise. When neuroscientists first began scanning the brains of research subjects to learn what structures of the brain worked together as they played music, watched scenes of combat on the news, or mourned the loss of a pet, the scientists assumed that when the subjects weren't asking the brain to do something, like name a color or solve a puzzle, the brain would be quiet.

Well, not exactly. They learned that the brain "at rest" is more active than ever — not just in certain brain regions but all over the brain. This has come to be known as the *default network mode* of brain activity: it's what the brain does on its own when we're not consciously focusing attention on a task. We can use this mode for what I call *deconditioning*.

4. Deconditioning

When you're not consciously engaging the brain's attention, it goes into default network mode and plays, creating its own associations and links, meandering where it wants to, and connecting the dots in new ways. This is the mode of processing involved in imagination and intuition. It is what's happening when you are lost in reverie or have a sudden insight or "aha!" moment.

Deconditioning exercises, using your imagination in guided visualizations and guided meditations, open up what Dan Siegel at the Mindsight Institute at UCLA calls "the plane of open possibilities" for your brain. You can harness the new insights generated from your brain's meandering and playing to create new behaviors.

I have two important cautions about using the default network mode of processing to recover resilience.

First, because the default network is where you process your social sense of self, activating it can tip you into worry and rumination: Do they like me? Do I belong? Did I just do something stupid in front of other people? What do they think of me? People who practice mindfulness meditation are familiar with the brain's tendency to slip into that pattern of rumination, sometimes called "wandering mind" or "monkey mind." For instance, while trying to focus attention on the breath or on a mantra, you'll find your brain drifting into thoughts about what's for dinner or next summer's vacation, an argument with a coworker, or worry about a friend's divorce. When you're carrying any shame, worry, or anguish about yourself or an unresolved, disturbing event, your brain can chew on those thoughts and emotions over and over.

Second, when a disturbing or painful memory that we have pushed out of awareness starts to come back into our awareness, the brain will sometimes avoid confronting it by dissociating: checking out, staying focused on something pleasant, or going into a fog. The potentially disturbing or painful memory is not present in conscious awareness at all. Dissociation is one of the brain's most powerful mechanisms to protect us from being overwhelmed by stress, pain, or trauma. Our brains can dissociate almost from the day we're born, and dissociation can indeed support our resilience when we're coping with traumas of violence or abuse from which there is no other escape.

We have probably all dissociated in small ways at some point in our lives: bored to death in third grade, you might have drifted off into daydream or a reverie; maybe you just mentally disappeared until the bell rang. There's no shame or blame here. But dissociation is not the same as consciously processing something in the default mode network in order to increase awareness and learn from it.

You can instantly pull the brain out of rumination or dissociation by focusing your attention on something in the present moment — the sensations of breathing or of your feet touching the ground. But you can also use the positive aspect of the default network, imagination and free association, to spontaneously and randomly create new insights and behaviors from your own deep, intuitive wisdom.

Conditioning, new conditioning, reconditioning, deconditioning: there's a particular wisdom to learning the processes of brain change in that order.

Conditioning creates neural circuitry in your brain all of your life. You want to become aware of previously conditioned patterns of response because those patterns, now stored in your implicit (out-of-awareness) memory, can be triggered by a current event and make you react as you have always reacted, before you have the chance to decide whether that's how you want to respond.

Sometimes your conditioned responses are still right on target; sometimes they are no longer so useful. The tricky thing is, implicit memories have no time stamp. When they come to the surface "out of the blue," they feel as real to you now as they did back then, and you may react as if the remembered events were happening right now, not realizing they are a memory. When you become aware of these patterns (something you will practice doing throughout this book), you can choose to rewire them or create new habits of response altogether.

New conditioning creates new neural circuitry and new, more skillful, more re-silient patterns of response. These new circuits run alongside or on top of the old circuits, giving you far more options when faced with new or recurrent challenges.

With more new options available and with more stability within the brain itself, you can choose to use *reconditioning* to deliberately rewire old patterns as you be-come aware of them. This process is powerful. When used consciously and carefully, reconditioning allows you to focus your attention and not only rewire old patterns but also deliberately create changes in brain structure.

When you become skillful at focusing the attention of your brain, you can learn to consciously defocus your attention, too, letting the brain play without the hov-ering guardianship of the prefrontal cortex, while knowing you can come back to focused attention in a heartbeat if you need to. In the default network mode, the brain creates its own associations and links, connecting dots in new and some-times very imaginative ways. This process of *deconditioning* generates our deep, intuitive wisdom. Exercises throughout this book help you practice accessing that wisdom.

As you become proficient at using these processes to create more resilience in your perceptions of events and your responses to them, you will begin to develop a sense of yourself as someone who *can* use these processes to effectively create brain change. You can see yourself as someone who can learn tools to cope with difficulty, disappointment, even disaster. You can realize that you can become more resilient; you can move into thriving and flourishing.

The Five Intelligences

Chapters 2–7 offer many tools using these three processes of brain change to help you strengthen what I call your five intelligences.

1. Somatic Intelligence

Accessing your somatic intelligence — the innate intelligence of your body — in-volves using body-based tools, such as breath, touch, movement, social engagement, and visualization, to manage the stress and survival responses of your nervous sys-tem, to engage the more comprehensive functioning of your higher brain, and to return the body-brain to its natural physiological equilibrium. Developing this intel-ligence strengthens your sense of safety and trust and primes the neuroplasticity of your brain for learning. Your "range of resilience" greatly expands; you are willing and able to try new behaviors and take new risks.

2. Emotional Intelligence

By developing your emotional intelligence, you acquire tools to manage powerful surges of anger, fear, grief, shame, and guilt; to cultivate the positive emotions that shift your brain out of contraction, reactivity, and negativity and into more openness, receptivity, and response flexibility; and to cultivate the practices of compassion, mindful empathy, and theory of mind that allow you to skillfully engage with and ride the waves of other people's emotions as well.

3. Relational Intelligence within Yourself

In accessing relational intelligence as it relates to your sense of self, you learn to claim the resilience you already have and the wisdom of your wiser self; to retire the inner critic who may threaten to derail your sense of competence, courage, and healthy connections with others; and to accept, integrate, and even embrace all the various inner voices and parts that make up your personal self. You recover and strengthen your "home base" of a secure, trustworthy, and courageous self, the foundation of your resilience, of anything you wish to be.

4. Relational Intelligence with Others

Relational intelligence involves learning how to engage with other people, in both intimate and social relationships, in ways that allow you to trust and connect with them as refuges and resources of resilience. You learn to connect with people without becoming enmeshed, as well as to differentiate yourself from them without becoming withdrawn or cut off; you develop a healthy interdependence with the common humanity of others, initiating and deepening relationships that are healthy, resonant, productive, and fulfilling.

5. Reflective Intelligence

Using reflective intelligence, you practice mindful awareness to see clearly what is happening and your reactions to what is happening, to intentionally shift and rewire habitual thought processes that block your brain's response flexibility, and to cultivate the mental equanimity that allows you to discern options and make wise choices.

The Three Levels of Disruption

Strengthening all five of these intelligences will help you navigate *any* level of disruption to your resilience. In this book I classify disruptions into three levels:

Level 1. Barely a Wobble

Wobble is what happens in life, moment by moment, but your inner base of resilience can be pretty stable. The response flexibility in your prefrontal cortex allows you to face any new situation, any unknown, and any uncertainty with calm confidence. No matter what is happening, you don't wobble very much. This book offers many tools for developing and stabilizing this inner secure base. No matter what is happening, you can return quickly and reliably to the felt sense of this home base.

Level 2. Glitches and Heartaches, Sorrows and Struggles

Shit happens. You're thrown off center briefly, or sometimes for longer, and your resilience is derailed for a time. But shift can happen, too. You use many tools and techniques that allow you to recover and respond capably. You choose to show up and use your skills to right yourself and regain your footing fairly quickly, fairly reliably.

Level 3. Too Much

Rarely do people get to face difficulties, let alone disasters, one at a time, at a time of their choosing, from a clean slate of no prior difficulties. Sometimes life hits us with more than we can handle. Maybe one terrible thing has happened, maybe many things are happening all at once. Maybe too many catastrophes or too much trauma happened too early in life. The defensive coping strategies we may have learned early on can compromise the natural development of the prefrontal cortex, hindering any new learning and limiting our ability to respond flexibly now. Maybe the effects of too many disasters have accumulated over time and weakened our resilience. When we face disruptions that seem like just too much, there's a potential for trauma. Learning to process and move through a trauma is foundational to recovering your resilience.

You may find yourself experiencing any of these three levels of disruption to your resilience at any time in your life. The tools offered in this book can help you navigate them all. You can figure out which tools you need, based on the level of resilience strengthening you need for the particular circumstances you are dealing with, and rewire your brain as you need to.

Accelerating Brain Change

In my work, I've discovered five practices that accelerate these processes of brain change.

1. Little and Often Works Best

The brain is always learning from experience, *any* experience, positive or negative. That's our neurobiology. Neuroscientists have also discovered that the brain learns best through a practice of little and often: small experiences repeated many times. In other words, you might be better off meditating for ten minutes a day, every day, than meditating for an hour only once a week. It may be more conducive to your brain's learning to shift perspectives if you notice and write down three to five things you are grateful for every evening rather than making a list of twenty things all at once on the weekend.

The neuroscientist Richard Davidson observes that mindfulness and self-compassion practices are two of the most powerful agents of brain change known to science. These practices operate precisely in the way that the brain learns best: through moment-by-moment-by-moment practice, repeated many, many times.

When we are trying to undo the effects of negative, harmful, or traumatic experiences, little and often is the way to go, working with one small part of the memory at a time. We take baby steps so that the brain doesn't get overwhelmed or retraumatized. This practice of little and often not only allows us to learn and reinforce new learning most effectively; it also helps us unlearn unhelpful patterns and lay down new ones most effectively.

2. Safety Primes Neuroplasticity

The need for resilience arises in the first place because we are facing something new or unknown, some difficulty or danger, some challenge or crisis. We develop our capacities for resilience each time we successfully engage with those unknowns, resolve the difficulties, and emerge on the other side of a crisis or trauma. But the brain also needs a perception (*neuroception*) of safety within itself in order to prime the neuroplasticity that does all of this learning and rewiring. A relaxed brain is better able to perceive and integrate what it learns from any experience than is a brain that is tense, contracted, and narrowly focused on survival.

In chapter 2, you'll learn about the natural physiological equilibrium of the brain and how to work with it skillfully. Being calm and relaxed, yet engaged and alert, allows the brain — you — to skillfully meet any upset, distress, potential danger, or life threat. You stay centered in that equilibrium, consciously present for the experience, able to keep calm and carry on.

This natural equilibrium in the brain is known in psychotherapy as the *range of resilience*, and in trauma therapy as the *window of tolerance*. There's a similar concept in the Buddhist wisdom tradition, where it's known as *equanimity* — the ability to witness the tumult of life with calm eyes. And there's a story from that tradition to illustrate the power of this kind of inner safety zone.

A Buddhist master and his disciples were meditating one day when a bandit and his gang, who had been terrorizing the countryside, burst into the temple. The monks fled, but the master quietly continued his contemplation practice. Furious at the master's lack of reaction to him, the bandit drew his sword, raised it above his head, and thundered, "Don't you understand? I could run you through with this sword and not bat an eye!" The master calmly replied, "Don't you understand? I could be run through by your sword and not bat an eye." The bandit was so unnerved by the master's equanimity that he and his followers turned and fled, never to be seen again.

That's a high bar for staying calm in the face of danger, but you get the idea. Learning to maintain that kind of equilibrium allows you to face a potential disaster full on without going into your automatic survival responses of fight, flight, freeze, or fold.

3. Positive Emotions Shift Brain Function

All emotions, negative as well as positive, are powerful signals from the body to the brain that say, "Something important is happening! Pay attention!" Chapter 3 offers you tools for managing the surges of even the most difficult — some would say destructive — emotions so that you can be informed and motivated by them without being overwhelmed or hijacked. You'll even learn how to rewire the habitual responses you may have when those negative emotions arise.

But first, you'll look at the power of positive emotions to shift the functioning of the brain out of contraction and reactivity and into more openness, receptivity, and optimism. The direct, measurable cause and effect outcome of this shift is greater resilience. You learn to cultivate positive emotions — gratitude, awe, and delight — not just to shift your mood and help you feel better but to enable your brain to *do* better, to be wise and more skillful in all your interactions.

4. Resonant Relationships Teach Us New Strategies

Being truly seen, understood, accepted, and validated by another person for who we truly are encourages us to understand, accept, validate, and value ourselves for who we are. It helps us develop the inner secure base of resilience that is essential to navigating the world with calm, courage, and competence. It's what allows us to trust other people both as refuges and as resources for our resilience.

Maybe you didn't get to experience or trust this valuing and appreciation early in your growing up. Close to half of us didn't. You may still be carrying patterns of mistrust (of yourself or others) from earlier in your life — patterns reinforced by repeated experiences of hurt, betrayal, neglect, abandonment, rejection, and criticism. Chapters 4 and 5 introduce you to many tools and techniques for undoing and rewiring those patterns, helping you fully recover that trust. They will help you develop the interpersonal skills — such as reaching out for help, negotiating change, and setting limits and boundaries — that allow you to engage in relationships, both intimate and social, that are a fundamental source of well-being and support for your resilience.

In her book *Love 2.0*, the positive psychology pioneer Barbara Fredrickson shows us how the foundation for resonant relationships might develop. When two people are in physical proximity, making eye contact, sharing positive emotions (kindness, serenity, joy) and a sense of mutual care and concern, their brain wave patterns begin to sync up, mirroring each other, creating a sense of resonance that I would call trust and she calls love.

This neural synchrony is probably fueled by the release of oxytocin, the hormone of safety and trust, which I talk more about in chapter 2. Oxytocin brings you into that safety zone that creates optimal conditions for neuroplasticity, and thus for learning and growth. We'll explore where it's possible to create these moments of relational resonance or neural synchrony — with parents or parental figures, siblings, friends, teachers, coaches, therapists, romantic partners, spouses, support groups, or therapy groups — to help resilience take root in your psyche and in your brain.

5. Conscious Reflection Helps Us See Clearly and Choose Wisely

The brain can process experiences without going through conscious awareness. Very often traumatizing experiences are encoded in a person's neural circuitry as implicit somatic memories from a time when the person was too young to form conscious memories of specific situations and events. But the same unconscious processing can happen with positive or neutral experiences. The brain does that all the time. Your commute route can be so deeply encoded in your brain that you can drive to work on automatic pilot, only "waking up" when you turn down the wrong street and suddenly everything looks different. The brain can register a vibe from someone at a party before you consciously remember where you've met them before.

When you want to create and install *new* patterns of perceiving and behaving in your brain, however, you need to engage in conscious reflection so that the resources of resilience you create are retrievable and usable. Conscious reflection is not exactly the same as thinking. It has more to do with knowing what you're experiencing while you're experiencing it. You're becoming aware of your perceptions of experience and your responses to experience all part of firing of your neural circuitry) so that you can rewire any patterns of beliefs, attitudes, identities, or behaviors that are blocking your resilience.

Cultivating a mindfulness practice is a reliable method of increasing your conscious reflection. Mindfulness not only focuses your attention and allows you to experience the consciousness that can hold and reflect on *any* content, but it also strengthens the structures of the brain that you use to focus attention, to reflect on experience, to shift your perspective, to discern options, and to choose wise actions. I present this invaluable, self-strengthening practice in chapter 6.

It may seem a stretch to claim that employing the tools that support these processes, intelligences, and practices can really enable you to cope with anything and everything, but that is what you will practice in chapter 7: integrating the practices that can lead to a rewired brain and full-on resilience.

The underlying theme of this book is that you can *choose to choose* experiences, moment by moment, that develop your neural circuitry and build greater resilience. You can learn to "change your brain to change your life for the better" in ways that are often immediate and permanent. And learning how the brain works to create those moments of choice and change gives you a genuine sense of mastery and competence.

Catch the moment; make a choice.

— Janet Friedman

Every moment has a choice and every choice has an impact.

— Julia Butterfly Hill

The goal of this book is precisely to give you these tools and choices.
Let's continue.

CHAPTER TWO

Practices of Somatic Intelligence

Breath, Touch, Movement, Visualization, Social Engagement

You can't stop the waves, but you can learn to surf.
— **SWAMI SATCHIDANANDA**

We've been talking about finding ways to cope skillfully when things go haywire. Our most basic responses to all of life's challenges and adversities begin in our bodies. So, to strengthen resilience, we begin with body-based tools, our practices of somatic intelligence.

Cast your mind back to high school biology and you may recall learning about the autonomic nervous system, or ANS. Your ANS constantly scans the environment, including your social environment, for cues of safety, danger, or threat to your physical survival or psychological well-being. This scanning and signaling comes from deep in the brain stem and spinal cord. It operates 24/7, even when you are asleep, and always outside of your awareness. Your higher brain can, however, become aware of this signaling. In fact, the oversight of your higher brain is necessary to interpret what the signals mean, based on your experience and conditioning. But while your higher brain is more complex and more comprehensive in its evaluation of what's happening and what you should do about it, it is also slower at its job. Whereas the body-based ANS responds to a signal in milliseconds, your prefrontal cortex takes more time to respond: a few seconds to many minutes.

You've probably learned along the way that the ANS has two branches, the *sympathetic* branch and the *parasympathetic* branch. The sympathetic branch revs you up to take immediate action when you feel uneasy or sense danger: the fight-flight response. This rapid, protective reactivity gets your body moving *now* to tackle or flee from the danger, to confront or flee from a person who seems unsafe or toxic.

Your lower brain tells your body to move before your higher brain is even aware that something has just happened. Your nervous system reacts to keep you alive before your conscious brain can even register that you might be in danger of being dead.

Along the same lines, you've probably learned that the parasympathetic branch of the ANS allows you to calm yourself down to "rest and digest" when the danger is over. These two branches operate like the gas and the brakes in a car: activating the sympathetic is stepping on the gas, and activating the parasympathetic is hitting the brakes.

There are many benefits to activating the sympathetic branch (SNS) when there is no danger. It's what gets us out of bed in the morning, makes us *want* to get out of bed in the morning, and motivates us to engage with people, explore the world, play, create, and produce. Thanks to the SNS, we create governments; we write symphonies; we design and construct buildings and work to solve the problems of climate change. Positive activation of the SNS, regulated by the prefrontal cortex, is the basis of human civilization as we know it.

Similarly, activating the parasympathetic branch (PNS) when there is no danger allows us to feel centered and grounded, at peace and at ease. Positive activation of the PNS, regulated by the prefrontal cortex, is the basis of personal well-being. This is the feeling you get when you take a nap on the beach, relax in a contemplative stillness, or fall asleep after making love.

It's when either the SNS or the PNS overactivates in response to a perceived danger or life threat that things can get tricky. A sudden spike of the SNS can rev you up into anger and rage or anxiety, fear, and panic. A sudden over-activation of the PNS can cause you to numb out, shut down, withdraw, or dissociate. That over-revving up or over-shutting down can derail the functioning of your higher brain altogether, at least temporarily. At that point you are reacting solely from your automatic survival responses and whatever conditioned learning has been encoded in your brain's neural circuitry early in life. This neurobiological response is instant, and it's potent.

This chapter introduces practices of breath, touch, movement, and visualization to strengthen your somatic intelligence so that you learn to recognize, interpret, and manage the signals sent by your nervous system to your higher brain. You can return to your baseline physiological state of well-being — your range of resilience, your window of tolerance, your equanimity. You are once again calm and relaxed, engaged and alert, coping just fine, humming along. In that state of equilibrium you have the response flexibility you need to interpret the signals coming from stressors in the environment (or even your own internal messages about those stressors, or about yourself in relationship to those stressors), discern additional options, and take resilient, wise action.

These days, rather than having to deal with acute threats to our physical safety, as generations of our ancestors did, modern humans more often face chronic threats to our psychological safety and well-being. Through these practices you'll also learn to strengthen the social engagement system in your brain (also unconscious) to regulate your nervous system specifically in response to those threats.

Stuck in "On" or "Off" Mode

A range of stressors can cause the SNS to get stuck in the "on" mode: relentless pressures at work; constant complaints and criticisms by people from whom you take your cues of self-worth — your partner, your boss, even your children; falling short in achieving goals, in comparison to others or to your own expectations. You rev up and don't take a break, don't get a break; you are constantly anxious, vigilant, and stressed and can't recover the sense of safety and calm that is essential to your well-being.

Other circumstances can cause the PNS to get stuck in the "off" mode: relentless boredom at work, too many losses or disconnections in too short a time, too much shaming and blaming, criticism and rejection — or experiences you *perceive* that way. Rather than showing up to engage and deal with the situation, you can fall into dissociation, denial, passivity, and despair; you can collapse into a state of learned helplessness or depression, unable to find the energy or motivation to try and try again. This response is part of our neurobiological legacy from millions of years of our ancestors playing dead so the lion wouldn't eat them, and hundreds of thousands of years of evolving in social groups, withdrawing from conflict or appeasing others so that the tribe wouldn't throw them out.

Just twenty years ago, the neurophysiologist Stephen Porges discovered a third branch of the ANS, the ventral vagus pathway, which he calls the *social vagus*: a neural pathway connecting the body and the brainstem, then connecting with nerves in the neck, throat, eyes, and ears. This pathway, communicating between the face and the heart, creates an unconscious neuroception of safety when you are with safe others. Human beings are social beings, born and raised in families, kinship groups, and communities. The brain has evolved to automatically reach out and connect with others to seek reassurance when its sense of safety and well-being has been disrupted. The social engagement system can perceive, even unconsciously, signals like "It's okay," "False alarm," "You're fine," or "You're safe." This is the neurobiological basis of secure attachment and an inner sense of safety and calm. It's also the neural foundation that enables us to take risks when necessary.

As Porges's collaborator Deb Dana says in *A Beginner's Guide to Polyvagal Theory*,

> In this [ventral vagal] state our heart rate is regulated, our breath is full, we take in the faces of friends, we can tune into conversations and tune out distracting noises. We see the "big picture" and connect to the world and the people in it. [You can experience yourself] as happy, active, interested and the world as safe, fun, and peaceful. This state includes being organized, following through with plans, taking care of yourself, taking time to play, doing things with others, feeling productive at work, a general feeling of regulation and a sense of management. We have the ability to acknowledge distress and explore options, to reach out for support and have organized responses.

Using your social engagement system to generate an inner sense of safety doesn't necessarily mean circumstances are safe — you may still be facing the threat of foreclosure on a house or your back going out just from bending over to tie your shoe, and you need to be resilient in coping with those threats — but there's an inner neuroception of calm and equilibrium.

When the ventral vagus pathway is fully mature and functioning well, it acts as a "brake" to modulate the surges of the sympathetic and parasympathetic branches, preventing you from spiraling upward into panic or down into the swamp of withdrawal. Your body may react, but your brain can maintain a sense of equilibrium and recover from a wobble fairly quickly. You trust yourself enough to say, "I've been through worse before; I can learn to deal with this now." You trust other people around you as resources: you return to calm because they are calm; you trust yourself to cope because *they* trust your capacities to cope.

The exercises in this chapter are designed to help you learn to use the many tools of your body-based somatic intelligence — which include breath, touch, movement, visualization, and social engagement — to return to your natural physiological equilibrium. Even in the face of repeated challenges, upheavals, losses, and traumas, when it can seem impossible to catch even a moment of equanimity, these tools can help you return to your range of resilience and prime the neuroplasticity of your brain for learning and coping. Here's an illustration of this return to equilibrium:

One Friday afternoon I picked up my five-year-old goddaughter, Emma, from school. I was carrying her in my arms to the car when I tripped on a crack in the sidewalk. I recovered my balance and didn't fall. Neither Emma nor I were hurt. On we went; business as usual. The next day I shared the incident with my yoga teacher, Ada, who said, "See, yoga isn't just for fitness. It's for life."

That's the point of *all* of these practices. Resilience training is not just a set of skills; it creates habits for life. You may trip but save yourself from falling. Even if you do fall, you can get up again. And even if you fall and break something and you can't get up again for a while — or ever — you can muster the energy, skills, and resources to recover your sense of well-being.

New Conditioning

These practices will help you respond to challenges with more resilience and flexibility. Even when things are going haywire, you'll be able to consciously create new choice points in your brain that enable you to manage your responses more flexibly.

Level 1. Barely a Wobble

These tools strengthen existing neural pathways that maintain a stable range of resilience, where you don't wobble very much. You can avoid being thrown off balance by an unexpected or unwelcome situation, or you can recover your balance quickly and return to your natural baseline of equanimity. You can more easily keep calm and carry on. One of the most fundamental tools is paying attention to your breathing.

> *Slow breathing increases vagal activation and parasympathetic tone, leading to better physical and psychological well-being. Slow, deep breathing can effectively inhibit distress. Slowing and deepening the breathing during moments of distress brings a return of ventral vagal control, and as our autonomic state changes, so can our story.*
>
> — DEB DANA, *Rhythms of Regulation*

You breathe all the time. To breathe is to be alive. Every inhalation activates the sympathetic branch of your nervous system just a little bit (or a lot, when you overreact to something and hyperventilate). Every exhalation activates the parasympathetic branch just a little bit (or a lot, when you feel scared to death and faint). You can learn to use this rhythm of breathing in and breathing out (longer exhalations) to cultivate more calm in the body and access a deeper sense of well-being.

EXERCISE 2-1: Mini Breath Meditation

1. Breathe naturally, gently, for five to ten breaths. Pay attention to the sensations of breathing in (notice the cool air in your nostrils or throat and the gentle expansion of your belly and chest) and breathing out (notice warmer air flowing out and the relaxation of your belly and chest). Remember the practical power of "little and often." Pause and repeat this practice many times a day.

2. If you wish, you can say these phrases from the Zen master Thich Nhat Hanh silently to yourself as you breathe: "Breathing in, I am home. Breathing out, I smile."

3. As you inhale, you can imagine "coming home" to yourself, saying, "I am here. I am home." As you exhale, imagine connecting safely with the world outside yourself, coming into ease and harmony with others. Imagine breathing in to the word *me*, breathing out to the word *we*. Repeat this rhythm for a full minute.

This exercise can help you relax into a comforting sense of well-being and connection, deepening the ease or calm in your body and in your mind. You may even notice a sense of safety in the moment: "Nothing is happening in *this* moment to undo my sense of well-being." Relax into that ease and safety, even if it's just for this moment.

EXERCISE 2-2: Affectionate Breathing

Here you use kind awareness of your breathing to strengthen a sense of safety and calm in your body and your mind.

1. Find a comfortable position in which your body is supported and you don't need to make an effort to remain in that position. Close your eyes if you wish, or allow your eyes to soften their gaze. Come into a sense of presence, relaxing in your body. Take a few slow, easy breaths to release any unnecessary tension.

2. Focus your awareness on your breathing, noticing where you perceive the breath most easily — perhaps through your nostrils, through your throat,

or through the rise and fall of your belly. Let yourself notice the simple sensations of breathing, just feeling your breath for a while.

3. See if you can orient toward yourself and your breathing with openness, curiosity, and care. If you notice any discomfort in your mind or body, see if you can simply be with that discomfort, soften toward it, accepting that this is so in this moment. Bring a sense of kindness toward yourself.

4. Notice how you don't have to remember to breathe. Your body breathes for you. Your body is breathing you.

5. See if you can feel your whole body breathing. Notice how your breathing expands into your entire body and nourishes every cell in your body.

6. Give yourself over to the breath. Let yourself become the breath. Rest in the ease of this moment for a minute or two.

7. Perhaps allow a moment of appreciation or gratitude for the breath that sustains your life in every moment.

8. Finally, release your awareness of your breathing. Allow everything that comes to awareness to be just as it is, for now. When you're ready, open your eyes.

This exercise can help you appreciate your own intentions and wise effort in creating or deepening a genuine sense of ease and equilibrium. Know that you are learning a tool that will help you reliably regulate the revving up and shutting down of your nervous system.

A gentle focus on the physicality of your body can ground your awareness in the safety of the present moment. Awareness of subtle movement in your body wakes up your brain and primes its neuroplasticity for curiosity and learning.

EXERCISE 2-3: Focusing on the Soles of the Feet

1. Stand up and focus your attention on the soles of your feet contacting the floor or ground. (Remove your shoes if you wish.) Notice the sensations in your feet as you feel the floor or ground.

2. Rock back and forth a little, and side to side. Notice any changes or shifts in sensation. Make little circles with your knees, feeling the changes of sensation in the soles of your feet.

3. When your mind wanders, simply focus your attention on the soles of your feet again.

4. Begin to lift one foot up and place it back down; lift the other foot up and place it back down. Notice how the sensations in your feet change as you lift each foot and return it to the ground while standing in place. Notice any sensations you feel in the rest of your body as you do this.

5. Begin to walk slowly, step by step, noticing the changing sensations in the soles of your feet. Notice the sensation of lifting each foot, stepping forward, and then placing the foot on the floor. Walk for thirty or sixty seconds (or longer if you wish, of course).

6. Return to standing. While standing still, notice the sensations in your feet, in your body now.

7. Recognize how the small surface area of your feet supports your entire body. Perhaps allow a moment of appreciation or gratitude for the amazing work of your feet, carrying you through your life, all day long.

You can apply this exercise while standing in line at the grocery store (you will have to get creative about step 5), or anywhere, to come into a sense of presence, calm, and safety in the moment. Even the subtle movements of this exercise will help reset your nervous system.

Level 2. Glitches and Heartaches, Sorrows and Struggles

We experience wobbles every day. Even if our inner base is stable, some distress or difficulty, even a minor crisis or major catastrophe, can cause us to lose our footing so that our resilience is derailed for a short time, and sometimes longer.

The following body-based exercises strengthen the social engagement system that reassures your nervous system, "You're fine; you're okay; everything will be okay," even when things don't look okay at all. They will help you recover your resilience and find the resources to try again.

According to Dacher Keltner, founder of the Greater Good Science Center at the University of California, Berkeley, the fastest way to restore ease and calm to your nervous system is through warm, safe touch. This is the "primary language of compassion, love, and gratitude, the central medium in which the goodness of one individual can spread to another." Warm, safe touch activates the release of oxytocin, the hormone of safety and trust, your brain's direct and immediate antidote to the stress hormone cortisol.

EXERCISE 2-4: Hugs

A warm hug may not be a new practice for you, but sometimes we forget its power to soothe our jangled nerves.

1. Identify people or pets in your life that you would feel comfortable hugging or asking for a hug. (I have borrowed my neighbor's dog on more than one occasion.)
2. Exchange a twenty-second, full-bodied hug with this person or pet. Twenty seconds (about three breaths) is enough to release the oxytocin in both hug-ees when there is a sense of safety and trust. It creates a self-reinforcing loop of bonding and belonging for each person.
3. Repeat, repeat, repeat with as many different people and pets as you feel comfortable hugging, as many times a day as you remember to.

Hugs are a "little and often" practice par excellence for your nervous system. With each hug, you'll become more relaxed and engaged, and you'll stay more relaxed and engaged as you move through your day. You are strengthening the neural pathways of your social engagement system in one of the most enjoyable ways possible.

Neural cells are part of the structure of your heart. Warm, safe touch activates those neurons; your body feels the comforting energy of your social engagement system.

EXERCISE 2-5: Energize Your Heart Center

1. Ask someone you feel safe with to sit beside you.
2. Place your hand on your heart. As you do so, ask the other person to gently

place their hand on the middle of your back, on a level with your hand on the front of your body. You can also experience the energy shift of this exercise by remembering the feeling of connection with another as you lean your back into a cushion while sitting on a firm couch or chair.

3. Breathe gently in and out. Feel the sense of stable energy in the center of your torso. Relax into the ease and comfort of an active social engagement system.

4. After a minute or two, you can switch roles with your partner if you wish.

The social engagement system works nonverbally. The warm, safe touch communicates safety, returning the nervous system to calm, even without words.

EXERCISE 2-6: Hand on Heart

This tool is powerful enough to calm down a panic attack in less than a minute.

1. Place your hand on your heart. Breathe gently, softly, and deeply into the area of your heart. If you wish, breathe in a sense of ease or safety or goodness into this heart center.

2. Remember one moment, just one moment, when you felt safe, loved, and cherished by another human being. Don't try to recall the entire relationship, just one moment. This could be a partner, a child, a friend, a therapist, or a teacher; it could be a spiritual figure. (Remembering a loving moment with a pet can work very well, too.)

3. As you remember this moment of feeling safe, loved, and cherished, let yourself experience the feelings of that moment. Let the sensations wash through your body. Let yourself stay with these feelings for twenty to thirty seconds. Notice any deepening in a visceral sense of ease and safety.

4. Repeat this practice many times a day at first, to strengthen the neural circuitry that remembers this pattern. Then you can repeat it any time you need to, any time at all.

Remembering a moment of feeling safe, loved, and cherished by another person or pet activates the social vagus, reassuring you that indeed you are safe, you belong, and you are welcomed. Your blood pressure decreases, and your heart rate stabilizes. You return to the sense of safety that comes from a feeling of connection and belonging with safe others, even when you are alone.

Of course, you can experience this bonding and belonging, this "calm and connect" feeling, whenever you are with people you trust and feel safe with. You can also activate the release of oxytocin whenever you remember or imagine such moments. I suggest you practice this exercise whenever you experience the first signal of a startle or an upset. With practice, it will enable you to back out of a difficult emotional reaction before it hijacks you. At a minimum, practice it five times a day for a full week to train your brain in this new response to any difficult moment. It's portable equilibrium.

EXERCISE 2-7: Savor a Moment of Connection

Note: This exercise works extremely well even in the midst of overwhelming trouble or tragedy.

1. Identify a trusted friend (or therapist). Sit face to face with this person, in comfortable physical proximity. Smile at each other in an open, friendly way, maintaining eye contact.
2. Feel a sense of care and concern for the welfare of the other person, and let your facial expressions convey that. Let yourself sense that this person cares for your well-being too; observe this caring in their facial expressions.
3. Savor the sense of relaxation in the connection. Focus on the experience for thirty seconds, and let the feelings deepen. Notice the felt sense of relaxation in your body.

Savoring connection is a neural exercise, using the ventral vagus pathway, that generates a resource of safety and thus resilience in your brain. Savoring gives your brain the time it needs to transform the positive experience into positive feelings.

Level 3. Too Much

Sometimes life whacks you really hard. "Fall down seven times, get up eight" is an inspiring Japanese proverb, but it's not always easy to pick yourself up from a trauma, a series of traumas, or a lifetime of traumas. When you've been dumped out of the boat and need help climbing back in, it's especially important to strengthen and use your social engagement system to find refuges and resources in safe connections with other people.

EXERCISE 2-8: Equanimity for Two

Each breath cycle gently exercises the rhythm of regulation of your social vagus. Breathing in, activating the SNS, supports social engagement and connection; breathing out, activating the PNS, evokes a sense of well-being. In this exercise, you synchronize your breathing with another person's to add interconnection to the practice.

1. Have your partner lie down comfortably on the floor with eyes closed. Sit comfortably on the floor nearby. Come into a sense of presence, of being with this person, here and now.
2. Place one hand on your partner's hand or forearm, the other hand on the crown of their head. Your partner breathes slowly and deeply.
3. Begin to synchronize your breathing with their breathing. Simply breathe together for two to three minutes, noticing the life force of the breath entering and leaving their body and yours.
4. After two to three minutes, you and your partner can switch roles.

    Repeated use strengthens your social engagement system. You can more easily drop into a shared equilibrium, an equanimity for two.

You gain stability and strength when you recognize your kinship with other human beings who are in the same boat you are — or who have been dumped out of the same boat you have. You realize the shared humanity of your situation. "I'm not the only one. I'm not alone."

EXERCISE 2-9: Join or Start a Support Group

1. Find a support group in your area for people who have experienced the same trauma as you have, or a similar trauma — a support group for people with cancer, for Alzheimer's caregivers, or for parents who have lost a child to violence, illness, or natural disaster. You gain support, encouragement, and role modeling from people who know what you're going through without your having to say anything, justify anything, or explain anything. These are people who, in the words of Brené Brown, have "earned the right to hear your story." Being with safe others strengthens everyone's social vagus; you are helping regulate one another's emotions even as you are supporting one another.

2. If no such group exists in your local area, consider starting one. The eighty-four-year-old mother of a friend of mine moved into a senior facility after she lost her husband of sixty-two years. She started a group there for recent widows in a similar situation. Sharing stories and offering support eased an otherwise painful transition.

   Decades of behavioral science research confirm the efficacy of support groups. However, reaching out to a larger number of people is a larger-scale experience of new conditioning. Apply the little-and-often principle even here. To find a suitable group, ask friends for recommendations. Try the experience once to see if it works for you. You might take a friend with you the first time you meet with a new group. If it does work for you, please continue. If not, try sharing your experiences with just one other person for now.

Reconditioning

Any time you move your body and shift your posture, you shift your physiology. Any time you shift your physiology, you shift the activity and state of your autonomic nervous system. You can experience this shift when you place and hold a pencil between your nose and your upper lip (which requires your facial muscles to frown a little) and then place the pencil between your teeth (which requires your muscles to smile). Notice the felt sense of the forced frown and the forced smile; notice the shift between the two. With practice, you can learn to notice the shift in your inner state from this shift in your physiology. (Thank you, Dan Siegel, for teaching me this practice.) You can use this kind of reconditioning — a juxtaposition of negative and positive physical movement — to return to the physiological base of your resilience. In the process, you may even rewire your experiences of your physical states.

Level 1. Barely a Wobble

The exercises below are simple tools with big effects. Practice them little and often to create the new pathways in your brain.

EXERCISE 2-10: Savor a Moment of Relief

Let your body sigh: exhale deeply, releasing tension from your body. A deep sigh (or several sighs) is the body's natural way to reset the nervous system. You can practice responding to any moment of tension, even a frightening one, with a deliberate sigh to shift your physiology into a relieved and more relaxed state.

The pairing of tense and relaxed states, when the relaxed state is stronger, strengthens the "muscle" of your vagal brake and allows more calm, even in tense moments.

EXERCISE 2-11: Progressive Muscle Relaxation

Because you cannot activate the sympathetic and parasympathetic branches of your nervous system at the same time, your body cannot be simultaneously anxious and relaxed. Progressive muscle relaxation activates the parasympathetic branch and helps you relax your entire body, step by step. These instructions work from foot to head, but you can also practice the sequence from head to foot. The entire exercise takes about seven to ten minutes and can be done lying down or sitting.

1. Begin by curling the toes of your right foot, holding that tensed position for a count of seven. Then relax that tension and uncurl the toes as you count to fifteen. Then curl the arch of your right foot as though pointing your foot, holding that tensed position for a count of seven. Relax and let

go of tensing the foot as you count to fifteen. Then flex your foot, raising the toes back toward your shin, holding that tensed position for a count of seven. Relax and untense the toes as you count to fifteen.

Counting to seven while tensing a part of your body and to fifteen while relaxing it ensures that you are relaxing more than tensing. That's part of the reconditioning. The counting also keeps your brain from wandering into the worry and rumination tendencies of the default network. When you breathe in on the tensing and breathe out on the relaxing you are activating the parasympathetic branch more than the sympathetic, bringing your body to more calm.

2. Continue tensing and relaxing various parts of your body, breathing in and counting to seven as you tense, breathing out and counting to fifteen as you let go and relax. Tense and relax your right calf, your right thigh, your right hip and buttock. Then tense and relax your left toes, your left foot, your left calf, your left thigh, and your left hip and buttock. Tense and relax your torso, your pelvis area, your belly, the muscles around your ribs and your spine. Tense and relax the fingers of each of your hands, the palms of your hands, your wrists, your forearms, your elbows, your upper arms, your shoulders and neck. Then tense and relax all your facial muscles in turn — jaw, throat, lips, cheeks, ears, eyes, nose, forehead.

3. End the session with another deep sigh; rest a full minute in the relaxed state.

Try practicing this tool at night: it's excellent for helping you get to sleep.

EXERCISE 2-12: Yoga — Child's Pose

One of the asanas, or poses, most appreciated by yoga practitioners for rest and restoration is *balasana*, or child's pose. After a good forty-five- to ninety-minute session of leading the body through many different poses and accompanying breath work, the practitioner gets to rest and integrate all of that physical activity into a calm, coherent resting state, nourishing the mind as well as relaxing the body. But you can use this pose to consciously relax your mind and body even if you never go to yoga class.

1.   Stand on a yoga mat, carpet, or other padded surface.
2.   Lower yourself to all fours, with your hands and knees supporting your body in a "table" position.
3.   Sit back. Stretch your derriere back toward your feet. Rest your butt on your heels (or on a cushion between your butt and heels, if that is more comfortable). Your arms will naturally stretch out in front of you. Rest your forehead on the ground (or on a cushion).
4.   Relax and rest in this position for two to three minutes, breathing softly, letting your mind focus on the ease in your body.

You can do child's pose after any physical activity, (or even if it's just been a long day). Experiencing the relaxation of your body helps you anchor in the natural baseline of your resilience.

Level 2. Glitches and Heartaches, Sorrows and Struggles

Your body naturally tenses when you experience distress or disaster, and that tension is part of what derails your sense of well-being. These exercises juxtapose that tension with the powerful relaxation of immersion in nature to shift your psychological state as well as your physical state.

EXERCISE 2-13: Friendly Body Scan

This exercise was originally designed as a core practice of the mindfulness-based stress reduction protocol developed by Jon Kabat-Zinn at the University of Massachusetts, Amherst, medical school to help patients better manage stress and chronic pain. If possible, do this practice outdoors, or with a clear view of a beautiful natural landscape. Research has demonstrated that even ten minutes being in or viewing a natural landscape relaxes the body and improves cognitive functioning.

1. Lie comfortably on your bed or on the floor, or on a blanket, yoga mat, or cushions outdoors. Feel the back of your head, your shoulders, your back, your hips, the backs of your legs, and your heels touching the ground. Let your body relax and sink into the ground supporting it. Breathe naturally, gently, deeply.

2. Begin by bringing your awareness to the sensations in your feet. Say hello to the big toe of your right foot, listening for any aches or pains in the toe, breathing gently into any tension in your toe, compassionately wishing it a sense of comfort and ease. Say hello to all the toes on your right foot, the arch, and the ankle and heel of your right foot, carefully noticing the sensations in each part of the foot, breathing a sense of comfort and ease into every part.

3. Do the same thing slowly for your left foot, for every part of your body up through your torso, hands, and arms, and every part of your face and head; to each ear, each eye, your nose, and all the tender parts of your mouth; to the hair on your scalp and to the phenomenal brain inside your skull that is allowing you to be mindful, compassionate, and steady in this moment.

4. As you scan your body, breathe in a compassionate caring and acceptance to any part of it that needs comfort and ease. You can slow way down, mindfully notice, and breathe compassionate caring to each knuckle if you have arthritis, or to scars from an old football injury. The body scan helps you mindfully and lovingly inhabit all parts of you, to become safely aware of every experience of your body.

5. Practice being especially mindful and compassionate toward sensations in your belly, your genitals, your heart center, and your throat and jaw, areas that may hold unconscious somatic memories of tension, shame, anger, or fear. Breathe compassionate acceptance now to hold any distressing sensations or memories. Say hello! Listen for aches and pains, physical or psychological, and send care and the intention for comfort and ease to any troubled memories held in your body.

6. End this practice by becoming aware of the energy field of your body as a whole — your whole body breathing, in equanimity, alive, relaxed, and resilient.

Through this exercise, you are creating a larger awareness and acceptance of your body. Later, if you begin working with any troubling somatic sensation or memory, the friendly body scan creates a safe setting for any feeling that arises and allows it to dissolve and move through.

EXERCISE 2-14: Forest Bathing

I go to nature to be soothed and healed, and to have my senses put in order.
—John Burroughs, *Studies in Nature and Literature*

As stress levels rise in our modern, urban, overly plugged-in society, people are seeking the calming effects of immersing the body-brain in nature, and science is documenting the validity of that intuitive wisdom.

1. Find a forest or a park with plenty of greenery to walk in for thirty to ninety minutes. (According to Florence Williams, author of *The Nature Fix*, longer periods have been shown to have a more positive effect on the brain.) You can walk by yourself; you can walk with a friend or with a group of people. But silence is also helpful to the brain in recovering its equilibrium: with less stimulation for the brain to process, there is more restfulness and restoration.

2. Begin to walk slowly, bathing in the input from all five senses:

    *   seeing the shape of a leaf, the variety of tree shapes, the clouds in the sky;
    *   smelling pine needles or the fresh air or the damp earth;
    *   hearing bird song or the rustle of the wind, and perhaps the lapping or babbling of water if there is a pond or stream nearby;
    *   touching moss on a twig or lichen on a rock or sand/pebbles beneath your feet;
    *   tasting a berry, if available (and edible).

3. Walk even more slowly, breathe more slowly, perhaps pausing to stand still, noticing the changes of light and shadow, movement and stillness around you. Pause to notice shifts within you, your energy, or your mood.

4. At the end of your walk, take a moment to reflect on your overall experience, especially any shifts in your bodily, felt experience.

This exercise can reliably produce decreases in blood pressure and cortisol levels. Researchers in Finland have found that immersion in nature for five hours per month (that's about ten minutes a day, or thirty minutes two or three times a week) is enough to yield positive long-term effects on physical and mental health.

Level 3. Too Much

It may seem counterintuitive to seek positive experiences in the midst of a tragedy, but juxtaposing positive experiences with negative ones is the basis of reconditioning and of all successful trauma therapy. It is essential to coping, healing, learning, and growing. The point is never to deny, push away, minimize, or forget what's happening. But even small positive, relaxing experiences, especially when things are truly going haywire, help shift the brain out of contraction, reactivity, and rumination into a sense of possibilities and a larger perspective.

EXERCISE 2-15: Skillful Distraction

1. Look for moments of positive experience even in the darkest, grimmest hours, especially body-based experiences, which will help you shift your psychological state by shifting your physiological state. These might include sipping a warm cup of coffee, feeling a cool breeze on your skin, returning the smile of a friend, walking in nature, or playing with a puppy. Let the felt sense of the experience register and linger in your awareness. Savor the refuge. Look for these experiences little and often. Even brief experiences can create an immediate shift.

2. When thoughts, feelings, or sensations begin to seem unworkable, shift the focus of your attention temporarily but completely away from the trouble of the moment. Again, the point is never to escape into denial or dissociation, but to consciously and deliberately switch to another channel of activity. Watch a favorite TV show, cook a good meal, go swimming

or bicycling or dancing, work out at the gym. Let your mind and heart have a respite without any guilt: this is essential self-care.

Consciously diverting your attention offers a temporary respite from difficulties and trials that need to be faced. You still have to reengage with your losses and trials afterward, but hopefully you'll be feeling recharged and able to fight the good fight again.

EXERCISE 2-16: Pendulation — Toggling between Tension and Ease

This exercise involves a deliberate, safe juxtaposition of negative and positive physical states to rewire somatic memories of a negative experience.

1. Identify a place in your body where you might be holding a somatic memory of a trauma, or just something that feels negative or unpleasant. Notice the physical sensations — a churning in the stomach, a tense jaw, a tightening in your back or shoulders.

2. Now locate a place in your body that is not feeling any distress or trauma at all — maybe your elbow or your big toe. Notice the physical sensations of being in the window of tolerance, feeling calm, relaxed, at ease. If you are currently experiencing the body-based sensations of any trauma, this window might be quite small. Focus attention on that calm, untraumatized place in the body, steadily feeling the sensations there of ease and relaxation.

3. Now intentionally toggle your attention back and forth between the pleasant physical sensations of the place in the body that is not traumatized and the unpleasant physical sensations of the place in the body that is holding the network of the traumatic memory. Focus your awareness on each of the two locations for thirty to sixty seconds, focusing on the unpleasant only as long as you can comfortably "hold" the experience without being overwhelmed.

4. Repeat the toggling between the unpleasant and pleasant sensations for

several rounds, gradually increasing the amount of time you spend focusing on the pleasant experience. Notice if the unpleasant sensation shifts or fades.

5. When the intensity of the unpleasant seems to have faded a bit, pause and reflect on the entire experience, noticing any shifts.

When you switch between awareness of these two different body sensations, you are practicing a technique called *pendulation*, so named because it resembles the pendulum of a clock swinging back and forth. Pendulation is an excellent way to safely recondition a trauma memory through body sensations alone. Do this exercise little and often. The effects can be immediate; they can be permanent.

Deconditioning

With deconditioning, you let your brain's attention relax into the spaciousness you naturally feel when your nervous system is in equilibrium. From this state of well-being, your brain can more readily play and generate new insights, new wisdom.

Level 1. Barely a Wobble

Fully 25 percent of your brain's real estate is devoted to visual processing in the occipital lobe. Researchers have observed that when we remember seeing a banana or imagine seeing a banana, the same neurons light up in the visual cortex as when we see a banana in real life. This means that visual memories and imagined scenarios can be as real to the brain as actual observations. You can use this power of visualization and imagination, as well as actual observation, to establish equilibrium in your neural circuitry, creating a safe base to come home to.

EXERCISE 2-17: Belly Botany

Years ago I was hiking in the backcountry of Yosemite National Park when I came upon a park ranger with a small group of hikers sprawled on the ground, face down, each of them completely absorbed in observing one square foot of ground from a height of six inches. The ranger called this a five-minute exercise in "belly botany." You can practice belly botany almost anywhere to create a shift in perspective between the small and the vast, and to sense your place in the overall scheme of things.

1. Find a one-foot-square patch on a favorite beach, in a meadow, in a forest, in your own backyard, or in a city park (just be very careful where you decide to lie down). Lie comfortably on your stomach so that your eyes can focus on your patch from a height of six inches.

2. Come into a sense of presence. Defocus your attention from any concerns for self; concentrate on what's happening in your patch. Notice the dirt or sand, the plants and bugs. Notice any activity, any stillness, any change of the light and shadows. Notice the relationship of things one to another; notice harmonies of colors and shapes; notice any oddities. Notice signs of life and death, aggression and beauty, all on a tiny scale. Observe your patch for two minutes or more.

3. After two minutes, stand up and refocus your attention on the horizon of the larger landscape all around you. Trace the shapes of the trees, hills, and buildings that you see. Observe this larger horizon for two minutes or more. Notice activity and stillness, changes in light and shadow. Notice the relationships of things one to another. Notice the harmonies of colors and shapes; notice any oddities. Notice signs of life and death, aggression and beauty, all on a vast scale.

4. You can toggle back and forth between these micro and macro landscapes as much as you wish. Let your mind play on its own for two minutes or more with the contrast of the small and the vast scale.

5. Return your awareness to the state of your own nervous system, noticing any felt sense of awe, any shifts in your perspective of your place in the world, and any changes in your sense of well-being.

Repeatedly shifting your visual perspective also builds the "muscles" of response flexibility in your brain.

EXERCISE 2-18: Memories of a Soothing Natural Landscape

This exercise can install a resource in your brain that can last a lifetime.

1. Go outside to a place that has been calming and soothing to you, or a place that has been the scene of moments of courage for you — an encouraging place.

2. Spend thirty seconds or more gazing at the landscape and committing the view to memory.

3. While still at the site, practice evoking the image repeatedly in your mind.

4. Practice evoking the image again later, when you are somewhere else. (If you can revisit your soothing or encouraging landscape several times to reinforce the experience, that's excellent.) Practice calling up the image many times until it becomes a reliable resource in your brain.

5. When you sense even the slightest whiff of a wobble, evoke this image in your mind's eye. (You can place your hand on your heart as you do so, if you wish.) Let the felt sense of the soothing or encouraging landscape help you steady your equilibrium now.

    You can, of course, create an entire library of memories of soothing landscapes, just like the memories of soothing and encouraging people, to help you recover your range of resilience even as circumstances change.

EXERCISE 2-19: Creating a Safe Place

This exercise uses visualization and your brain's neuroplasticity to create a reliable refuge and resource for coping.

1. Sit comfortably and quietly. When you are ready, imagine that you are standing in front of a gate. Imagine in rich detail how tall the gate is, how wide, how thick, what it's made of, what color it is. Make this gate as real as you can in your mind's eye.

2. Then imagine yourself opening the gate and walking through. When you are on the other side, visualize what lies ahead: a path, a hallway, a trail, a sidewalk, or a street that will lead you to a place that is very special, just for you. This is your safe place.

3. Begin to walk along the path. As you walk, notice what you are seeing, hearing, smelling, and anything else you are experiencing.

4. After a while, you come to a place that you know is your safe place. It may be a meadow, a cottage, a favorite room in your home, a garden court-yard, or a table in a café with a friend — anywhere that is a special place for you. Allow yourself to walk up to your safe place and enter.

5. Take time to look around: notice all the things that help you feel safe and comfortable here. Relax and enjoy being here; savor the sense of confidence and inner strength your safe place gives you.

6. If you like, find a place to sit down. Add anything you want to this space to help you feel safer and more at ease. Remove anything you don't want. You can change anything you want. Then simply relax, feeling at ease, enjoying your safe place. You might let yourself feel a moment of gratitude that your safe place exists and that you can feel safe here anytime you need to.

7. When it's time to leave, imagine standing up, saying a word of thanks to your safe place for being there, and then leaving it by the way you came in, walking back along the same path or walkway you took to get there, eventually passing through the gate, turning around, and closing it. Your safe place is on the other side, but you know you can return there anytime you need to.

8. Practice evoking this safe place in ordinary, nonstressful moments so that it is available to you when the flak hits the fan. Recognize that you are using your brain's neuroplasticity to create a new and reliable resource for coping.

Your safe place may change over time; that would be natural. By practicing this exercise, your brain is learning how to create refuges and resources for coping any time you need them.

Level 2. Glitches and Heartaches, Sorrows and Struggles

When my eighty-year-old dad had a stroke serious enough to land him in the hospital and a skilled nursing facility after that, my anxiety level went right through the roof, and my higher brain was really not driving the bus very well at all. My meditation teacher, Howie Cohn, advised me to simply stop, lie peacefully in bed, and allow whatever body sensations were present to come into my awareness, but not to feed them with stories and what-ifs. He advised me not even to label them as fear, panic, or terror, but just to let the body sensations be there. These sensations might be uncomfortable, disturbing, or scary, but they weren't going to do anything except be there.

I practiced noticing the agitation in my chest, the contraction around my heart, the tensing of my jaw, without trying to change or fix it. Just being with the sensations created the space for them to loosen up and shift on their own. It wasn't that the shifting solved my dad's health issues: it simply helped me avoid creating my own emergency about his emergency. I could come back to my good-enough regular state and make wise choices from there.

EXERCISE 2-20: Soften, Soothe, Allow

This exercise helps you access a kind of spacious awareness that allows whatever is disturbing your nervous system, and thus your functioning, to arise, be recognized, sit there for a while, and then move through.

1. Let your body find a comfortable position, sitting or lying down. Gently close your eyes and take three relaxing breaths. Being comfortable physically helps you manage difficult sensations or emotions as they arise in your body.

2. Place your hand on your heart for a few moments to remind yourself that you are present and safe in this moment, and that you too are worthy of kindness.

3. In the spaciousness of this kind awareness, identify any situation or circumstances that might be disturbing your equilibrium and well-being right now, and let it come into your awareness.

4. Notice and label whatever emotions are being triggered by those circumstances — perhaps fear, anger, sadness, loneliness, or shame.

5. Then focus your awareness entirely on the sensations in your body being triggered by these circumstances. Let the story go for now. Let the emotions go for now. Just focus on your experience of the sensations. You can name the sensations in a gentle, warmhearted, understanding voice as though you were validating a friend's feelings: "That's tension," "That's constriction," "That's an ache."

6. Expand your awareness to your body as a whole. Scan your body for places where you are most aware of these difficult sensations. Choose a single location where you feel a sensation most strongly, perhaps as a point of muscle tension. Incline your awareness gently toward that spot.

7. Now let the muscles holding the sensation soften, as if you were applying heat to sore muscles. Softening…softening…softening. You are not trying to make the sensations go away, you are just holding them in a tender embrace.

8. If the discomfort of noticing the sensation becomes too great, return your awareness to the sensation of breathing. When you feel calmer, you can try again. If it works better for you, just soften around the edges of the sensations. There's no need to go all the way in.

9. Now offer yourself some soothing words and comfort as you struggle with these sensations. "Ooh, this is hard. This is truly unpleasant. May I be kind to myself in this moment. May I accept this moment, these sensations, exactly as they are. May I hold them in loving awareness." Soothing… soothing…soothing.

10. Then simply *allow* the discomfort of the sensations to be there. Let go of the wish for the discomfort to disappear. Allow the discomfort to come and go as it pleases, like a guest in your home. Allowing…allowing… allowing.

11. *Soften, soothe, allow.* Repeat these words like a mantra, holding the discomfort of the sensations in a larger spacious awareness.

As you allow the sensations in your body to simply be there, and approach your experience of them with a relaxed kindness and curiosity, any feelings of tension or contraction will eventually ease on their own, and move through.

EXERCISE 2-21: Focusing (adapted from an exercise by Ann Weiser Cornell)

Focusing is a process of listening to your body in a gentle, accepting way and hearing the messages your inner self is sending you.

1. Find a place to sit comfortably where you will not be interrupted for about twenty minutes. Take some time to find a comfortable, supported position. Gently close your eyes if you wish.

2. Take the time to become aware of your whole body, here and now. You might notice your hands and what they are touching. Notice your feet and what they are touching. Feel the contact of your body on what you are sitting on. Allow yourself to rest into the support that is there. Become aware of your breathing.

3. Gradually let your awareness travel inward, focusing on the inside of your body, including your throat, your chest, your stomach and belly. Just let the awareness arrive and settle in there.

4. Now quietly ask yourself, "Is there something in my body, in my life, that feels off, or wrong, or uncomfortable?" Wait until you get a feeling response. If the answer is no, and that feels good, just enjoy that feeling.

5. Most likely, if you have a felt sense that something isn't quite right in your life, whatever that might be, a memory or story of it will probably arise in your awareness. Let the story go for now. Just allow the bodily felt sense to become stronger. This often takes a little time. The body is slower than the mind.

6. When you begin to feel something, say, "I am feeling something." And now describe it in physical terms, exactly as you feel it right now. Acknowledge the feeling. Let it know you feel it. You get it. Allow the feeling to be exactly as it is. Stay with it for a while, just feeling it, and being open to anything more that comes into your awareness, like images, thoughts, or more feelings.

7. Notice if something changes. (It may not, and that's okay. After a while, it will be time to stop. Do this slowly, thanking your body. Become aware of the room around you. When you are ready, open your eyes.

8. You may want to write down anything that you learned and any shifts that you noticed.

Your bodily felt sense not only conveys what is important in your life right now; it can also begin to indicate new directions in which you might want your life to be going. New responses create new choices.

Level 3. Too Much

In every other exercise in this chapter, you have chosen to engage in practices designed to shift the state of your nervous system and return you to a more balanced, body-based state of being. That proactivity, even with a good outcome, takes effort. In the exercise below, you give yourself permission to fully disengage, to unplug, to take a break from coping or having to do anything else. It's another kind of wise effort. You use the positive process of the default network to drop into as much ease and relaxation as you can; you use the positive side of the parasympathetic branch of your nervous system, the "rest and digest" branch, to slow down or even stop. By metaphorically hiding under the covers for a while, you take refuge from everything that is bombarding and overwhelming you, to just lie still and do nothing as a way to replenish yourself so that you can go on.

EXERCISE 2-22: Taking Refuge

1. Set aside three or four hours on a day when other people are showing up to deal with whatever is happening and you don't have to.

2. Find a physical place where you feel safe and comfortable and won't be interrupted: your bed, the bath, your living room, going for a drive in the countryside, or sitting on a bench in a park or on a hill overlooking the ocean.

3. Turn off all devices that keep you connected to your world. Leave them somewhere else for now, in another room if you're at home, at home if you are out.

4. Simply let your mind empty itself of all worries, duties, and obligations. That's not simple, but give yourself permission to let go of as much as you can. You can walk somewhere during this break if you wish, but you don't have to. Let your awareness fill with whatever is pleasant and uncomplicated in this moment. You are alive and breathing. The electricity is on (if it is). You already walked the dog, who is now comfortably napping while you are taking this break. Let yourself experience something other than the constant overwhelm you have been experiencing. Let your senses savor any pleasant sensations you notice: the cushiness of the bed or couch you are lying on, the quiet of the house when no one else is at home,

the smell of fresh air. (You may find that you fall asleep during these rare moments of refuge, and sleep may be exactly what you need. Do notice whether you feel restored by the nap or still feel overwhelmed. Taking this kind of refuge is meant to "fill up the well" so that you can return to your circumstances with renewed energy.)

5. When the three or four hours are up, you may be reluctant to leave your refuge and return to whatever you must face. But you will face it from a more rested, balanced state. This exercise of deconditioning may even bring new and potentially useful perspectives on the dilemma.

Take this kind of break as often as you can. It's not a complete break from your troubles, but a little break is far better than none. You will reset your nervous system, recharge your energy and revitalize your coping. You are rewiring your resilience.

This chapter has offered many tools for accessing your somatic intelligence — through breath, touch, movement, social engagement, and visualization — that reliably reduce your brain's reactivity to any level of challenge or stress. With greater resilience, you'll have more choices about how to respond.

That the birds of worry and care fly over your head, this you cannot change; but that they build nests in your hair, this you can prevent.

— CHINESE PROVERB

When you practice these body-based tools, little and often, you strengthen the neural pathways of feeling safe, centered, grounded, and at ease. These feelings prime the neuroplasticity of your brain, making it receptive to further learning and able to try new, more flexible behaviors and take new risks.

This inner equilibrium, achieved by accessing your somatic intelligence, becomes the basis for exercising all of your more complex intelligences — emotional, relational, and reflective.

CHAPTER THREE

Practices of Emotional Intelligence

Self-Compassion, Mindful Empathy, Positivity, Theory of Mind

Just simply living evokes emotions, and we experience one emotion or another every single moment of the day — unless we are clinically depressed and have effectively blocked feeling any emotions. We register delight in watching a sunrise, frustration at getting stalled in gridlock traffic, resentment when a coworker takes credit for an idea we came up with first, terror for the future when a spouse or a child gets a life-threatening diagnosis. Whether we like having these emotions or not, whether we trust them or know what to do with them or not, our feelings constantly filter our perceptions and guide (or sometimes misguide) our responses to all of our experiences. Thus they play an integral role in how well or poorly we bounce back from any adversity. Learning to *manage* our feelings, rather than let them hijack us or shut us down, is the practice of emotional intelligence you will learn throughout this chapter.

It's very normal to be upset with yourself sometimes for even having emotions or not knowing how to manage them very well. Today, however, we can integrate data from twenty-five years of neuroscience research and twenty-five years of behavioral science research to revolutionize our thinking about what feelings are and how we can work with them. Here are some of the latest discoveries most relevant to strengthening our resilience.

1. Emotions are signals to act.

Emotions are sensations flowing up from the body to alert the brain to notice and pay attention to something. Whether it's the first shy glimmer of falling in love or the deep heartache of losing someone you love, the emotion itself is a signal saying, "Pay attention! Something important is happening here!"

Every emotion, even the ones we deem negative, disturbing, or destructive, is also a signal to move. The very word *emotion* is from the Latin *emovere*, meaning to move or to act. We're learning that all emotions have *adaptive action tendencies*. Anger may signal you to protest an injustice, a betrayal, or the sting of a humiliation; it is often the first catalyst that lifts a person out of shame or depression. Sadness signals you to reach out to others for comfort and support, or to comfort and support others. Fear signals you to move away from danger or toxicity. Guilt, when it leads to healthy remorse, may lead you to make repairs and amends. Joy can spark the urge to play, to push the limits and be creative. Interest can spark the urge to explore, take in new information and experiences, and expand the sense of self in the process. Laughter breathes some space into grief. Contentment creates the urge to savor your current life circumstances, even when they're less than ideal. Your emotions are the catalysts of every move you make and thus are intricately woven into the fabric of your resilience.

2. Your pre-frontal cortex manages your emotions.

Through guidance from the prefrontal cortex, your CEO of resilience, you *skillfully read and manage the signals of your emotions* and decide what action to take. Managing the entire range of your emotional landscape, from slight whiffs of feelings to a full-on emotional cascade — keeping you not too revved up, and not shut down — is one of the most important functions of your prefrontal cortex, a task very similar to regulating your nervous system. When the self-regulating capacity of your brain is functioning well, you can inhabit or quickly recover a felt sense of centeredness, ease, and well-being. From there you can perceive clearly what's triggering your emotions and discern what a wise response to those triggers would be, thus accessing a wellspring of resilience.

We know it's not resilient to be hijacked by floods of emotions: you can't think straight, and your responses may be useless or harmful. And it's not resilient to try to repress or split off your emotions. For one thing, it takes an enormous amount of physical and psychological energy to do that, energy you would be better off using to respond to the situation or to other people wisely. Secondly, when you try to repress or split off any specific emotion (anger, grief, and shame are common targets), you can wind up damping down all of your emotions, even the helpful ones. You can go flat in your being and lose the motivation to do anything at all. So the task is to *manage* your emotions rather than be hijacked or shut down by them.

3. Emotional memories from the past can trigger powerful reactivity in the present.

It's often difficult to tell whether our emotional responses are based on present or past events. *Emotional memories*, especially those formed in early childhood, can be deeply buried in implicit (unconscious) memory. When these implicit emotional memories come up into conscious awareness again, they carry no time stamp. There's no sense that they are a memory from the past. These emotions feel completely real, and often you can react as though you have to deal with them right now. (That reactivity itself may be a learned conditioned response buried in implicit or unconscious memory.)

You may give up at the first sign of failure, sometimes rationalizing that you didn't really want that job or friendship anyway. You may find yourself getting tense and irritated, then blowing your top at the slightest additional provocation, even when you really do know better. You may hang back, hesitant to embark on the new adventure you want for yourself, not because you're shy but because deep down you believe you're unworthy and don't want anyone else to find out.

You may not even consciously know *why* you're behaving the way you're behaving. You just are, even if consciously you know that you want to — and know how to — act differently. There can be layers and layers of implicit memories stored in our brains, making us react in the present to some hurt or wrong from the past. The exercises in this chapter show you ways to rewire these implicit memories so they don't trigger less-than-resilient responses.

4. Negativity bias skews our reactions.

In order to survive, as individuals and as a species, we have in our brain a built-in *negativity bias*, evolved over millions of years, that leads us to pay more attention to negative and dangerous experiences than to positive and safe ones. You are more likely to pay attention to and store memories of negative experiences and negative emotions — irritation, loneliness, embarrassment — than positive ones — awe, satisfaction, tranquility. As my friend and colleague Rick Hanson puts it, "We have Velcro for the negative, Teflon for the positive."

This tendency to pay more attention to the negative than the positive, originally hardwired into your brain to protect you from physical danger, now serves to protect you from social and emotional danger: the threat of being disconnected from those you depend on for survival and well-being. This is why you are likely to pay more attention to the one negative comment made by your boss in a meeting or your lover at the dinner table than you will to the nineteen positive comments made to you that same day. The brain is a social brain, and you are a social being. This negativity bias is a permanent predisposition of your brain.

What you can do, however, is learn to work with or work around this feature by managing surges of negative emotions (finding the upside of their dark side) and by intentionally cultivating positive emotions. We practice kindness, gratitude, generosity, delight, and awe not just to feel better but to *do* better. Positive emotions shift the brain out of the contraction and reactivity of the negativity bias into the receptivity and openness that increase your response flexibility. The direct measurable outcome of these practices is resilience.

5. Emotions are contagious.

Through *emotional contagion*, we pick up the emotional signals of other people (and even pets) very easily when we're not defensively guarding against them. You can sense your spouse's or child's frustrations about their day as soon as they walk in the door, without them having to say anything. You can sense the anger or loneliness of someone standing in line near you at the grocery store, even though you're not feeling that way yourself. This is the neurological basis of empathy. Some evolutionary psychologists believe it was the need to empathize and communicate accurately with fellow members of our tribe tens of thousands of years ago that drove the development of language and thus the evolution of the higher (conscious) cortex of the human brain we have today. A well-developed theory of mind, discussed below, helps us manage emotional contagion: it helps us recognize whose emotions are whose and relate to our fellow human beings, intimately or socially, with healthy boundaries.

Four major practices of emotional intelligence allow us to manage our own emotional roller coasters and respond skillfully to other people's emotions too. These practices are the foundation of all the tools presented in this chapter.

Emotional Intelligence Practices

Mindful Self-Compassion

Mindful self-compassion, a practice developed by Chris Germer at Harvard University and Kristin Neff at the University of Texas, Austin, simply brings awareness and acceptance to your emotional experience, no matter how upsetting or crazy-making it is. At an even deeper level in your brain, it brings awareness and acceptance of yourself as the *experiencer* of the experience.

It's hard being a human being. Life tosses you about, sometimes even throwing you right out of your boat. And you are inevitably going to lose your emotional equilibrium, your inner sense of well-being, from time to time, no question. Practices of mindful self-compassion help you understand that this is true for everybody. You are not the only one. You are not alone. Mindful self-compassion is a very important and sometimes essential practice. It supports mindful empathy, which is another practice that brings you back into an emotional equilibrium.

Mindful Empathy

Mindful empathy is actually a sequence of three skills — attending, attuning, and making sense — that allows emotions (your own or another person's) to arise in your conscious awareness, alert your brain to pay attention, deliver their important message, and then subside, leaving your higher brain free to listen to the message and decide what wise action to take in response. Your emotions don't get to drive the bus, but they play an important role in deciding where the bus is going to go.

Positivity

Deliberately cultivating practices of compassion, gratitude, trust, and other positive, prosocial emotions can reverse the constricting effects of negative emotions like envy, resentment, regret, and hostility on your nervous system and your behaviors.

These practices refocus your attention away from stress and worry. They can reverse the impact of anxiety, depression, learned helplessness, and loneliness and help you feel more enthused, energetic, and alive. Experiencing more positive emotions increases your curiosity and engagement with circumstances and supports more optimistic, creative coping. These emotions strengthen the capacity to approach, rather than avoid, challenges and catastrophes. They can even help resolve traumatic memories.

Focusing on positive and prosocial emotions is not meant to bypass or suppress dark, difficult, afflictive emotions. Your experiences of angst, pain, and despair are very real. By persevering in your practices of mindful empathy, you learn to acknowledge, hold, and process those emotions. You deliberately cultivate positive, prosocial emotions as a way to broaden your habitual modes of thinking or acting, and to build enduring, resilient resources for coping. These include increasing social bonds and social support and deepening insights that help place events in a broader context. You strengthen your capacity to cope, find a way through, and come out the other side.

Theory of Mind

Theory of mind simply means an awareness that I am me, and you are you, and that I may be having an emotional experience (or a thought, belief, or plan) that you are not experiencing. We are two different people with two different experiences, and that's okay.

As with all capacities of your brain, you develop the capacity for theory of mind by experiencing it with other people. You come to recognize that at any given moment, you may be having an emotional experience that is different from the emotional experience another person is having, and that's okay. And you get to experience that the other person also recognizes that your experience is different from theirs, and that that's okay with them. Experiencing theory of mind through others helps develop theory of mind in your own brain.

According to developmental psychologists, most children develop the capacity for theory of mind by the age of four. Depending on your experience with your earliest caregivers and role models, maybe you did, and maybe you didn't. But it's one of the essential skills of emotional intelligence. You need to be able to sense and accept what you are feeling: that's mindful self-compassion. You need to be able to sense and accept what other people are feeling while they are feeling it: that's mindful empathy. And you need to be able to differentiate what they are feeling from what you are feeling: that's theory of mind.

Your brain, specifically your prefrontal cortex, develops the neurological capacities needed to attend, attune, make sense of, and respond wisely to your emotions and maintain your emotional equilibrium through the experience of having those emotions attended to and mirrored by people around you. In more technical terms, this process involves initial mirroring and validation of your emotional experience and dyadic regulation of your emotional equilibrium. That's the neurobiology of how your brain develops these basic life skills. If your caregivers were not able to provide these experiences, you may not have learned to regulate your own emotions and recover your own emotional well-being when you were young. If that's the case, this chapter will show you how you can develop these capacities and maintain that equilibrium now.

New Conditioning

These tools strengthen the response flexibility you need to manage your own emotions and the impact of other people's emotions on you. Regular practice in using these tools will create the neural circuitry in your brain that will almost miraculously shift the functioning of your brain from negativity to positivity. That includes the full range of your emotions needing your attention.

Level 1. Barely a Wobble

These exercises strengthen your ability to simply be with your emotional experiences and those of others, deepening a sense of trust and confidence that you *can* do this.

EXERCISE 3-1: Attending

This exercise focuses on paying attention to the bodily, felt sense of an emotion. You are not thinking about it but simply being with it. The goal is to develop awareness of what you are experiencing while you are experiencing it, allowing, acknowledging, and accepting that this is what's happening.

1. Sit quietly in a place where you won't be interrupted for at least five minutes. Come into a sense of presence, knowing you are here, in your body, in your mind, in this moment, in this place.

2. Notice whatever comes to the forefront of your conscious awareness for the next five minutes — and things spontaneously will. Whatever body sensation, feeling, or thought comes up, simply notice it, acknowledge that it has shown up on your radar, allow it to be there, and accept that it is there. At this point you're not wondering about it or trying to figure it out, just attending to it enough to register the experience in your awareness.

    This exercise can deepen your capacity to become present to and consciously aware of your own experience without needing to leave or push away that experience to maintain your emotional equilibrium.

    To be present is far from trivial. It may be the hardest work in the world. And forget about the "may be." It is the hardest work in the world — at least to sustain presence. And the most important. When you do drop into presence, you know it instantly, feel at home instantly. And being home, you can let loose, let go, rest in your being, rest in awareness, in presence itself, in your own good company.

    — Jon Kabat-Zinn

3. At this stage in the exercise, you have come to a choice point.

    a. You can let go of attending to the experience of the moment and to any subsequent experience that arises in your awareness, and refocus your attention on the quiet, background, spacious awareness that allows you to be aware — the "home ground" of your well-being; or

b. You can attune to the felt sense of the experience to decipher its message.

EXERCISE 3-2: Attuning

This exercise entails discerning the particular flavor of an emotion. Attuning allows you to label complex, subtly nuanced emotions, such as those of feeling lonely or suspicious. This labeling is part of the capacity of emotional literacy, your capacity to read your emotional experience, and attune to and read the emotional experience of others as well.

Two meditation teachers of mine have shared their stories about attuning to the felt sense. Guy Armstrong tells of a time when he was having great difficulty settling into a long, silent meditation retreat. Feeling restless and agitated, he was finally able to notice and name what he was experiencing: "Oh, despair!" Despair is not a pleasant emotion to feel, but as soon as Guy could name it, he was no longer embedded in it: he could observe it and begin to let it be, let it unfold, and then let it go. When you notice and name the experience of the moment, you engage your prefrontal cortex. Noticing and naming allowed Guy to reflect and come to a resolution without feeling caught or trapped.

In a different vein, Anna Douglas tells of a time she was experiencing something she couldn't quite put her finger on. Finally she realized, "Oh! This is calm!" It's important to be able to recognize and attune to the ease of well-being in yourself, too.

Often you can sense a disturbance in the force field — a gut reaction to something, a sudden shift in the balance of your nervous system, before you have any clear idea of what you're experiencing or what to call it. You simply notice that there is something to notice.

1. When you notice a disturbance, focus on and drop into the felt sense of the experience in your body. Begin to label the felt sense — shaky, tight,

churning, bubbling, contracting, expanding. Try not to create a story about it. Just feel it and name it. From previous experience, you might already have a word for this particular feeling.

2. Sometimes it's a challenge to put your finger on the exact nuance or flavor of the message. Try to find a "good enough" label for your emotions for now: maybe "This is contentment," "This is aggravation," or "This is despair."

Whatever feeling you are attuning to, and however you choose to label it, this feeling is what it is. All you have to know at this point is that you *can* know what it is and label it in a way that is useful to you. (If you can name it, you can tame it.) You can trust in your ability to know and label a feeling even if you change your mind later about what it is.

Once you can name an emotion, you are on the way to making sense of it. All emotions are understandable if we put in the time and the wise effort to discern them: "Given what is happening, and given my previous conditioning, it makes perfect sense that I would feel the way I do." For example, on your first morning at a new job, depending on your conditioning, you may feel vulnerable, or you may feel exuberant. But either way, what you feel makes sense. All emotions — the ones you dislike and dread as well as the ones you welcome and enjoy — can guide your behaviors in resilient ways, self-protecting or self-enhancing. You don't have to be afraid of your emotions, be stuck in them, or be swept away by them. You do have to take responsibility for how you experience and express them.

EXERCISE 3-3: Making Sense

1. Anchor in your own emotional equilibrium as much as possible, and sit quietly with whatever emotion you have been attending and attuning to.

2. Let yourself acknowledge that whatever emotion you are sitting with, and whatever further emotions you might be feeling about feeling this emotion, given the circumstances and your previous conditioning around coping resiliently (or not), of course you are feeling exactly what you are feeling; it makes perfect sense.

3. Begin to engage your prefrontal cortex, the meaning-making structure of your brain. This doesn't involve thinking per se, just opening your mind to any learning from previous experience that would make sense of your current experience. When have you experienced anything like this before? What did it mean then? How did you respond then? Did that response work? Have you ever misjudged or misinterpreted this feeling? Have you made any mistakes because of how you responded before?

4. This form of inquiry may trigger deeper feelings that are more difficult to manage. The tools of mindful self-compassion offered in later exercises will help you manage them and return to your emotional equilibrium.

5. You may want to ask friends, colleagues, mentors, teachers, therapists, or coaches to assist you with this inquiry. Learning from other people's experiences and mistakes is a valid form of learning and can be helpful in returning you to your own emotional equilibrium.

    Making sense of your experience can be an exciting process and a high art. As you increase your capacities to make sense of what's going on and why you are responding as you are, you become more competent at choosing the wisest possible response.

The point of these exercises is not just to get you using your higher brain to manage your emotions so that they don't get in the way of your decision-making. You're learning to manage them so they can be included and valued in your decision-making. Simply listen, get the gist, and then use what you've learned from the emotions to take wise action.

EXERCISE 3-4: Taking Action

1. Begin this exercise in a state of emotional equilibrium if you can, with your prefrontal cortex already online, calmly minding the store.

2. Choose one small moment of an emotion you want to work with, positive or negative. Choose something familiar in your daily life: the ripple of

annoyance at dishes left overnight in the sink or tools left out in the rain, again; the "Oh no!" you feel when the tax document you're working on disappears into cyberspace; the mounting concern when your teenager hasn't come home and hasn't called. For this exercise, avoid choosing the most overwhelming negative emotion you feel. Give your brain a chance to succeed and strengthen its response flexibility first.

3. Feel the emotion wherever you feel it in your body. Notice whatever thoughts and other emotions are triggered when you sense this emotion. Notice any possibilities that arise for acting in some way that will relieve this emotion (if negative) or amplify the emotion (if positive).

4. Take some time to let your mind brainstorm five other options for taking action. Let your mind play with those possibilities for a moment.

5. Imagine the possible consequences of any of these possibilities. Notice whether you are especially drawn to or repulsed by any of them.

6. You can either end the exercise now, or you can choose to follow one of the possible courses of action you've come up with. If you choose to act, you can notice not just what happens but whether the emotion was useful to you in asking for your attention and guiding your choices.

You can apply the principle of little and often to developing your emotional intelligence. Slow down. Take the time to anchor in your emotional equilibrium. Work on one emotion at a time, or just one little aspect of a single emotion. Practice attending, attuning, and making sense again and again until these skills become the new habits of perceiving and responding to your emotional landscape. Then you can choose your response. You're creating the space to respond to challenges and crises in a new and more resilient way.

Ninety-three percent of all emotional communication happens through facial expressions, body language, tone, melody, and rhythm of the voice, and only 7 percent through words. Do you need words to formulate and express your understanding of your emotions and other people's? Absolutely. But emotional intelligence emerges from the bottom up, as emotions do, and emotional literacy is based on attuning to and nonverbally reading the felt sense of your experience and that of others.

EXERCISE 3-5: Attuning to and Conveying Basic Emotions

You strengthen the capacity of the prefrontal cortex to attune to and recognize the flavors of the emotions you experience through practice, like doing reps at the gym. This exercise involves communicating with a partner without using words to strengthen the capacities of your prefrontal cortex to perceive and interpret nonverbal expressions. Practicing with five of the most basic emotions — anger, fear, sadness, joy, and disgust — builds your capacities for attunement, which can then be refined later to read more nuanced emotions such as disappointment, jealousy, guilt, or awe and wonder.

1. Recruit a partner to participate in this exercise with you. Allow thirty minutes for you each to have a turn.

2. Decide the order in which you will evoke these five emotions — anger, fear, sadness, joy, and disgust — without telling your partner. Recalling previous experiences of each emotion is a quick and easy way to experience the emotion again internally.

3. Tune in to your own experience of the first emotion you've chosen to work with, and then let your body wordlessly display the chosen emotion for ten seconds. Maintain eye contact with your partner. You can use gestures, facial expressions, and sounds — just not words. You may find yourself exaggerating your expressions at first; that's okay. Your partner notes which emotion he is reading from your expression but doesn't disclose it yet. Notice what happens inside of you — self-attunement — as you communicate your own feelings to someone else. Notice whether the felt sense of the emotion increases, decreases, or changes into something else.

4. Without discussion yet, turn your attention inward again. Release the emotion you've been expressing with a few gentle, deep breaths into your heart center. Evoke the next emotion on your list, and display it to your partner for ten seconds. Again, your partner notes the emotion, but the two of you don't discuss anything.

5. Still without any discussion, refocus your attention inward, evoke the next emotion on your list, and display the feeling to your partner. Repeat the process for each emotion.

6. Before discussing anything yet, switch roles, so that your partner now displays five emotions in sequence. As you observe them, notice what signals you pay attention to — facial expressions, body language, the tone or rhythm of sounds — to distinguish one emotion from another. And notice what happens inside you as you perceive your partner's feelings.

7. When your partner has finished, you each share your best guesses at the emotions the other person was trying to convey, and explain how you each identified each emotion.

If all the guesses were accurate, congratulations to both of you! If there were discrepancies, take the opportunity to discuss what you perceived in each other's expression of emotion that led you to a different interpretation. This exercise strengthens the prefrontal cortex's capacities for expressing and attuning to emotions, which are the foundation of building more competence in communicating what you need, developing the skills you need to get those needs met, and empathizing with others as they express their own needs.

EXERCISE 3-6: Feeling Empathy for Fellow Human Beings

We often have reactions or judgments about the ways others choose to behave. This exercise cultivates your capacity to empathize with the emotional experience of other people by attuning to and empathizing with the felt sense of your own experiences in similar situations.

1. Take a moment to identify a behavior you've observed in someone that you don't like very much, at least in the moment. Maybe the driver in the lane next to you on the freeway is yelling at another driver who just cut her off. Your daughter puts off paying the credit card bill until she's racking up late fees and jeopardizing her credit rating. Your best friend arrives fifteen minutes late to pick up his son from soccer practice and picks a fight with the coach to cover his chagrin.

2. Notice your own internal reaction to this behavior, including any opinions or spontaneous judgments you may have about this behavior. Set those reactions aside for the moment.

3. Begin to be curious — you're activating your prefrontal cortex here — about what might be going on in that other person to cause them to act this way. Could they be already stressed, swamped with too many things to attend to, or acting out of inexperience, lack of skill, or low self-esteem?

4. Remember a time when you have acted similarly. I might yell at a driver who cuts me off on the freeway, too. Then I remember times when I've inadvertently done the same thing. I can understand and forgive the other driver if I put myself in their place and can understand and forgive myself.

5. Remember that any behavior you're witnessing now — in yourself or others — is rooted in learned conditioned responses that originally served some survival purpose. Knowing this, you can bring some understanding, compassion, and forgiveness to the other person now.

6. If possible, communicate your empathic understanding of the other person's experience to them — maybe not the driver on the freeway, but to your daughter or your friend — to make sure that your understanding is accurate and that the care offered in the empathy "lands" or registers with the other person. The other person's perception of this empathy can help them rewire their encoded patterns of themselves and become receptive to changing their behavior. Your own practice of empathy can help strengthen your prefrontal cortex so that you can accomplish further rewiring, too.

Empathy is one of the key skills in emotional intelligence, and emotional intelligence is more predictive of your success in life than IQ. As you become more competent in connecting to other people through understanding their struggles, you build the relational resources you can call on to deal more resiliently with your own.

Level 2. Glitches and Heartaches, Sorrows and Struggles

When you intentionally and continually evoke experiences of positive and pro-social emotions, you strengthen the parts of your brain that allow you to respond to life events with an open heart rather than a contracted one, with resilience and care rather than fear, with willingness and acceptance rather than withdrawal and shutting down. Resilience and well-being are direct, measurable outcomes.

EXERCISE 3-7: Sharing Kindness

Kindness is more important than wisdom, and the recognition of that is the beginning of wisdom.

— Theodore Rubin

Doing a kindness produces the single most reliable momentary increase in well-being of any exercise we have tested.

— Martin Seligman

1. Invite a friend, an acquaintance, or a friendly coworker to do this exercise with you. Take two minutes each to share a moment of kindness that you have experienced — today, earlier in the week, earlier this year, even back in the third grade. It might be a moment when someone held open the door for you, picked up something you had dropped, smiled as you walked down the hallway, or sent a supportive email when you were going through a hard time — something that registered in your consciousness as support from the universe and gave you just a little lift or steadiness.

2. Then, for two minutes each, describe what it's like for you to be sharing your story with your partner now, receiving kind attention, resonance, and support — even, or maybe especially, nonverbally. And describe what it's like for you to hear your partner's story, empathizing with the feelings and understanding the meaning of it for them.

3. Then pause silently to notice any effects in your body-mind from doing the exercise, such as a sense of buoyancy, comfort, or relaxation.

4. You can do this exercise with variations — recalling moments of courage, patience, or serenity — with great benefit to your brain and to your capacities for resilience. Each time you explore a quality necessary for resilience, you are inscribing that quality more deeply in your neural circuitry.

Sharing positive emotional experiences with others, in a setting of friendliness and mutual care and concern, evokes the neural synchrony Barbara Fredrickson describes in *Love 2.0*. The shared resonance brings warmheartedness and delight to everyone present. This practice is very self-reinforcing: you learn firsthand how cultivating positive emotions shifts the functioning of the brain.

EXERCISE 3-8: Practicing Gratitude for the Web of Life

At times our own light goes out and is rekindled by the spark from another person. Each of us has cause to think with deep gratitude of those who have lighted the flame within us.

— attributed to Albert Schweitzer

Cultivating the experience of gratitude — thankfulness for any blessings and good fortune in your life — is one of the easiest ways to bring about the shift in your brain functioning that comes from practicing positive and prosocial emotions. In this exercise, you extend your gratitude beyond the most immediate blessings to the larger web of life — people who keep your life going even though you may never have met them.

1. Take five to ten minutes to pause from the ongoing demands of your life to recall people who have helped you keep going: someone who helped you find your reading glasses when you were distracted by rushing on to the next thing; a friend who sent a supportive email when your nephew wrecked your car (though thankfully not himself); the grocery clerk who promptly swept up the jelly jars your exuberant three-year-old knocked off the shelf; a coworker who took over your duties for the day when a nasty flu simply would not let you get out of bed.

2. Take a moment to focus on any felt sense of thankfulness these recollections evoke. As you let the sensations resonate, notice where in your body you feel any sense of gratitude.

3. Expand the circle of your awareness to gratitude for the people you have not yet met who also help keep your life going. Think of the people who are staffing your local hospital right now, ready to help if you slip on a rug on the way to the bathroom, break a bone, and have to be rushed to the emergency room. You might include people staffing airports, pharmacies, fire stations, and gas stations, and those who test water quality at the municipal reservoir so that when you turn on the kitchen faucet you have safe water to drink. (For years my brother Barry was on call in his hometown to drive the snowplow at 3 AM so that folks could get to work in the morning. I know how deeply he appreciated it when people acknowledged that

service.) Practice gratitude for the people growing your food and recycling your garbage, for the entire web of life that supports you.

4. Reflect on this experience of practicing gratitude and empathy for helpful people in your life and for the larger web of life. Sense the feelings your practice evokes. Notice any changes in your own emotions or thoughts about yourself as you focus on cultivating gratitude.

5. If you wish, set the intention to do a three-minute gratitude practice every day for thirty days, focusing your attention on the people, circumstances, and resources that sustain your well-being every day.

Over time, this practice will cause you to experience not only more gratitude but more of other positive emotions as well — joy, tranquility, contentment — enhancing your well-being overall.

EXERCISE 3-9: Awe Practice

Awe is the larger-than-life feeling we experience in the presence of something vast and extraordinary — the glory of a panoramic sunset, a star-studded night sky, a total solar eclipse, or the aurora borealis. It can also be inspired by the novelty, complexity, and harmony of a great creative work, such as the magnificence of the Taj Mahal, and by small things, such as the miraculous blooming of a flower.

> *The most beautiful thing we can experience is the mysterious. It is the source of all true art and science. He to whom the emotion is a stranger, who can no longer pause to wonder and stand wrapped in awe, is as good as dead — his eyes are closed.*
>
> — Albert Einstein

Awe is not a luxury. Experiencing awe promotes resilience by challenging our usual ways of seeing the world and our place in it. Awe promotes curiosity and exploration while simultaneously soothing the nervous system. It puts our day-to-day concerns into perspective and broadens our horizons; we feel more interconnected with others.

To see a World in a Grain of Sand,
And a Heaven in a Wildflower;
Hold Infinity in the palm of your hand,
And Eternity in an hour.

— William Blake, "Auguries of Innocence"

1. Immerse yourself in nature — a park, a garden, a forest — and notice everything as if seeing it for the first time. Bring a wide-eyed curiosity to every tree and blade of grass, every bend in the road, every cloud in the sky.

2. Visit a good museum or art gallery, or attend a top-notch concert or play. Let the expressions of others who have experienced awe transmit that experience to you. Notice shifts in your own perspective and sense of possibilities.

3. Review your own past experiences of awe: photographs from hiking in a national park or touring one of the great cities of the world, or the birth of your first child. This review can be especially helpful when the daily grind is getting you down: it reminds you that the world is still a magical place, full of mystery and potential.

4. Find an online video of an inspiring speech or performance or describing a scientific discovery. Watch it with an attitude of openness and readiness to be inspired and uplifted, and to notice and savor the moments of awe when they happen.

Opportunities to experience awe are practically infinite. Experiencing awe creates a new habit to pay attention, shift the functioning of your brain, and nourish your spirit.

EXERCISE 3-10: Taking In the Good

1. Pause for a moment, and notice (attend to) any experiences of kindness, gratitude, or awe that you have experienced today or remember from the past. Maybe your neighbor transported you to and from work for three

days while your car was in the shop, or you saw a blue heron rise up from a pond at dusk.

2. Attune to the felt sense of the goodness of this moment — a warmth in your body, a lightness in your heart, a little recognition of "Wow, this is terrific!"

3. Focus your awareness on this felt sense of goodness for ten to thirty seconds. Savor it slowly, allowing your brain the time it needs to really register the experience and store it in long-term memory.

4. Set the intention to evoke this memory five more times today. This repeats the neural firing in your brain, recording the memory so you can recollect it later, making it a resource for your own sense of emotional well-being, and thus strengthening the inner secure base of resilience.

As you experience and reexperience the moment, register that not only are you doing this, you are learning *how* to do this. You are becoming competent at creating new neural circuitry for resilience.

Level 3. Too Much

Too many crises or catastrophes, all at once or too close together, can trigger a cascade of overwhelming emotions, the experience of "too much." The deepest existential fears for your future take up permanent residence. Overwhelming emotions can become self-reinforcing, triggering a relentless cycle of panic, rage, guilt, and shame. Sometimes we react by shutting down all feelings and retreating into numbness and depression. When emotions run amok or get buried six feet under, we're vulnerable to experiencing trauma, not just from the external events but from the derailing of our emotional resilience as well.

Compassion — giving and receiving care and concern in times of pain and suffering — is a balm to a distressed heart. Being listened to compassionately activates the social engagement system in the brain and soothes the nervous system. The reassurance of being part of the human community restores a sense of emotional equilibrium. Even if the external problem or trauma is not resolved, compassion helps us feel we deserve to have it solved.

EXERCISE 3-11: Meeting Your Compassionate Friend

This guided visualization creates a feeling of being listened to, heard, and cared about, which can become a resource for the mind and heart. Whatever upset or distress we are experiencing, we can also experience the tenderness of care.

1. Allow yourself to sit or lie down comfortably, coming into a sense of presence — being aware of being in your own body, in this moment, focusing your awareness on the gentle rhythm of your breathing, coming into a sense of relaxation and peacefulness. Then, when you're ready, imagine that you are in your own safe place, a comfortable place where you can feel protected, at ease, and content. This may be a room in your own home, a favorite bench in a park or on a hill overlooking the beach, or in a café with a friend. Let yourself settle into the security and comfort of being in your safe place.

2. Then, let yourself know that you are going to receive a visitor, someone older, wiser, and stronger, someone who knows you well and cares about you a great deal. This figure may be someone you already know; it may be someone completely imaginary. It could be simply a sense of warm, loving presence. However this works for you, this figure wants you to be happy, and they want to visit with you for a little while.

3. As you imagine this compassionate friend coming to visit you in your safe place, imagine in detail what they look like, how they're dressed, and how they move. Imagine what it feels like for you to be in their presence, in their energy field.

4. Imagine how you meet and greet this figure: do you stand up and shake hands, do you hug, do you bow?

5. Then imagine how you will have a conversation with this compassionate friend: sitting face to face, sitting side by side, going for a walk.

6. Begin to share with this compassionate friend some current worry, some upset, or some distress. Imagine what it feels like to share this concern with your compassionate friend. Does your energy shift or change in any way as you begin to share it ?

7. Imagine your friend listening receptively, openly, understandingly. Imagine

how you feel being listened to and understood and accepted by this compassionate friend.

8. Imagine any words of acceptance or encouragement or support your compassionate friend might have to offer. If you could hear whatever you need to hear right now, what would those words be? As you imagine listening, sense what you feel as you hear these words.

9. When the conversation is complete and it's time for your friend to depart, imagine how you say good-bye, knowing that you can visit with this compassionate friend again any time you wish to.

10. When you are in your safe place by yourself again, take a moment to pause, notice, and reflect on your experience. Reflect on any shifts in your experience of yourself or the upset you were working with, knowing that you have tapped into your own deep, intuitive wisdom.

As you evoke your compassionate friend, you are activating your own caregiving system, which calms your nervous system and restores your physiological and emotional equilibrium. As evoking your compassionate friend becomes a reliable habit in your brain, you deepen your sense that you are not alone, which can be very nurturing to your resilience.

EXERCISE 3-12: Priming the Flow of Compassion

Researchers have found it's far and away easier for people to feel compassion for other people than for themselves. This exercise primes the flow of compassion by extending it to others first, then lets compassion for ourselves slip in almost through the back door.

1. Bring to mind a moment when it was relatively easy for you to feel caring, compassion, concern for someone else's heartache or sorrow. Your neighbor was struggling to carry heavy bags of groceries up the driveway with a recently broken ankle. Your cousin lost his luggage before he arrived at your house for a weekend visit. Your eight-year-old came home in tears because he was late for the class picnic, and the school bus took

off without him. Your cat sprained his hip jumping down from too high a kitchen counter and limped around the house for three days.

2.   Imagine this person or pet sitting with you. You might imagine a child or pet sitting in your lap. Notice any warmth, concern, and goodwill arising in your own heart as you sit with them. Feel the empathy, compassion, and love flowing from your body, your heart to theirs.

3.   When these feelings are steady enough, shift gears a bit and remember a moment when you were facing pain or trouble of your own. However big or small it was, let yourself feel that pain for a moment.

4.   Then return to the feelings of warmth, concern, and goodwill you felt for the other person or pet. Without changing anything, simply redirect this flow of empathy, compassion, and love for them toward yourself. Accept your own care and concern, your own empathy and compassion for your own pain, for whatever has happened or whatever you've done or failed to do, at any age or level of your psyche that needs to receive it. You may express this feeling toward yourself in words: "May this suffering pass.... May things resolve for me.... May I feel less upset over time."

5.   Let yourself take in the feeling of being understood and nurtured. Let the self-compassion soak in and settle in your body. Let your heart relax into a more peaceful sense of understanding, compassion, and forgiveness. Let it rewire your sense of yourself in this very moment.

6.   Reflect on your experience of this exercise. Notice any sense of openness or a shift in your approach to your own experiences now. Notice whether this stance opens up possibilities for change and resolution of these difficulties.

As you offer yourself genuine compassion for whatever pain you are experiencing, you shift the functioning of your brain toward more openness and engagement with the world. As you cultivate a more open "approach" stance toward experience, you are creating more response flexibility in your brain, thus creating the conditions for more resilience.

Reconditioning

You've learned that all emotions are cues to pay attention because something important is happening. Two of the most difficult emotions to tolerate while waiting for the message are anxiety and shame. The exercises below offer tools for rewiring anxiety into action, for rewiring shame into compassion and self-acceptance, and, finally, for rewiring any negative emotion into its opposite, including the emotional shutdown of depression and despair.

If you discover [within yourself] a very black hole, a thick shadow, be sure there is somewhere in you a great light. It is up to you to know how to use the one to realize the other.

— SRI AURIBINDO

Level 1. Barely a Wobble

Whenever you're about to venture into something new — moving across the country, getting married again, starting a new job, finally fixing the leaky shower head — you may feel a hesitancy, a withdrawing — a somatic feeling of "Uh-oh! Strange territory! Don't know if I should be doing this!" — even though, consciously, you might very well want to forge ahead. Your resilience goes on hold.

You can interpret this feeling of unease as anxiety, which can automatically lead to refusing or deferring new challenges. It feels like a risk to try something new. You can choose to "feel the fear and do it anyway," as Susan Jeffers suggests. You can reinterpret the signal anxiety as a sign that you're about to grow, as the meditation teacher Jack Kornfield suggests. Or you can rewire anxiety into action, as was the practice of Eleanor Roosevelt, doing "one thing every day which scares you."

You gain strength, courage and confidence by every experience in which you really stop to look fear in the face. You must do the thing which you think you cannot do.

— ELEANOR ROOSEVELT

Practicing dealing with anxiety as a cue to act retrains your brain to respond differently to the signal and dramatically strengthens your response flexibility and resilience. And when you call to mind the moments when you *did* manage to rewire your anxiety, you already have a head start on dealing with the next scary thing.

EXERCISE 3-13: Doing One Scary Thing a Day

1. Start small. Start by simply identifying moments of signal anxiety as you experience them throughout the day. Maybe your normal route to work is

blocked by an accident, so if you want to get to work on time you'll have to find another way. A friend suggests trying a new ethnic restaurant or seeing an avant-garde play. You discover that doing your taxes is suddenly more appealing than meeting a potential romantic partner.

2. Choose one moment of signal anxiety as a cue to respond with action rather than stopping or pulling back. Choose to act in a way that actually involves turning your hesitancy into acting on that signal, not just avoiding what's scary by doing something else less scary but unrelated. (Go on the date rather than doing your taxes.)

3. Notice any shift in your emotions from doing the scary activity. Notice any shift in your view of yourself for having found the courage to act.

4. Do one scary thing every day for a week. Little is fine; often is necessary for the brain to rewire its old responses and for the new behavior to take hold. Notice whether you experience new feelings about the activity or about yourself and whether those feelings take hold.

By repeatedly practicing doing small scary things, you're laying the groundwork for the brain to choose to respond with action when bigger scary things come along. By continuing the practice, you can gradually take on the truly difficult things: having that serious conversation with your spouse or asking your boss for a raise.

EXERCISE 3-14: Sure I Can!

Very often you can find the courage to do something scary because you know you've succeeded at doing it before. That feeling of confidence is a fine resource for your resilience. Researchers have found that you can also generate a sense of self-confidence from having done *anything* well before. The present and past accomplishments don't have to be remotely similar. It's the feeling of confidence and trust that carries forward into the current moment. Further, the successful accomplishment doesn't have to be big or dramatic to create confidence for facing a new challenge. Little and often truly works well here.

1. Identify areas of your life where you would like to have more of a felt sense of "Sure I can!" Maybe you're contemplating returning to school after thirty years in the workforce, buying into a business franchise, or facing the empty nest when your youngest child moves away.

2. Identify three moments in your life where you actually believed and felt "I can!" — a visceral sense of confidence arising from a previous moment of competence. Reflect not so much on what you did to cope, because that will change with circumstances, as on how you felt when you realized that you had done it. Remember, we're talking moments here, not major events: opening a stuck jar lid for your mom, intuiting where to find the train station in a strange city, knowing just what to say when your child experienced a disappointment.

3. For now, don't worry at all about the size of the success; focus on the genuine sense of mastery. How does that sense of mastery feel in your body now as you remember it? Take in the good of "I did; I can" as a body-based resource.

4. Experiment with bringing that visceral sense of "I did; I can" into the present moment and applying it to the challenges for which you are seeking confidence now.

You're choosing to bring a sense of trust and mastery forward into a realm where you want to feel it now. Even the slightest success at doing this reconditions your brain for greater resilience.

Level 2. Glitches and Heartaches, Sorrows and Struggles

Shame is one of the most powerful emotional threats to your resilience and well-being. Practices of mindfulness and compassion, two of the most powerful agents of brain change, are among the most effective tools you can use to shift and heal from shame.

Mindfulness brings awareness and acceptance to whatever is happening right now that you wish with all your heart wasn't happening. Self-compassion brings care and concern for yourself as the one experiencing it. When that experience is a shaming one, you may wish you weren't reacting the way you are, even while you can't seem to change your reaction. The acceptance and concern of mindful self-compassion help you hold and shift the entire experience of shame to something more tolerable, more workable.

EXERCISE 3-15: Giving Yourself a Self-Compassion Break

At times when any emotional upset or distress is still reasonably manageable, taking a self-compassion break helps create and strengthen the neural circuits that can steady you when things are really tough.

1. Any moment you notice (by attending and attuning) a surge of a difficult emotion — boredom, contempt, or remorse — pause and put your hand on your heart. This gesture activates the release of oxytocin, the hormone of safety and trust.

2. Empathize with your experience. Say to yourself, "This is upsetting," "This is hard," "This is scary," "This is painful," or "Ouch! This hurts," to acknowledge and care about yourself as someone experiencing distress.

3. Repeat these phrases to yourself, or substitute words that work better for you:

    May I be kind to myself in this moment.
    May I accept this moment exactly as it is.
    May I accept myself exactly as I am in this moment.
    May I give myself all the compassion I need.

4. Continue repeating the phrases until you can feel your compassion, kindness, and care for yourself becoming stronger than the original negative emotion.

5. Pause and reflect on your experience. Notice whether any possibilities of wise action arise.

6. I often practice an expanded variation of the traditional mindful self-compassion phrases:

    May I be kind to myself in *this* moment, in *any* moment, in *every* moment.
    May I accept *this* moment exactly as it is, *any* moment, *every* moment.
    May I accept myself exactly as I am in *this* moment, in *any* moment, in *every* moment.
    May I give myself all the compassion *and courageous action* that I need.

This variation, like the traditional self-compassion break, is completely portable: it's effective anywhere, anytime. And this variation helps extend the practice of mindful self-compassion into an ongoing way of being.

EXERCISE 3-16: Recovering from a Shame Attack

1. The instant you recognize the disturbance in the force field that is the signal of distress or upset, place your hand on your heart and begin to say the mindful self-compassion phrases to yourself: "May I be kind to myself in this moment." Interrupt your automatic reactions to any experiences of shame you might be automatically experiencing for the reactions you are having.

2. Take a few deep, relaxing breaths. Attune to your emotional experiences as they arise, exactly as they are in this moment. Gently begin to label them: "This is fear." "This is my shame about being a scared ninny." "This is my anger." "This is my shame about going ballistic (again!)." "This is my envy; this is my shame about still being vulnerable to envy after all these years."

3. Allow any feelings to be there, just as they are, held in your kind, compassionate awareness.

4. Evoke a sense of shared humanity to help hold these feelings. "I'm a human being. These feelings are perfectly normal human feelings. I'm not the only person on the planet who has ever felt this way. Probably millions of other people are feeling this way, too, right now. I'm not alone in having these feelings. I don't have to feel alone because I am having these feelings. I'm a work in progress, and I'm doing the best I can."

5. See if you can locate a place in your body where you feel the shame most strongly. In your jaw? In your chest? In your belly? Focus your attention kindly, tenderly on that spot.

6. Say the mindful self-compassion phrases to this particular spot. "May I be kind to *you* in this moment. May I accept *you* exactly as you are in this moment. May I give *you*, and myself, all the compassion we need."

7.   Spend as much time as you need offering compassion to this feeling of shame, and to yourself for experiencing this shame, until it softens and dissolves. Focus on accepting yourself in this moment exactly as you are.

We don't necessarily practice mindful self-compassion to feel better, though the practice may have that effect over time. We do it so that our brain functions better, with less contraction, more openness, less reactivity, more receptivity. We do better when our brains are more open to learning and to the big picture. That openness helps us respond to whatever is happening with more flexibility and wiser choices.

EXERCISE 3-17: Cultivating Compassion with Equanimity

"Empathy fatigue" is a very real concern among health care professionals and family caregivers. People who care for others can burn out, becoming depleted by the emotional overload.

Neuroscientists have discovered that the brain processes compassion in different parts of the brain than it does empathy. When you attune to other people's emotions (or experience them through emotional contagion) and take them on, take them in, and take them home with you, without a strong enough theory of mind to distinguish the other person's experience from your own, you can experience what scientists now call *empathy fatigue*. Compassion activates the sensory motor cortex of the brain as well as other structures, motivating you to move, to act on someone's behalf. Movement, which activates the sympathetic branch of the nervous system, is energizing and actually acts as a buffer against the depletion of the overactivation of the parasympathetic branch.

This guided visualization is a practice in being with another person's emotional pain, exactly as it is, using compassion for both of you while maintaining your own emotional equilibrium.

COMPASSION
Have compassion for everyone you meet,
even if they don't want it. What seems conceit,

bad manners, or cynicism is always a sign
of things no ears have heard, no eyes have seen.
You do not know what wars are going on
down there where the spirit meets the bone.
　　　　　　　　　— Miller Williams, *The Way We Touch: Poems*

1. Sit comfortably, closing your eyes, and take a few deep, relaxing breaths. Allow yourself to feel the sensations of breathing in and breathing out. Notice how your breath nourishes your body as you inhale and soothes your body as you exhale.

2. Let your breathing find its own natural rhythm. Continue feeling the sensations of breathing in and breathing out. If you like, place your hand over your heart or any other place on your body where touch feels soothing, as a reminder to bring not just awareness but *loving* awareness to your experience, and to yourself.

3. If you become aware of any stress you are carrying in your body, inhale fully and deeply, drawing compassion inside your body and filling every cell in your body with compassion. Let yourself be soothed by inhaling deeply, and by giving yourself the compassion you need when you experience discomfort.

4. Now focus your attention on your in-breath, letting yourself enjoy the sensations of breathing in, one breath after another, noticing how your in-breath nourishes every cell in your body, and then releasing your breath.

5. If you like, you can also carry a word or phrase on each in-breath, such as *nourishing*, *loving*, *compassion and care*, *deep ease*, or *inner peace*. Give yourself whatever you need in this moment. You can also imagine inhaling warmth or light — whatever works for you.

6. Now, bring to mind someone to whom you would like to send warmth, kindness, care, and goodwill, either someone you love or someone who is struggling and needs compassion. Visualize that person clearly in your mind.

7. Shift your focus now to your out-breath. Feel your body breathe out, and send warmth, kindness, care, and goodwill to this person with each exhalation. If you like, you can add a kind word or phrase with each out-breath — *soothing*, or *ease*, or an image of caring and compassion.

8. Now, feel your body breathe both in and out — breathing in for yourself and breathing out for another. Repeat a phrase like "Nourishing for me; nourishing for you," "Soothing for me; soothing for you," or whatever words work for you. Eventually, you can simply repeat, "One for me; one for you." Feel the breath of kindness flowing in and flowing out.

9. As you maintain that rhythm, let these words gently roll through your mind:

Everyone is on his or her own life journey.
I am not the cause of this person's suffering,
Nor is it entirely within my power to make it go away,
Even if I wish I could.
Moments like this are difficult to bear,
Yet I may still try to help if I can.

Still breathing in for yourself and breathing out for another, feel the breath of kindness flowing in, flowing out.

10. You can focus a little more on yourself, or a little more on the other person — whatever you need. Repeat the phrases again.

11. Gently bring your awareness back to breathing in and out, in this moment, in this place. When you are ready, open your eyes.

12. Reflect on your experience. Notice any shifts in your feelings for yourself or for the other person.

Attuning to the feelings of another person in distress or emotional pain can make you vulnerable to emotional contagion and empathy fatigue. You want to stay engaged and respond skillfully and compassionately to other people's difficulties. This exercise allows you to use your theory of mind to take care of yourself at the same time.

Level 3. Too Much

When the pains and pressures of life events really are too much, and when the emotions that might guide you to wise action are too chaotic to be of any help, or you are too mired in depression or despair to act at all, you want to be able to shift those emotions into something more tolerable, more resilient. The exercises below are among the most powerful in the book in their capacity to rewire your brain circuitry instantly and permanently. As always, practice little and often, and practice with awareness, curiosity, and self-care.

EXERCISE 3-18: Rewiring a Negative Emotion through Movement

You can use this tool to shift any difficult negative emotion—anger, fear, sadness, disgust, and even nuance emotions such as resentment and disappointment. Here I suggest you practice with shame to experience a felt sense of recovering your emotional equilibrium and your inner secure base of well-being.

1. Stand up in a place where you have space to move. Settle into a posture of feeling comfortable and at ease in your body.

2. Let your body move into a posture that embodies or expresses shame. You might stand with head bent forward, chest collapsed, in a shrinking stance. Let yourself feel just enough shame in this posture that you can work with it to rewire it, but not so much that you become overwhelmed. This may take some experimentation to find the Goldilocks spot of just enough to feel, deal, and heal.

3. Remain in this posture for thirty seconds or so, modifying it and returning again as you need to stay regulated.

4. Now, without thinking at all, let your body move into a posture that feels the opposite of the emotion you're examining. You don't even have to know what this posture is or what to call it. Just let your body find its way—perhaps standing up straighter and taller, perhaps lifting your head higher, perhaps raising your arms over your head. Stay in this posture for thirty seconds or so, slightly longer than the original shame position.

5. Let your body return to the original posture. Hold that posture for twenty seconds or so, noticing any shifts in your inner feelings.

6. Let your body return to the second, opposite posture. Hold that posture again for thirty seconds or so, longer than the original posture.

7. Let your body find a posture that is somewhere in between the original posture and the second posture. Hold this intermediate posture for thirty seconds.

8. Pause and reflect on your experience of the entire exercise, noticing any shifts in your inner feelings, labeling any of the three postures you have experienced if that's helpful to you. You may be surprised at how your higher brain now labels those experiences.

This exercise helps you shift from any problematic emotional experience to a more grounded one, creating a more secure base for your resilience.

EXERCISE 3-19: Power Posing

Power posing is your self-directed neuroplasticity in action.

1. Before going into any situation that might evoke feelings of anxiety or shame — a job interview, a business meeting, a court hearing, a tax audit, a confrontation over serious misbehavior by a family member — find a quiet, private place where you can practice the power pose for at least five minutes. Stand tall and erect, feet about hip width apart, chest lifted and head held high, your arms either akimbo (like Superman or Wonder Woman) or held high over your head (the Toyota feeling, the mountain pose of yoga).

2. Let yourself feel strength and energy in your body. Experiment with different poses to learn what allows you to experience these feelings most reliably.

3. Practice embodying the difficult feelings that might derail your resilience, too. Let your body experience the anxiety or shame or anger you might actually be feeling. Then return to your power pose.

4. Practice your power pose in the moments before you enter your challenging situation, and then walk mindfully into that situation with more inner strength and energy.

With frequent practice, your power pose becomes a natural way to develop and tap into your inner strength, courage, and resilience.

EXERCISE 3-20: Creating a Wished-For Outcome

Sometimes you need to sit with your feelings and offer yourself compassion for feeling them. You can also use reconditioning to rewire challenging feelings that you still carry from difficult experiences in the past. This exercise is a powerful tool for reconditioning any feelings of regret, guilt, or shame about past events, any less-than-intelligent reactions or less-than-resilient coping. This exercise does not change what happened, but it does change your relationship to what happened. It doesn't rewrite history, but it does rewire the brain.

Start with one small memory, so that your brain has a chance to succeed at reconditioning it and you develop a sense of competence in using this tool.

1. Find a place and time where you can sit uninterrupted for ten to fifteen minutes. Come into a sense of presence, knowing that you are in your body, in this moment, in this place. Let yourself feel energy and strength in your body, without any sense of strain.

2. Close your eyes and take three deep, relaxing breaths. Place your hand on your heart for a few moments to evoke a sense of safety, anchoring yourself in your emotional equilibrium and well-being. Bring a sense of openness, kindness, and curiosity to your experience.

3. When you are ready, bring to mind one small memory of a moment when an interaction between you and another person went awry and you wound up feeling shame, guilt, or regret about yourself or your behavior. Stay anchored in your own mindful self-compassion — your awareness and your acceptance of yourself — as you evoke this memory.

4. Start recalling all the details of this interaction: where you were, who you were with, what you said, what they said. Take your time remembering, until the feeling from that event is fully evoked. This recollection activates all the neural circuitry involved in recording the original experience.

5. See if you can locate that visceral, felt sense of the experience somewhere in your body now. Try to locate it clearly enough to feel it so that you can work with it but not so strongly that you get overwhelmed by it now.

6. Notice any negative thoughts you may have about yourself now because of

what you experienced then. Make the evocation of this negative experience as vivid as you can: behaviors, words, feelings, body sensations, thoughts. You're "lighting up" the entire memory so it can be rewired.

7. Set the negative memory aside for the moment. Now you'll begin to create the positive resource that you will juxtapose with this negative memory to do the rewiring.

8. Begin by imagining a different, more satisfactory ending to the negative scenario, even if this wished-for ending could never have happened in real life. Remember, whatever you can imagine is real to your brain. You'll be using this imaginary outcome to rewire the brain.

9. Imagine something different you might have said during the scenario. Imagine something different the other person might have said. Again, it doesn't matter if this conversation could never have happened in real life. Let your brain do its own imagining and its own rewiring.

10. Imagine something different you might have done. Imagine the other person doing something differently, even if that never could have happened in real life. You can even imagine someone who wasn't there at the time coming in and doing something helpful. Let your imagination create a more satisfying resolution of the entire event.

11. Bring this scenario to its new, wished-for conclusion. And now, notice how you feel as you imagine this ending. Notice what emotions you feel; notice where you feel those emotions in your body. Notice the visceral, felt sense of this new ending. Notice any new, more positive thoughts you have about yourself. Let these feelings, bodily sensations, and thoughts about yourself now be as vivid in your imagination as possible in order to strengthen this new experience of yourself.

12. Now begin toggling back and forth between the feelings of this new outcome and the feelings of the original event or the feelings of remembering that event now.

13. Gently recall the original, negative feelings. Touch them lightly. Then let those feelings go, and return to feeling strongly the new, more positive feelings of the wished-for ending. Rest in the new positive for a moment. Then recall the negative feelings again, just lightly; notice any shift in those feelings. Let them go again, and return to the newer, more positive

feelings. Recall the negative feelings again one more time, then let them go. Rest completely in the new feelings of the new ending.

14. Take a moment to reflect on your experience of the entire exercise, noticing shifts in your view and experience of yourself now.

With frequent practice of this exercise, you will notice that the original, negative feelings about yourself are less intense, and the new, positive feelings about yourself feel more real. Repeat the exercise as many times as you need to.

This is not about being disloyal to who you were at the time of the event or dismissing what you felt at the time. It's about rewiring your feelings about yourself for having had those feelings, being able to feel differently about yourself now about what happened then.

You can use this exercise again and again with memories of the same interaction or other interactions with this same person, or similar interactions with other people. You don't have to rewire all 4,957 interactions that have ever gone awry in your life. Eventually your brain learns to generalize the processing of similar difficult emotions. You can use tools like this to work intelligently with any overwhelming emotion. You are learning that you can cope resiliently with all the emotional ups and downs of your life.

Deconditioning

This chapter has presented many tools of focused processing to help you attend to and make sense of your emotions, to manage and rewire difficult negative emotions, and to use positive emotions to shift the functioning of your brain and to shift your moods and states of being. You can continue using those tools whenever necessary, but now we're going to look at a different process of brain change: deconditioning.

With deconditioning, you temporarily suspend all that (wise) effort. You use the spaciousness of the defocused default network mode to let your emotions "dissolve" into a peaceful, easy tranquility — the home base of emotional well-being that all of these practices return us to.

Level 1. Barely a Wobble

You may have experienced moments of well-being when you feel centered, grounded, at peace, and at ease. These result from the positive activation of our parasympathetic nervous system when there is no danger. We are calm and relaxed, able to REST — relax and enter into safety and trust. "God's in his heaven; all's right with the [inner] world." You can deliberately evoke that sense of well-being with the exercise below and, with practice, sustain it over time.

EXERCISE 3-21: Resting in Well-Being

1. Lie down on a bed, a couch, the floor, or the ground, somewhere you feel comfortable and safe and won't be interrupted for five minutes. Slowly let your body relax. Let the weight of your body drop, feeling supported by the surface beneath you. You don't have to "carry" yourself for the moment.

2. Breathe slowly, gently, and deeply, taking slightly longer on the exhalations. Breathe in a sense of ease, calm, and tranquility. Breathe out, one by one, all the worries, thoughts, and feelings you might still be carrying. Breathe in and breathe out, as many times as you need to.

3. Notice a spaciousness inside your body, even inside your skull. Feel the space between any lingering tension, any lingering thoughts, any lingering feelings, like the space between notes of music. Notice the ease, the calm of the spaciousness.

4. Begin to gently focus your awareness on the presence of the spaciousness more; notice the absence, the emptiness around the feelings, thoughts, and tensions. Rest in the presence of this spaciousness for a few moments.

5. Name this feeling of spaciousness to help you evoke it later. Call it peacefulness, tranquility, calm, ease, or well-being — whatever works for you.

6. Return to your focused awareness and reflect on your experience of this exercise.

We often notice the storms of emotions in our lives, but we don't always pay attention to the blue sky of well-being they are blowing through. Cultivating and deepening an awareness of that background equilibrium is a way of strengthening your resilience. The spaciousness allows your brain to hold bigger, more challenging, more difficult emotions as you move through your life.

Level 2. Glitches and Heartaches, Sorrows and Struggles

When my client Sean was going through a particularly tough time, waking up every morning in a state of existential panic, I suggested he set the intention to not get out of bed in the morning until he could bring his mind and body to a state of calm and come into the spaciousness of his emotional well-being. A few weeks later, when Sean came in to report his progress with this practice, he acknowledged that he had had to practice self-empathy and self-compassion, too, to keep going in the practice. At first, his body-brain needed more than an hour to come to the state of ease and emotional equilibrium from which he wanted to launch his day. But within a week, he was able to achieve that state of calm in forty minutes; soon he was able to reduce the time to twenty minutes, then five minutes, then just a few breaths. What a grand day it was when he woke up already in that state of calm. With practice, he learned that he could reliably sustain it.

EXERCISE 3-22: Holding Turbulent Emotions
in the Equilibrium of Well-Being

Here's a variation of Sean's practice that can help you recover your well-being when difficult emotions arise.

1. First evoke a sense of your own emotional well-being as best as you can. Steady yourself in the experience of inner calm, ease, and tranquility.
2. Then practice deliberately evoking a (small!) feeling of anger, sadness, or fear — enough to recognize it, but not enough to be overwhelmed by it.
3. Let the spacious sense of well-being contain whatever feeling you have evoked, and notice that it can. The noticing helps deepen your trust in this process. The sense of well-being is larger than whatever feeling has come up.
4. Let the smaller, difficult feeling dissolve again, and simply REST in your emotional well-being.
5. Repeat this exercise as many times as necessary to deepen your trust in your own equilibrium as a resource for your resilience.

Over time, you can learn to wake up in and abide in a sense of well-being as you move through your day, always able to return to it whenever you wobble. Your prefrontal cortex is still on duty, too, to manage emotions as they arise. You can toggle back and forth between focused and defocused processing as needed to maintain your emotional equilibrium.

Level 3. Too Much

Chapter 2 introduced you to many tools for managing the revving up and shutting down of your nervous system and returning to a physiological equilibrium from which you could discern options and make wise choices. This chapter, too, has presented many tools to manage emotional roller coasters — the many flavors of mad, bad, sad, and glad so common in human experience — and return to an emotional equilibrium of well-being from which you can face challenges and be resilient in dealing with them.

When you're being challenged by a flood of difficult emotions, and the tools you have practiced so far don't seem to be working, simply stop and rest. Giving yourself the gift of rest is a form of self-compassion. Stop trying. Take refuge. Let yourself be held, soothed, and comforted by someone else, at least until you can recover your own resources to manage your emotions yourself.

EXERCISE 3-23: Just Rest

1. When the feelings flooding through you seem to be more than you can handle at the moment, take time to notice what is happening. Simply noticing your experience pulls your higher brain back online a bit.

2. Find refuge in the presence of someone who is securely anchored in their own emotional well-being, who can handle being with you without wobbling themselves, and who can offer you compassion with equanimity. This can be a real person who is physically present; it can be someone you can remember or imagine being with; or it can be a resource from your imagination, like your compassionate friend (see exercise 3-11).

3. You don't have to do anything here except be with your experience and receive the comfort of someone else. Let the calming and compassionate presence, even an imagined one, calm you.

4. Notice the calming; notice the return to your own equilibrium, or at least to the memory that this equilibrium is available to you. With practice and repetition, you'll get there.

Emotional contagion can work in a positive direction as well as a negative one. Experiencing someone else's emotional well-being can help you recover your own.

This chapter has introduced many tools to help you ride the waves of your own emotions and manage the effect on you of other people's emotions, guiding you toward more resilient, flexible, skillful responses and behaviors.

As you master the use of positive emotions like compassion and gratitude to shift the functioning of your brain out of contraction and reactivity into openness and receptivity, and as you deepen your skills in practices of mindful empathy and theory of mind, you're strengthening the stable neural circuits you need to return to your emotional equilibrium and well-being. And you are learning to trust that you *can*.

Working these muscles of your emotional intelligence will help you grow into a more robust relational intelligence as well.

CHAPTER FOUR

Practices of Relational Intelligence within Yourself

Self-Awareness, Self-Acceptance, Inner Secure Base

The curious paradox is, when I accept myself just as I am, then I can change.
— **CARL ROGERS**

Self-awareness, self-acceptance, and trust in your inner capacities are essential to resilience. These capacities create a home base, a secure sense of self from which you can respond flexibly to all of life's difficulties. When you turn your focus inward, you feel safe, at home, and at peace, trusting your capacities to engage skillfully and competently with the outer world. When you face a challenging situation, even when you have no clue of how to best respond to it, this inner secure base of resilience allows you to move forward and risk trying something new.

The neural circuitry for this inner secure base initially develops, as all capacities in the brain do, through your earliest interactions with your caregivers. It can be modified and rewired later with the help of encouraging and supportive others.

> *The roots of resilience are to be found in the felt sense of being held in the mind and heart of an empathic, attuned, self-possessed other.*
> — DIANA FOSHA, *The Transforming Power of Affect*

Just as we first learn to regulate our nervous system through others regulating it for us — just as we learn to manage our emotions by having those emotions validated for us by others, soothed if negative and amplified if positive — we develop a healthy sense of self when we experience being truly accepted, valued, seen, heard, and understood by people around us for who we truly are. Acceptance by people on whom we depend and from whom we learn our essential sense of self-worth enables us to trust that we matter and that we are competent.

We do not believe in ourselves until someone reveals that deep inside us there is something valuable, worth listening to, worthy of our trust, sacred to our touch. Once we believe in ourselves, we can risk curiosity, wonder, spontaneous delight or any experience that reveals the human spirit.
— ATTRIBUTED TO E. E. CUMMINGS

Our earliest experiences of feeling seen, accepted, and trusted not only shape a healthy sense of self and its inner secure base; they also kindle and strengthen the maturation of the prefrontal cortex, which in turn sustains that development. The central challenge of parenting is to help children develop an inner secure base by accepting them as they are; the central challenge of maturing into our resilience is to discover and rediscover that inner secure base and become who we are meant to be.

The turning point in the process of growing up is when you discover the core of strength within you that survives all hurt.
— MAX LERNER, *The Unfinished Country*

That larger, authentic experience of self is actually an integration of many inner parts, voices, or facets. An inner warrior, inner flirt, inner pleaser, and inner critic, for example, are subpersonalities that coexist, interact, and work together to form your personal self. Just as you have learned to value and manage all emotions as signals of something important to pay attention to, you can choose to value, integrate, and even embrace all inner parts of yourself as contributing to who you are — including those parts with the bad habit of disrupting your resilience. It's the prefrontal cortex that integrates these various parts of the self, fostering an authentic sense of wholeness and allowing you to experience your integrated self as more and more capable, flexible, and resilient.

This chapter presents tools to help you strengthen your self-awareness, self-acceptance, and trust in the capacities and strengths of your inner secure base, as well as to help you work skillfully with your inner critic or inner judge, who is the biggest disrupter of your inner secure base. You'll learn how to integrate all inner parts into the magnificent complexity that is your authentic self.

A BRIEF ASIDE ON SHAME
AND THE INNER CRITIC

Strengthening self-acceptance and trust in yourself as resilient, turning momentary experiences into reliably steady states and then into long-term permanent traits, can be a daily practice. Learning to hum along in your range of resilience, and to recover when you're thrown about by choppy seas or full-scale hurricanes, is literally a lifelong practice. You practice, little and often, forever. You hope to eventually preempt being thrown.

Challenges to your sense of self-acceptance and self-trust can come at any moment. You might hear negative messages about yourself from others, whether they know you well or not at all. You may carry very powerful negative messages about yourself that come from early or recent experiences. You are vulnerable to messages from your inner critic or inner judge because, as human beings, we are universally vulnerable to the powerful, conditioned messages of shame.

Shame is one of the emotions intrinsic to being human — like anger, fear, sadness, surprise, and delight. We are hardwired to want to feel safe, to feel loved and lovable, to belong, to feel accepted and valued. These feelings are not about ego; they're part of being a social animal. We depend on the love and affection of others to experience love and affection for ourselves. We need to feel we belong, to feel comfortable with our place in the tribe and in the world. When we feel rejected or excluded by others — when we're blown off by a friend, passed over for a promotion at work, criticized in front of coworkers, or ridiculed at a family gathering, we are hardwired to feel shame.

Experiencing shame occasionally is inevitable. All tribes, clans, cultures, and societies have to teach their young the norms of acceptable (and lifesaving) behaviors and how to stay deserving of the group's protection, if not love. Shame arises when we pick up signals from people around us, especially people we depend on for our survival, that we have done something they don't approve of, or that we *are* something they don't approve of.

It's impossible to be perfect and meet other people's expectations or plans for us all the time, and it's impossible not to feel shame when we feel we have done, or we are, something wrong or bad. That sense of being wrong or bad is easily internalized: we begin to hear others' negative messages as our own; we begin to listen to and believe the voice of our own inner critic. Every human being on the planet is vulnerable to the harsh messages that can come from a well-practiced inner critic or inner judge.

The derailing of resilience that results from shame is what most of my clients come into therapy for, what my workshop participants are most curious about, and what draws the most responses to my blog posts about recovering resilience.

Shame has been called the great disconnector; the inner critic is its relentless messenger. You can begin to counteract the effects of both shame and the inner critic by practicing self-awareness, self-compassion, self-acceptance, self-appreciation, and self-love.

> *Just that action of paying attention to ourselves, [knowing] that I care enough about myself, that I am worthy enough to pay attention to, starts to unlock some of those deep beliefs of unworthiness at a deeper level in the brain.*
>
> — ELISHA GOLDSTEIN

New Conditioning

Learning to integrate all the diverse components of yourself, including the sometimes corrosive inner critic, involves directing your own neuroplasticity to develop a healthy new relationship with yourself, based on deepening self-awareness and self-acceptance. You harness the integrative capacities of your prefrontal cortex to form all these inner voices and parts into a coherent and resilient inner secure base that supports further reconditioning and rewiring.

Level 1. Barely a Wobble

If you feel you know your strengths pretty well and generally accept yourself lovingly and courageously, these exercises can deepen your trust that you are capable and resilient. You begin by identifying core strengths and core values you already have, or aspire to have, in order to strengthen the inner secure base and begin rewiring your relationship to other parts of you that are less easy to accept.

EXERCISE 4-1: Identifying Personal Traits of Resilience

1. From this list, identify five traits you know and trust you already have, or list other traits of your own.

accountability	focus	patience
approachability	forgiveness	perseverance
calm	friendliness	perspective
cheerfulness	frugality	playfulness
clarity	generosity	prudence
commitment	gratitude	purposefulness
compassion	happiness	reliability
composure	honesty	resourcefulness
confidence	humility	respect
connectedness	idealism	responsiveness
cooperation	imagination	reverence
courage	industriousness	self-acceptance
courtesy	joyfulness	self-awareness
creativity	kindness	self-compassion
curiosity	knowledge	selflessness
dependability	love	sincerity
determination	loyalty	spontaneity
discernment	magnanimity	thoughtfulness
discipline	mercy	tolerance
enthusiasm	modesty	tranquility
equanimity	open-mindedness	trust
fairness	optimism	warmheartedness
flexibility	organization	

2. For each trait you identify, write down three specific memories of moments when you actively expressed these traits. Maybe you were generous to a coworker, your neighbor, or your brother; you were prudent about paying your utility bill on time, driving within the speed limit, filling up the gas tank, and so on. For each example, consciously acknowledge that indeed you were exhibiting that trait.

3. After you've written three memories for each of the traits you've identified, set your reflections aside for a few hours or days, and then reread them.

4. As you reread these recollections of your own traits of resilience, notice any shifts in your view of yourself. Can you accept these traits as real, valid, and integral parts of you, as contributing to your own inner secure base of resilience? Practice and repeat steps 1–3 until this feels real to you.

5. Reflect on how these five traits of resilience might reinforce and strengthen each other, building your inner secure base of resilience and deepening your trust in yourself.

As you experience and claim your traits of resilience, you deepen your trust that they are parts of who you truly are.

EXERCISE 4-2: Deep Listening to Core Strengths

Being accepted for who you are by others kick-starts the self-acceptance you need for resilience. Allow thirty minutes for this exercise — the time deepens the practice, the learning, and the rewiring.

1. Recruit a partner — a friend or a colleague — to do this exercise with you. You can switch roles later, if you wish.

2. Tell your partner which of your five traits of resilience you want to explore first.

3. For each of your five traits of resilience, your partner will ask you, "When have you experienced [your trait] in difficult or challenging times?" and listen quietly as you answer.

4. Answer the question with examples that feel authentic to you. You may want to share your reflections from exercise 4-1, if they seem appropriate.

5. Your partner listens receptively and acceptingly to your answers, without commenting. Then she repeats the same question again and again for about five minutes. This repetition allows your brain to go deeper into memory and into your own wisdom.

6. When you have finished answering the question about this first trait, identify for your partner the second trait you want to explore.

7. Repeat this exercise for all five traits, with your partner asking you the question, repeating the question and listening receptively.

8. When you have responded to the question for all five traits, take another five minutes to silently reflect and notice any shifts in your view of yourself, any deeper integration of your sense of yourself, and any stronger awareness of your own inner secure base of resilience.

By recalling traits of resilience you have already called on, you are reinforcing the sense that this is, in fact, who you are.

Most of the time, you receive far more positive than negative messages about yourself as you go through your day. You hear "Thank you" as you open the door for someone, or "That's very kind of you"; "Good catch!" as you almost trip but don't; a friendly smile from a stranger on the sidewalk; a puppy trustingly waggling up to you to be petted.

The trouble is, you may not notice or take in these positive messages, these affirmations that you exist, that you're noticed, that you matter. It's easy to get caught up in your own worries or negativity and miss them completely. But each of these messages and moments has the potential to create a resource of self-acceptance in your brain.

EXERCISE 4-3: Taking In the Good, Reprised

You learned in exercise 3-10 to take in the good of moments of kindness from others or awe about the world we live in. Here you practice taking in, accepting, and treasuring the goodness of your own self.

1. Pause for a moment and reflect on any message of acceptance and belonging you encountered today. Your five-year-old took your hand as you crossed the street; your neighbor brought over some extra tomatoes from his garden. Your friend emailed a "miss you" message and suggested getting together for brunch.

2. Notice the felt sense of receiving this message: a warmth in your body, a lightness in your heart, a little recognition of "Wow, this is terrific!"

3. Focus your awareness on this felt sense for ten to thirty seconds. Savor it slowly, allowing your brain the time it needs to register the experience and store it in long-term memory.

4. Set the intention to evoke this memory five more times today. This repeats the neural firing in your brain, recording the memory so you can recollect it later, making it a resource for your sense of self-acceptance and self-worth, thereby strengthening your inner secure base of resilience.

As you register and take in these experiences, you can also register and take in the fact that you are learning how to do this. You are becoming competent at creating new circuitry for resilience in your brain.

EXERCISE 4-4: Working with Symbols of Traits of Resilience

You can use reminders of your growth and learning to prompt your brain to refresh and strengthen the neural circuitry associated with these changes.

1. For each of the five traits of resilience you are working with, which may change over time, begin to gather symbols that represent you expressing that trait. They might include

   - a photograph of you and a person to whom you are loving
   - a postcard from a trip where your flexibility really showed up
   - a stone with a word relevant to the trait carved in it
   - the printed agenda of a city council meeting where you found the courage to speak about an important neighborhood issue

2. Gather these symbolic reminders of your traits in a box, a bowl, or a bag. Or display them on a windowsill, a bookshelf, a kitchen counter, or your desk. You might even label the collection "Reminders of My Resilience."

3. Revisit these symbolic reminders once a day for a month. Then revisit them whenever you want to strengthen your sense of yourself as a stable, secure, resilient person.

Repetition, little and often, lays down and strengthens new neural circuitry. It doesn't rewire old circuitry, but it creates the resources needed to do that rewiring.

Level 2. Glitches and Heartaches, Sorrows and Struggles

If we don't experience being fully loved and cherished for who we are, we can sometimes hide or split off parts of ourselves that we have been told, or have come to believe, are less than acceptable. It takes an enormous amount of the brain's energy to maintain this splitting off.

By letting yourself become aware of these "unlovable" parts of yourself, accepting them and reintegrating them into conscious awareness and into your sense of yourself, you free up that energy to let yourself be more fully engaged with your world and to be more resilient when facing any problems.

EXERCISE 4-5: Seeing the Goodness That Others See in You

This exercise creates a resource to heal your sense of self when your view of your self is already "less than."

1. Sit in a comfortable position where you won't be interrupted for at least five minutes. Allow your eyes to gently close. Focus your attention on your breathing. Rest comfortably in the simple presence of awareness. When you're ready, let yourself become aware of how you are holding yourself in this moment. Are you feeling kind toward yourself? Are you uneasy with yourself? Are you feeling critical of yourself? Just notice, just be aware and accepting of what is, without judgment — or if there is judgment, noticing that.

2. When you're ready, bring to mind someone in your life who you know loves you unconditionally, someone in whose presence you feel safe. This could be a teacher or dear friend; a partner, parent, or child; or a beloved dog or cat. It could be a spiritual figure — Jesus or the Dalai Lama, or your compassionate friend. Or it could simply be a memory of anyone, living or no longer living, who ever accepted you for exactly who you were in that moment. When a client occasionally insists that no one has ever loved them in this way, I ask them to make someone up in their imagination. That imagined someone can be as real to the brain as a real person, and we go from there.

3. Imagine yourself sitting with this person face-to-face. Visualize the person looking at you with acceptance and tenderness, love and joy. Feel yourself

taking in their love and their acceptance of all of who you are. Nothing needs to be hidden.

4. Now imagine yourself being the other person, looking at yourself through their eyes. Feel that person's love and openness being directed toward you. See in yourself the goodness, the wholeness that the other person sees in you. Let yourself savor this awareness of your own goodness.

5. Now come back to being yourself. You are in your own body again, experiencing the other person looking at you again, with love and acceptance. Take the love and acceptance deeply into your own being. Notice how and where you feel that love and acceptance in your body — as a smile, as a warmth in your heart — and savor it.

6. Take a moment to reflect on your experience, noticing any shifts in your relationship to yourself.

This exercise helps you create new pathways of self-acceptance in your brain. Set the intention to remember this feeling any time you need to.

EXERCISE 4-6: Allowing Inner Parts to Be There

This exercise helps you not only see and integrate the positive traits that others see in you but also acknowledge and allow parts of you that you don't necessarily want other people to see, and which you may not want to acknowledge either. This process frees up some of the enormous psychic energy that it takes to keep these parts hidden or split off, so that your brain will be less fatigued. It also frees up the energy it takes to clean up the messes that these parts of you can create when they act out and derail your resilience, so that you have more energy to live your life.

Your larger, wiser self (see exercise 4-15 below) can manage the behaviors of your various inner parts when you are aware of them and tolerant enough of them to stay in charge of them, even when they really, really want to act out and run the show.

1. Find a place to sit and work where you won't be interrupted for five to ten minutes. Come into a sense of presence. As much as possible, come into

a felt sense of your own inner secure base of resilience, stable yet open-minded and flexible.

2. Read over this list of traits commonly deemed negative, the parts of the self that are related to these traits, and the related messages that can derail your resilience. This is not an exhaustive list; I learn new examples from clients and workshop participants every week.

TRAIT	PART	MESSAGE
Giving up	Discouraged part	I might as well not try; this is too hard.
Grouchiness	Curmudgeon	Life sucks, and it's not going to get any better.
Complaining	Whiner	I don't like this, and I'm not happy.
Rigidity	Stubborn part	I refuse, and you can't make me.
Being judgmental	Inner critic	Who do you think you are?
Lacking confidence	Smallifyer	Better to settle for less than to risk another failure.
Creative block	Procrastinator	No worries; I'll show up for this tomorrow, maybe.
Shyness	Withdrawer	If I don't engage, I won't be disappointed.
Pretending	Fantasizer	If only [whatever] were true, I would be happy.

3. Identify one example from this list that is relevant to you. You wish it weren't a part of you, but you know it is. You may choose instead to work

with a trait that's not listed here; if you do, identify the related part of self and its message.

4. Notice any reaction in your nervous system or felt sense of your emotional landscape as you begin to work with this trait. If these reactions become overwhelming, you may want to use tools from chapters 2 and 3 to regulate the reactivity and return you to your physiological and emotional equilibrium.

5. Recall one specific experience in the past when this part of you was triggered. Remember the message this part was sending at the time, whether it was one of the messages listed here or something completely different. When this part is triggered, what is it likely to say to you?

6. Notice your reactions now as you remember this experience. Can you simply allow the part of you and its message to be in your awareness, without further judgment or criticism? It is what it is, and there's always an understandable and forgivable reason for it being what it is.

7. Try to identify one possible positive contribution this part might make to your larger self. No worries if you can't yet; additional exercises in this chapter will assist you. If you can do this, you might express a preliminary sense of gratitude to this part of you for its contribution.

8. When you feel comfortable acknowledging and allowing this part and its habitual messages to be part of your sense of self, repeat the exercise with other memories of this part and its message, or with other traits on the list, or with other traits altogether.

9. Notice and reflect on your experience of this exercise. Claim your own growing capacity to skillfully acknowledge and allow any part of you to simply exist, to be there. This is an important step toward accepting and integrating that part into your sense of self and recovering your resilience and well-being.

Integration — one of the main functions of the prefrontal cortex — frees up an enormous amount of psychic energy, enabling you to move toward a more coherent, resilient sense of self. The prefrontal cortex gets to drive the bus, no matter how intrusive or rambunctious these inner parts of you may be.

EXERCISE 4-7: Finding a True Other to Your True Self

Oh, the comfort — the inexpressible comfort of feeling safe with a person — having neither to weigh thoughts nor measure words, but pouring them all right out, just as they are, chaff and grain together; certain that a faithful hand will take and sift them, keep what is worth keeping, and then with the breath of kindness blow the rest away.

— Dinah Craik, *A Life for a Life*

Your entire self can gel and blossom when every facet of it is seen by someone else as acceptable, and when you yourself come to believe that all of these facets are acceptable. This rewiring of your neural circuitry to enable self-acceptance happens most efficiently and most reliably with the help of another, trusted person.

A true other is someone who sees the inherent goodness of who you are and accepts you exactly as you are, even in moments when that goodness is obscure. This true other is often someone close to you — a parent, spouse, or child — but not necessarily. Family dynamics can sometimes be too fraught. Fortunately, many people in other roles — friend, teacher, coach, therapist, or mentor — can also function as a true other. Even strangers can act as true others in the "moments of meeting" we'll explore in exercise 5-2.

1. Ask a trustworthy friend to help you with this exercise, somebody you already feel safe and comfortable with. You're looking for an empathic, attuned, and self-possessed other, someone who can stay anchored in her own secure base and won't be triggered or need anything from you during this exercise.

2. Come into a sense of safety and trust with this person. The safety primes the neuroplasticity of the brain for learning and rewiring.

3. Choose one of the traits that you identified in exercise 4-6, or any other trait you're concerned about.

4. Begin to share your experience of this trait, its associated part of self, and its associated message with your partner. Share anything that feels relevant; if possible, share details of your experience that you may feel reluctant to share. This exercise is the opportunity for those qualities and their messages to come out of the shadows into the light of awareness and acceptance.

5. Your friend listens deeply and empathically, without offering a lot of comments.

6. Notice your own reactions to the sharing, feeling heard, and feeling accepted. Notice your own opening to acknowledgment and acceptance.

7. When you are ready, take a moment to reflect on the entire experience of this exercise. Notice any shifts in your relationship to this part and to yourself as a whole.

8. You can repeat this exercise with as many parts of yourself and as many true others as you wish.

This exercise helps you build your inner secure base, strengthening your secure attachment to yourself and your resilience in the world.

EXERCISE 4-8: Expressing Loving-Kindness Even for Unlovable Parts

About 2,600 years ago, the Buddha taught his followers the practice of loving-kindness, *metta*, as a way to keep the mind and heart open to any of life's experiences in any circumstances, including pain and suffering. This practice recognizes and honors the deep nobility and worthiness of every sentient being. We can learn to wish all beings well, including ourselves, no matter what our personal opinions may be about the other people, or ourselves at the moment.

The acceptance and honoring at the base of loving-kindness practice interrupts whatever automatic thoughts and opinions you may be having and refocuses your attention on keeping the mind and heart open to what is happening right now.

1. Find a few quiet moments in your day to pause and say these traditional phrases to yourself:

May I be safe from inner and outer harm.
May I be happy and deeply content.
May I be healthy and strong in body and mind.
May I live with the ease of well-being.

2. Repeat the phrases five to ten times; repeat the practice five times during the day for a full week or longer.

3. Notice any shifts in your energy, your mood, as you deepen the practice. You may not notice any immediate shifts from practicing the phrases per se; instead, you may notice that an incident that might previously have caused you to tip into shame or collapse now causes barely a blip on your radar. Notice whether this trend continues as you deepen the practice.

4. You can adapt this practice and phrases to offer loving-kindness to parts of yourself as well. All are worthy and deserving of love and attention.

> May my whiner find soothing and ease.
> May my stubborn part feel acknowledged and relax.
> May my inner critic feel appreciated for the job it's trying to do.
> May my smallifyer trust the growth of my capacities and strengths.
> May my withdrawer feel safe and able to stay engaged.
> May my procrastinator trust that the capacities are there to begin this project right now.
> May my fantasizer rest in and enjoy this moment.

5. Modify the phrases over time as necessary to keep your mind and heart focused and open. Besides learning *how* to do this new conditioning, you are learning that you *can*.

I suggested this practice, with these updated phrases, to a client. Not only did she notice a change in her response when her computer crashed over the weekend, but she reported to me that after she had coped with that disaster pretty resiliently, she had bounded down the stairs saying excitedly, "I'm growing new neurons! I'm growing new neurons!" Indeed, she was.

Level 3. Too Much

At this level of new conditioning, you're learning to shift your entire philosophical stance toward the inner critic (see the aside on shame and the inner critic, p. 99). That shift is the most effective way to cope with your inner critic in the long run.

The most potent way to change your relationship with your inner critic is to understand that it believes it has a very important job to do — to protect you from making mistakes and failing in front of other people (and thereby provoking who knows what unbearable humiliation or rejection). And so it hammers at you — admittedly at some of us more than others — about doing better and not messing up. In its overzealousness, it endlessly reminds you of every fault and screwup, just in case you hadn't noticed. The biggest difficulty with the inner critic is that it blames *you* for every mistake, labeling you as bad, irresponsible, and worthless. And when you listen to and believe the inner critic, when you hear its messages as true, you stop being able to see your inner critic as an overworked, underpaid part of your whole self.

Arguing with your inner critic, trying to persuade it of your worth, doesn't work well. There will always be some imperfection it can pounce on to prove you wrong. (And your goal, in any event, is to accept your imperfections as part of your particular flavor of being human.) And you can't ignore the inner critic. It will never go away on its own, because it thinks its self-imposed job is essential to your survival. Trying to ignore it takes an enormous and exhausting amount of psychological energy.

What works is to retire it, to rewire your view of it, to shift your perspective — the gold standard of response flexibility — and to relate to it as one part of your larger self. You can work with any grain of truth in the inner critic's message as you would work with negative emotions, saying, "Thank you for the signal to pay attention to something important. I trust that I will. Now please go back to your room."

When you choose to relate to the inner critic as just another part of yourself, it will settle down to being listened to, and you can settle down to listening without being derailed.

EXERCISE 4-9: Meeting with the Inner Critic

1. Settle in a comfortable place where you won't be interrupted. Allow thirty minutes for the exercise.

2. Imagine your inner critic as a character in your multiplicity of selves, as you imagined different parts of yourself in exercise 4-6. Imagine having a meeting with your inner critic, just as you imagined a meeting with your compassionate friend in exercise 3-11. In fact, you may invite your compassionate friend to this meeting for support.

3. Imagine your inner critic as a person, a figure, a presence. Visualize who

or what they look like. Imagine meeting and greeting them and the place where you will sit or walk and talk. Remember, you're the one running this meeting.

4. Begin the dialogue by acknowledging that you know the inner critic has been trying really hard to protect you from actions and traits it believes are harmful. You can set some guidelines for this dialogue: it is not an invitation to the inner critic to deliver its own message. Convey your understanding and appreciation and even compassion for how hard the inner critic has been working.

5. As you convey your appreciation to the inner critic for the job it is still trying to do, let yourself feel your own wholeness, your ability to do this important job of protecting yourself from harm. Anchor in your own inner secure base of resilience. Trust that your own capacities for resilience are quite solid now. Let your inner critic know that you expect it to trust you too. The inner critic can retire now, with thanks for its service.

6. Imagine your inner critic taking in your empathy for it and your trust in your own competence. Try! This imagining is *real* to your brain. Imagine your inner critic acquiescing in your new relationship to it and to its new role as inner adviser.

7. Imagine saying goodbye to your inner critic for now. Savor your own skill in shifting your view, rewiring your relationship with your inner critic, and retiring it to a new, more workable role.

8. Repeat, repeat, repeat, little and often, for as long as you need to. It's *your* choice to retire the inner critic.

Realistically, the inner critic will probably never fully disappear. It's part of our deeply ingrained arsenal of survival strategies. But you can shift your relationship to your inner critic, not take its message so personally, not believe it so readily. Over time, the voice of the inner critic can be muted. It may still be annoying at times, but it will no longer derail your resilience.

Reconditioning

Whenever a whiff — or even a whack — of shame wobbles your inner secure base, you want to stabilize that base as quickly as possible. A critical comment from another person, or even from yourself, may contain a grain of truth. But you want to explore that opportunity for learning (AFGO — another frickin' growth opportunity) from a place of strength and confidence, not from a smallified place of shame and self-doubt.

Level 1. Barely a Wobble

Developing an inner secure base is the best protection we have against later stress, trauma, and psychopathology. You want to recover and maintain that base.

EXERCISE 4-10: Carrying Love and Appreciation in Your Wallet

1. Begin to gather appreciative comments about yourself from birthday cards, holiday cards, random emails from friends and colleagues, comments you notice in conversations with friends. Write them down on a "Genuine Appreciations" list.

2. You can even ask two or three or five or seven friends, people you trust to express their appreciation of you, to send you an email, card, or text listing two or three things they appreciate about you. Add these comments to the list.

3. Type up the comments on a single sheet of paper. Tape the list to your computer monitor or on the bathroom mirror, carry it in your wallet or purse, or enter it on your phone: put it somewhere you can read it every day.

4. Read these comments three times a day, every day, for thirty days. Each time you read them, take another thirty seconds to take in the good of receiving this support and appreciation from people who know you and care about you. Repeatedly taking in the appreciation of others does create a new appreciation of yourself in your brain.

5. Any time a sense of shame, failure, inadequacy, unworthiness, self-doubt, or unlovability threatens your inner self-acceptance, pull out the list and read it, or recite it from memory. Use it to counter the negative self-talk that might be arising.

This exercise trains your brain to counter any possible derailing of your resilience caused by shame, by immediately shifting to and remembering positive perceptions of you. That response flexibility becomes the new, more resilient pathway in your brain.

Level 2. Glitches and Heartaches, Sorrows and Struggles

Review the previous discussion of shame and the inner critic (p. 99) if you wish. When you experience any collapse into shame, any hounding from the inner critic, it's important to right yourself as quickly as possible, and reinforce your sense of yourself as fully lovable and acceptable, to prevent any further derailing of your resilience.

EXERCISE 4-11: Loving and Accepting Yourself, Even Though...

1. Practice saying this phrase: "Even though... [you'll fill in the blank in a moment], I deeply and completely love and accept myself," over and over again until it feels natural and believable to you. You're creating the positive message you will use to rewire a negative one. This phrase may feel unnatural to say at first, but it can become more familiar and comfortable with practice. If "I deeply and completely love and accept myself" is too much of a stretch, start with "I'm willing to consider thinking about trying to love and accept myself."

2. When the positive phrase begins to feel realistic, you can begin to juxtapose it with a current or previous example of a negative one. Start small! "Even though I forgot to email Janet and Don about changing dinner plans for Saturday, I deeply and completely love and accept myself." "Even though my feelings were hurt when both Janet and Don forgot to email me about changing dinner plans for Saturday, I deeply and completely love and accept myself." "Even though my boss wasn't too crazy about my idea of putting up a stop sign in the parking lot, I deeply and completely love and accept myself." "Even though Bill was a bit harsh in his criticism of how I disciplined George today, I deeply and completely love and accept myself."

You get the gist. Repeat over and over and over.

This exercise trains your brain to create the responses that will rewire old negative messages about yourself and prevent any new ones from arising.

EXERCISE 4-12: Turning Enemies into Allies

You may have noticed that a food you couldn't stand when you were younger (pickled herring for me) has become a favorite now. Or a type of music that used to drive you bonkers (rhythm and blues for my neighbor Bob) has grown on you; you find it quite respectable and engaging now. Similarly, parts of ourselves that we used to disdain, ignore, or be ashamed of can begin to occupy their rightful place as part of ourselves as we mature and gain resilience. We don't let them take over, but we can be present for any gifts they have to offer.

1. Identify one particular part of yourself to work with in this exercise. It may be a part you explored in exercise 4-6, it may be another part on the list, or it may be a different part altogether.

2. Begin to explore the gift that this particular part of yourself might bring. Your lazy part may be protecting you from getting involved with projects or people you really don't want to engage with but don't know how to say no to. Your stubborn part may insist that you be seen and understood for who you are and what you believe before you go along with someone else's plan. Your inner critic may be trying to shape up your behavior before other people criticize you for it. Your smallifying part may be trying to maintain a healthy humility about your place on the planet. Your fantasizer part may simply want to be fully alive and engaged. Let your imagination help you find the gift that this part brings you.

3. If you find this process hard, recruit a friend to brainstorm with you.

   - Share with your friend the concerns you have about the part you've chosen to work with.
   - With your friend, brainstorm ten possible ways this part might be useful or have something to contribute — to anyone, not necessarily to you personally.
   - From these ten possibilities, identify one that might be relevant to you. See if you can identify a moment when this part might have benefited you in this way.
   - Thank your friend for helping you see new possibilities.

4. Now remember a specific time when the gift of this part really *was* a gift, when some aspect of this part actively supported your resilience. For

example, your stubborn part may have helped you when your insurance company denied your disability benefits after a car accident. You persisted and argued and talked to supervisors and managers and C-level staff until you were blue in the face — and until you got your benefits approved. Notice this reframing of stubbornness to persistence. If you wish to, write this memory down and save it among your "Reminders of My Resilience."

Recognizing the gift offered by a challenging part of yourself can radically shift your overall view of, understanding of, and relationship to the part. It is now available to support your resilience.

EXERCISE 4-13: Sifting and Shifting Parts

1. Spend one entire day (or longer) noticing various traits and parts of yourself as they come into your awareness, perhaps through noticing an inner message or a habitual behavior.
2. Pay attention to all of these traits — such as upbeat, discouraged, openminded, playful, irritable — whether you deem them positive or negative and whether you relate to them positively or negatively.
3. Notice how long each one lingers, whether it's moments or hours.
4. Notice how these traits and parts shift on their own, coming and going. Notice whether any one part seems to dominate for very long.
5. Practice deliberately choosing to shift from one trait or part to another. The purpose is not to deny or repress, or to dislike or disdain, but to learn to discern the different aspects of yourself and do the shifting.
6. Repeat this exercise many times, noticing what aspect has shown up, and shifting it if you choose to.

Parts of the self do come and go and do shift on their own. You're strengthening the flexibility of your prefrontal cortex so that you never have to be stuck with any one part taking over for too long, and you're learning that you are in charge. You can choose to return to the sense of your larger, whole self.

Level 3. Too Much

Tools of reconditioning can rewire our relationships to *any* stubborn, recalcitrant, acting-out part of us that seems to insist on derailing our inner secure base. We enable this rewiring through strengthening the response flexibility and functioning of the prefrontal cortex. We have to be mindful, compassionate, patient, and persevering in the process.

How long should you try? Until.

— JIM ROHN

EXERCISE 4-14: Writing a Compassionate Letter to Retire the Inner Critic

The rubber meets the road here. In this exercise, you use the focused attention of your prefrontal cortex to shift your relationship with the most powerful derailer of your inner secure base: your inner critic.

1. Identify just one negative message you typically hear from your inner critic, such as "You're so lazy!" or "You sure are out of shape these days!" Write the comment down. Write down also the tone of voice your inner critic uses, such as harsh, angry, or nagging. And write down the reaction in your own nervous system when you hear that message and that tone of voice, like tensing up or cringing.

2. Write a letter to a trusted friend — perhaps a true other, perhaps an imaginary friend. (You won't mail this letter.) Explain to your friend the circumstances in your life that usually trigger this negative comment from your inner critic. Share with your friend how you react when you hear this message: include the body sensations you notice, your feelings, and your thoughts when you hear this message delivered in this tone of voice.

3. Share with your friend any fears about any grain of truth in the critic's message.

4. Ask your friend to convey understanding and support for you as you struggle with this message from your inner critic.

5. Set this letter aside. Begin to write a second letter, this time from your friend to you, conveying understanding and support.

6. Have your friend convey their empathy for the misery of this pummeling

by your inner critic and their empathy for your experience of it. Have the friend reaffirm your many strengths and capacities to deal with your inner critic and to deal with the situation or behavior your inner critic is complaining about.

7. Have your friend convey love and acceptance of you, exactly as you are, regardless of what the inner critic says, regardless of your vulnerability to hearing that same message from your inner critic for the umpteen-thousandth time.

8. End the letter with your friend's sincere wishes for your anchoring in your own wholeness, your own inner secure base of resilience, your own strengths and gifts. Include, too, their sincere wishes for the lessening of your vulnerability to believing or being bothered by the messages of your inner critic.

9. Set this second letter aside for a while. After a few hours or days, reread your friend's letter to you. Take in the understanding and compassion you have given to yourself through your friend. Let this understanding and empathy shift your view of yourself and your relationship with your inner critic.

Repeat this exercise as often as you need to, addressing as many different messages from your inner critic as you hear, to prevent the negative messages from derailing your resilience or even taking up much of your attention any more. As these messages become less frequent and less bothersome, you'll have more mental bandwidth to cultivate the positive messages of acceptance and appreciation that strengthen your inner secure base.

Deconditioning

You may not have expected to use your imagination so much for coping with real-life disappointments, difficulties, and even disasters, so I'll reiterate here that whatever you can imagine is *real* to your brain. (This is precisely why your fears and worries can be so troublesome.)

Here you practice using your imagination to install reliable inner resources in your neural circuitry that you can call to mind and draw support from again and again and again.

Level 1. Barely a Wobble

Throughout this book I have emphasized response flexibility, being able to shift gears and perspectives to respond to challenging circumstances or internal messages differently than you have before. The inner resources created in your imagination by the two exercises below still foster flexibility but attempt to balance that response flexibility with response *stability*. You remain anchored in your inner secure base, with these resources to support you.

EXERCISE 4-15: Cultivating the Wiser Self

Cultivating the sense of a wiser self is somewhat de rigueur these days in many therapeutic and coaching modalities that help people strengthen their resilience. The wiser self is an imaginary figure who embodies the positive qualities that lead to more resilience and well-being: wisdom, courage, patience, perseverance. This wiser self is someone who truly cares for you and offers you understanding, support, and guidance to help you change and grow. Your wiser self could be drawn from a composite of many people who have been helpful to you already — role models, mentors, and benefactors. It could be a visualization of yourself five or ten years from now, when you have fulfilled your aspirations for developing strength, competence, and empowerment. However you imagine this figure, you can pose a particular problem or question to your wiser self and then listen for the answer, which comes from your own intuitive wisdom.

The beginning steps of this exercise resemble the compassionate friend exercise in chapter 3. It's a similar process that creates different resources.

1. Find a comfortable position for sitting quietly. Allow your eyes to gently close. Breathe deeply a few times into your belly, and allow your awareness to come more deeply into your body. Allow yourself to breathe comfortably. Become aware of relaxing into a gentle state of well-being.

2. When you are ready, imagine you are in your safe place, somewhere you feel comfortable, safe, relaxed, and at ease. This could be a room in your home, a cabin in the woods, a place by a pond or lake, or a café with a friend.

3. Let yourself know you are going to receive a visit from your wiser self,

perhaps an older, wiser, stronger version of yourself — someone who embodies the qualities you aspire to and is mature and settled in them.

4. As your wiser self arrives at your safe place, imagine the figure in quite some detail. Notice how old your wiser self is, how they are dressed, how they move. Notice how you greet your wiser self. Do you go out to meet them? Do you invite them in? Do you shake hands, bow, or hug?

5. Imagine yourself sitting and talking with your wiser self, or going for a walk together. Notice the way their presence and energy affect you.

6. Then, begin a conversation in your imagination with your wiser self. You can ask your wiser self how they came to be who they are. Ask what helped them most along the way. What did they have to let go of to become who they are? Can they share examples of when and how they triumphed over adversity?

7. You may choose to ask about a particular problem or challenge you are facing. Listen carefully to their response. Notice what advice your wiser self offers that you can take with you. Listen carefully to all they have to tell you.

8. Imagine what it would be like to embody your wiser self. Invite them to become part of you. Notice how it feels to experience your wiser self within you, how it feels to be your wiser self. When you are ready, imagine your wiser self becoming separate from you again.

9. Imagine that your wiser self offers you a gift — an object, a symbol, a word or phrase — to remind you of this meeting. Take this object in your hand and place it somewhere in your clothing for safekeeping. Your wiser self will let you know their name; remember it well.

10. As your wiser self prepares to leave, take a few gentle breaths to anchor your connection with them. Know that you can evoke this experience of encountering your wiser self anytime you choose. Thank your wiser self for the time you have spent together, and say goodbye.

11. Take a moment to reflect on this entire meeting and conversation. Notice any insights or shifts from the experience.

12. You may choose to write down your experience with your wiser self to help integrate it into your conscious memory and to have it ready to use any time you need guidance from within about how to be more resilient.

As with any use of imagination to access our deep intuitive knowing, the more you practice encountering your wiser self, the more reliably you will be able to embody this wisdom as you respond to the challenges and difficulties of your life.

EXERCISE 4-16: Befriending the Many Parts of Yourself

This being human is a guest house.
Every morning a new arrival.
A joy, a depression, a meanness,
Some momentary awareness comes
As an unexpected visitor.
Welcome and entertain them all!
Even if they're a crowd of sorrows,
who violently sweep your house
empty of its furniture,
still, treat each guest honorably.
He may be clearing you
out for some new delight.
The dark thought, the shame, the malice,
meet them at the door laughing,
and invite them in.
Be grateful for whoever comes,
because each has been sent
as a guide from beyond.

—Jalaluddin Rumi, "The Guest House"

Now you're ready to draw on the intuitive wisdom of your own wiser self to integrate the gifts offered by many parts of yourself, positive and negative, into an acceptance of all of who you are. This process helps your inner secure base become more stable and reliable.

1. Sit comfortably. Allow your eyes to gently close. Relax into the awareness of being at home in yourself.

2. When you're ready, imagine you are standing on a sidewalk outside a theater. Imagine the building, the marquee, the people walking by. Walk up to one of the main doors, open it, and walk into the lobby. Walk through the lobby — it's empty — to the door into the theater. Open it and walk into the theater — it's also empty. Walk all the way down to the third or fourth row and take a seat in the center of the row. An empty stage lies in front of you. All is quiet.

3. In this visualization, a series of characters will come out on to the stage representing your wiser self and various inner parts. You will be able to have a dialogue with each of these parts.

4. The first character to come out onto the stage is your wiser self from exercise 4-15. This character embodies all the qualities of resilience you identified in exercise 4-1. This wiser self creates the safety for all of the other characters in this exercise to come on stage. Temporarily, your prefrontal cortex doesn't have to be in charge; it can relax and enjoy the play.

5. Now imagine other characters coming onto the stage one by one. Each of these imaginary characters embodies a particular part of you. Each part might be represented by someone you know; yourself at a different age; someone you know from the movies, history, or literature; an animal; or a cartoon character.

6. The first character embodies a part of yourself that you really, really like. It's truly a part of you, and you are proud that it is. Let that character take the stage and remember it (perhaps make a note).

7. A second character joins the first on the stage, embodying another positive part of yourself. Again let that character materialize on the stage and remember it.

8. Now bring a third character onto the stage that embodies a part of yourself that you really don't like all that much. In fact, you wish it weren't part of you, but you know that it is. Let this character materialize and take a moment to remember it.

9. Bring a fourth character onto the stage that embodies another negative part of you. Observe and remember it.

10. Now you have on stage your wiser self, two parts of yourself that you really like, and two parts that you don't like so much, that you maybe even dislike

or disdain. You may even wish these last two weren't part of you at all, but they are.

11. One by one, ask each character what particular gift they bring to you by being part of you. Ask the parts you like first, and then the parts you don't like as much. Listen receptively, open-mindedly, to the answers from each part. Thank each part in turn for their answers, and sit with the answers you've heard for a moment, noticing any grain of truth or wisdom in them.

12. Ask your wiser self what gifts each of these parts may bring to you. Listen receptively to these answers, which may be different from the answers from the characters or your own perception of these characters.

13. Briefly thank each character for participating in this exercise with you. Watch as they leave the stage one by one, the wiser self last.

14. Imagine yourself getting up out of your seat and walking back up the aisle, through the lobby, and back outside. Turn around to look at the theater where all this happened. Then slowly come back to the awareness of sitting quietly. When you're ready, open your eyes.

15. Notice and reflect on your experience of this exercise. Notice any insights or shifts. Remember and embrace the lessons of each of these five characters, especially the ones you originally didn't like so much. Each one is an integral part of you, essential to your wholeness. This time of reflection helps your brain integrate the learning into long-term memory.

In this exercise, you release the energy it takes to repress or split off negative parts of yourself because you aren't repressing them anymore. They are recognized and accepted as part of the family system.

That energy is now available to you to grow, thrive, and flourish.

Level 2. Glitches and Heartaches, Sorrows and Struggles

When things get a little rougher and you need more inner resources to draw on, you can recruit someone who can be a true other to your true self, or you can use the power of your imagination to create those resources.

EXERCISE 4-17: Singing Your Song Back to You

A friend is someone who knows your song and sings it back to you when you have forgotten the words.

— passed on to me by Shoshana Alexander

Friends — anyone who knows something of your history — can act as true others to your true self when you feel overwhelmed by stress and can't find your way back home.

1. Ask a trustworthy friend who has been around the block with you a few times, or at least knows your stories of how you've found your way around the block before, to help you with this exercise.
2. Come into a sense of presence and acceptance together; let the social engagement evoke a neuroception of safety and trust.
3. Ask your friend to remember, or help you remember, moments of previous competency at coping, of response flexibility, and of resilience, even if you can't remember them right now. (These could be the "Sure I can!" moments you identified in exercise 3-14. Small is fine.)
4. Let one memory lead to another. In the safety of the social engagement, your brain can shift into the default network mode to start exploring, and it will.
5. Integrate several of these memories to recover the "song" of yourself as a competent, resilient person. Let yourself take in this sense of competence as a core part of who you are.

With the recovery of one memory, the default network of the brain can begin to meander and uncover other memories. Even if these memories are not particularly relevant to the stressor you are coping with now, your sense of being competent and resilient *is* relevant. That can be reintegrated into a sense of yourself as a competent, resilient person.

EXERCISE 4-18: Imagining a Good Inner Parent

This exercise is a highly modified variation of a form of group therapy now known as psychodrama, in which members of a group assist someone in reexperiencing and rewriting old, implicitly encoded internal models or old mental scripts of a past relationship with a neglectful, dismissive, or critical parent. One group member acts the role of that parent; another acts the role of a new, empathic, responsive "good inner parent." Other members play other roles as needed. In this version of the exercise, you create the characters you choose to work with entirely in your imagination. You can ask friends to assist you if you wish, or you can use furniture, pillows, or other objects to stand in for the characters you want to evoke.

1. Sit quietly and comfortably in a place where you won't be interrupted for ten to twenty minutes. Come into a sense of presence, breathing gently and deeply to reduce any body tension. You may place your hand on your heart at any time to remind yourself to bring a kind, loving awareness to your experience.

2. Evoke the presence of your wiser self to act as a witness in this exercise, who can mirror and reflect your experience back to you. You may also imagine your compassionate friend (or a representational object like a pillow or stuffed animal) sitting near you to help with this exercise, not saying anything but offering presence, connection, and comfort.

3. In your imagination (or using another representational object in the space around you, such as a chair or a lamp), evoke the parental figure you wish to work with — mother, father, stepparent or grandparent, aunt, or uncle if they were significant in shaping your sense of yourself as unworthy and unimportant. Share with your wiser self your visceral, felt sense of being in the presence of this remembered person (or the object representing them). Notice feeling heard and accurately understood by your wiser self. Notice any safety or ease that comes from hearing your wiser self empathically and accurately reflect your experience back to you.

4. Bring in any other characters who are relevant in re-creating this earlier experience — siblings, neighbors, friends, or teachers. Trust your imagination to evoke the characters most needed in this scenario, even if your conscious brain is not entirely sure why they are there.

5. Now imagine the character of a good parent — the ideal or better parent you can feel safe with, who understands, accepts, and appreciates you.

Take your time to evoke the character of this good parent until it feels real to you. This figure may be an imagined version of someone you know who does act like a good parental figure. Notice your experience of being in the presence of this good parent, and share it with your wiser self. Take the time you need for this experience of sharing to emerge. Notice your own felt response to having your experience understood and mirrored by your wiser self.

6. You can imagine interactions with this new parent, witnessed by your wiser self. Notice whether you feel any increased sense of worthiness or acceptance. Notice and share with your wiser self your experience of these interactions.

7. Spend as much time as you wish with your good parent. Let yourself take in the good of the encounter.

8. You can explore a juxtaposition of the "old" parent with this new, good parent if you wish, always sharing your experience with your wiser self and having it witnessed and reflected back to you.

9. When you feel complete, let all of the characters dissolve, your wiser self last. Reflect on the entire experience, noticing any shifts in your sense of yourself.

The creative imagination called for in this exercise is quite a stretch for your default network. The new scenarios you imagine (which most likely will evolve if you choose to do this exercise again) can become powerful inner supports of your resilience.

Level 3. Too Much

Sometimes too many experiences of being thrown off center leave you abiding long-term in a sense of shame, rather than spending most of your time centered and only occasionally being thrown off into shame. If this is the case, it may seem extremely difficult, or impossible, to find your way back to your secure stable base.

Other exercises (6-15 and 7-6) offer additional tools to deal with the feelings of being lost, confused, and overwhelmed that come up when you are derailed. Here, for practice, we explore the use of tools for recovering from the shame engendered by feeling like a failure too often, over too long a time, or starting when you were very young.

We personify your experiences as the archetypal wounded inner child who has too often felt neglected, criticized, rejected, abused, humiliated, abandoned, and shamed. These are painful experiences that occurred at times or in circumstances when you did not have enough inner resilience or support from others to avoid the feeling of shame. This wounded inner child is found in the mythology of every culture and many modern therapeutic modalities, and most people recognize and resonate with the experience of it instantly.

Recovering resilience involves using tools to help that inner child at last feel seen, heard, understood, accepted, and loved when that didn't happen the first time around, or not often enough or deeply enough, with parents, peers, colleagues, friends, and romantic partners. This inner child is not who you are, but it is very often part of who you *have been*. Recalling moments of social rejection and embarrassment or the failure of relationship can activate the pain as though it were happening right here, right now.

It doesn't always require therapy to recover the resilience of the inner child, though a skillful relational therapy certainly can help. *Any* attuned, understanding, accepting, loving relationship can do this rewiring and recovering. It's the seeing, understanding, and accepting of the inner child by any older, wiser, and stronger (more resilient) parental figure that does the healing.

In practicing this skill of relational intelligence, you're evoking your own wiser adult self to provide the seeing, understanding, acceptance, and even embracing and love that will help your inner child heal from shame and recover its inner secure base of resilience — its birthright.

EXERCISE 4-19: Dialogue between Your Wiser Self and Your Inner Child

Conducting an imagined dialogue between your wiser self (or good inner parent) and your emerging, wounded inner child draws on your powers of imagination and your capacities of awareness and acceptance to create a new experience of an inner relationship between your wiser self (or good inner parent) and another part of yourself. This relationship allows you to create new patterns of responding to your inner self.

1. Evoke a sense of your wiser self (or good inner parent). Imagine that wiser self sitting somewhere that feels safe for your inner child too: on the floor at home, on a bench in a park, on a blanket on the beach.

2. Evoke a sense of your inner child at a time when that child felt a little lost, confused, and unsure of belonging. I've noticed that for many folks, thinking about being back in the third grade or in middle school or junior high reliably evokes this state of being.

3. Imagine your wiser self and inner child sitting together, perhaps saying hello, perhaps saying nothing and simply coming into an awareness of the presence of the other. Let your wiser self be open and receptive, trusting and relaxed. Let your inner child be exactly however they are, with whatever comforts they need (teddy bear, stuffie, toy car, beloved poodle) to feel safe enough to sit with the wiser self.

4. Imagine a sense of connection developing between your wiser self and your inner child, however shy or wary the inner child might be about the contact. Imagine a conversation developing between the two, however hesitant or superficially courteous that might be at first. Imagine the inner child feeling safe, comfortable, and familiar enough with the wiser self to settle into a genuine conversation about whatever needs to be seen, heard, and known.

5. Imagine your wiser self and your inner child settling into getting acquainted: "So this is who you are. Glad to finally meet you. This is okay." This encounter is neither idealized nor idealizing, not fantasy perfect. Whatever arises, love that.

6. Let your wiser self and your inner child reflect separately on their experiences of this conversation. (Toggling back and forth between the two is fine.)

7. Imagine your wiser self and your inner child saying goodbye and parting company for now, knowing they can come together again whenever the inner child wishes.

8. Reflect on your experience of this entire exercise, noticing any shift in your sense of self and accepting this part of yourself.

Acknowledging and relating to the inner child with kindness, interest, curiosity, and care rewires some of our earliest internal working models of self and creates the neural platform for earned secure attachment, which you experience as your inner secure base. This is the strongest inner foundation you can have for your resilience.

EXERCISE 4-20: Empowering Your Inner Child to Evoke Your Wiser Self

Building on the previous exercise, here you use your imagination to rewire a moment when your inner child felt dropped or forgotten by others, with no inner resources available at the time to remedy the situation or prevent a collapse into shame. But now your inner child can become empowered to evoke the wiser self to step in, evoking self-acceptance and a sense of inner goodness, to prevent that shame response.

1. Imagine your wiser self and your inner child getting together for another conversation. This time, your inner child feels and expresses appropriate anger from a time when an adult in charge didn't connect with or protect the child. Maybe it was a time when a parent forgot to pick the child up after school, a teacher failed to stop bullying on the playground, or a best friend turned mean and snotty. At the time, the child didn't have the inner resources to respond resiliently to the situation, and your wiser self, not yet a part of your psyche, wasn't present to intervene.

2. As your inner child relates the story to your wiser self, the child may express some anger. "Where were you when I needed you? How can I trust you to show up now?" And your wiser self (or good inner parent) listens empathically and understandingly. "Of course you would be upset; that's perfectly understandable." The wiser self reassures your inner child that they are here now and will be here whenever needed from now on.

3. Your inner child receives and trusts this reassurance from your wiser self as best they can. This building of trust is the repair and the rewiring your inner child needs: the realization that they have the power to evoke the wiser self anytime they need to, and the wiser self will show up and help.

4. Notice any shifts in your inner child's experience: is there a sense of becoming more empowered, more resilient?

This exercise doesn't change what happened, but it does change the inner child's relationship to what happened. It doesn't rewrite history, but it does rewire the brain. Repeat this exercise as many times as is necessary to firmly establish the sense of the inner child's empowerment to evoke the help of the wiser self.

This chapter has introduced many tools of self-awareness, self-acceptance, and inner integration to recover and strengthen your own, powerful inner secure base of resilience. These practices allow you to meet the challenges and stressors of your life with your own core strengths of resilience, guided by the intuitive wisdom of your wiser self.

Feeling more trusting and secure within yourself creates more flexibility and resilience in your brain to meet the challenges of relating to others. We'll address those in the next chapter.

This deeper resilience in relating to people allows you to receive more support from them. You can come to see other people as useful refuges, resources, and role models who can foster your own growing capacities, competence, and courage.

CHAPTER FIVE

Practices of Relational Intelligence with Others

Trust, Shared Humanity, Interdependence, Refuges, Resources

*I've learned that people will forget what you said, and people will forget what you did,
but people will never forget how you made them feel.*

— **ATTRIBUTED TO MAYA ANGELOU**

Human beings are social beings, evolutionarily hardwired to connect. We are born, raised, schooled, and rewarded or repudiated in kinship families, tribes, societies, and cultures, for better or worse. We don't have much choice about how that neural wiring evolved in the first place.

We do have choices about how we perceive other people and the dynamics of our relationships with them, and how we respond to those connections, interactions, and disconnections. We've all had the experience of relationships that derail our resilience: we've been let down, had our feelings hurt, been betrayed, been treated unfairly. We may be part of communities that have been oppressed and discriminated against or that have oppressed and discriminated against others. As the revered meditation teacher Jack Kornfield says, "We hurt people, and are hurt by people, because we are people."

Yet people can also provide both the best refuges and the best resources for healing from any pain we have ever experienced, especially the pain we've experienced in relationships. Deepening our skills of relational intelligence, connecting safely and resonantly with other people, reliably helps us recover our resilience. We can learn to install new wiring and to recondition or decondition old neural pathways in our brain that might be blocking that resilient relating.

We learn "rules" about interacting with others — how to safely connect with and disconnect from others — in our earliest relational experiences. The brain installs those models of relating in our neural circuitry by eighteen months of age (before we develop the capacity for conscious processing). And these conditioned patterns, unless we choose to change them, operate robustly well into adulthood.

If you learned healthy patterns of relating to others early on, including the ability to find refuges and resources in other people, you can reliably connect and engage safely with other people: you can be who you are and allow them to be who they are. (This is theory of mind at work. You are you and I am me, and we are different people, and that's okay.) You can safely differentiate yourself and disengage from other people and comfortably return to your own home base, being and enjoying who you are. You develop a base of healthy interdependence from which to navigate relationships with others. You can be affiliative and join in; you can be autonomous and stand on your own. You can be intimate; you can be independent. A healthy interdependency allows you to shift your focus between yourself and others as needed.

This healthy interdependency supports your resilience in three important ways:

1. *Trust.* When you trust yourself and your inner secure base (initially nurtured by true others to your true self), when you know how to be both stable and flexible in your responses to people and events, and when you have learned to trust the processes of relating, you then can trust being interdependent with others. Knowing how to safely engage and disengage, you can risk trusting another person. You can be open and receptive, experiencing a nourishing connection as a two-way street, enjoying common ground, common interests, and your shared humanity with someone else. And if that connection isn't happening or doesn't feel trustworthy, you can safely disengage and be comfortable in your own good company.

2. *Refuges.* You can trust other people to act as genuine refuges, offering respite and sanctuary from pain or grief, especially pain and grief caused by other people. The empathy and understanding offered by compassionate companions allow you to regroup; restore your faith in yourself, in other people, and in life itself again; and recover your resilience.

3. *Resources.* You learn response flexibility and recover your resilience from role models, advisers offering wise counsel based on their experience, and from people who provide material resources (such as financial or logistical assistance) or links to those resources. People create safety nets — in families, communities, and societies. Whenever a difficulty or disaster strikes, that safety net is already in place.

When Relational Intelligence Didn't Quite Gel

Sometimes the models of relating to others that you learned early on, or models of relating that you have learned since, don't quite gel into the healthy interdependency that supports resilience in relationships or allows healthy relationships now to rewire inadequate patterns encoded in the past.

Your brain may have encoded patterns of being pulled off center by becoming enmeshed or codependent with others, needing to take care of someone to get their attention or approval in order to feel good about yourself. Maybe that sense of self never quite fully coalesced because another person needed you to be someone other than who you really were, so that you can now focus on a demanding other person all right, but not so easily on yourself. Maybe you learned to focus exclusively on yourself in order to gel that sense of self, to avoid being distracted or hurt by people who couldn't quite see, respect, honor, or embrace you for who you are. You may have learned to cut off or withdraw from others to protect that sense of self.

This chapter will help you learn to rewire those patterns by choosing to relate to people now who can relate to you from their own healthy sense of interdependency, their own inner secure base. You will also practice relating to other people from the stability and flexibility of your inner secure base so that you can safely engage with and disengage from the dynamics of relationship with another person as needed, whether that person is coming from a healthy interdependency in the moment or not. Not everyone has worked on developing their response flexibility and resilience. Even those nearest and dearest to you can sometimes lose it temporarily.

You will learn to skillfully dance in relationship with others, with both affiliation and autonomy, intimacy and independence, resilient relating and recovering resilience through relationships.

New Conditioning

Strengthening your brain's capacities to engage with other people in healthy interdependency requires you to engage in healthy interactions with other people that install new neural circuitry or amplify existing circuitry. You engage in these new experiences specifically to strengthen your response flexibility.

Level 1. Barely a Wobble

Trust is foundational to any safe, skillful, and successful engagement with other people. To develop it, you want to deepen your trust of yourself (through the exercises in chapter 4 that help you develop an inner secure base) and your trust in your competence at relating, so that you can negotiate your relationships successfully even when other people are not completely trustworthy.

The following exercises strengthen the circuitry in your brain that deepens that capacity to trust.

EXERCISE 5-1: Deep Listening to Develop Resilience

The most basic and powerful way to connect to another person is to listen. Just listen. Perhaps the most important thing we ever give each other is our attention.... A loving silence often has far more power to heal and to connect than the most well-intentioned words.

— Rachel Naomi Remen

When we shift our attention toward listening, our whole world changes. Learning to listen is equal to learning to love.

— Ruth Cox

Here you revisit the skill of deep listening (exercise 4-2), expanding the conversation to new topics. Allow thirty minutes for this exercise: time deepens the practice, the learning, and the rewiring.

1. Recruit a partner (a friend or colleague) to do this exercise with you. You can switch roles later, if you wish.

2. From the list of questions below, or similar questions of your own, tell your partner which question you would like to answer first.

   - What brings you joy in your life?
   - What brings you sorrow?
   - What worries you now?
   - When have you found courage in dark times?
   - What are you grateful for?
   - What are you proud of?

3. Your partner asks you the question, listens quietly to your answer, not commenting but thanking you for your response, and repeats this process, asking the same question, for about five minutes.

4. Answer the question as honestly as you can. Notice how it feels to be listened to and received. Let your inquiry deepen with each repetition of the question.

5. When you have finished answering the first question, pause to reflect on your experience of yourself and of the exercise.

6. Continue to answer as many of the questions as you wish. Then you can also switch roles with your partner, starting with whichever question they would like to answer first.

7. When you and your partner have answered as many questions as you each wish, debrief together. What was it like for you to share your answers? What was it like to be listened to? What was it like to hear your partner's answers?

The repetition of the questions allows your brain to delve more and more deeply into them and produce richer answers. The "little and often" practice of inquiry allows you to bring the processing of your brain into conscious awareness, creating a new, clearer sense of yourself and your resilience. The safety you experience in doing this exercise strengthens the brain's social engagement system for both you and your partner. Being listened to and received deepens your trust in yourself, in your partner, and in the process of relating.

EXERCISE 5-2: Moments of Meeting

A "moment of meeting" is a moment when two people traverse a feeling-landscape together as it unfolds in real time. They achieve a "felt sense" of each other; they share a sufficiently similar mental landscape so that a recognition of specific fittedness is achieved — they each know what the other is experiencing.

The authentic, mutual responses of this shared feeling voyage create a shared private world that reorganizes the relationship and [initiates] an irreversible shift into a new state. The two people sense an opening up. There is a newly expanded intersubjective field that allows for different possibilities of ways-of-being-with-one-another.

These shared feeling voyages are so simple and natural, yet very hard to explain or even talk about (outside of poetry). Moments of meeting are one of life's most startling yet normal events, capable of altering our world step by step or in one leap. People are changed, and they are linked differently for having changed one another.

— Daniel Stern, author of The Present Moment in
Psychotherapy and Everyday Life

Moments of meeting can happen with people you already feel closely connected to. They can sometimes happen randomly, with people you have met only once and may never meet again. My friend Rob Timineri calls these spontaneous moments of meeting "brief affairs." They are not sexual encounters but moments of feeling deeply connected and resonant.

This exercise helps you develop the skill to notice these moments of meeting when they happen (or to realize and appreciate retrospectively that they happened) and to use the experience or memory to deepen your trust in connection.

1. Think back on relational moments when you experienced a sudden feeling of close connection with another person, even if it wasn't acknowledged at the time. These moments of connection can happen with pets, too.

2. Acknowledge the moment now. Get the felt sense of it in your body now. Savor the moment.

Like exercise 2-6, in which you generate a sense of safety and trust by remembering a moment of feeling loved and cherished, this exercise helps you create a sense of safety and trust in the process of relating. Experiencing and recollecting these moments create a safety net in the brain for taking risks in relationships.

EXERCISE 5-3: Monitoring the Rhythm of Resonance

When you experience moments of genuine connection, you typically want more. You certainly want to trust that you can create them again or anew. Tools of mindful empathy, anchored in theory of mind, can foster the rhythm of relating that allows a connection to continue, expand, and deepen.

1. In your everyday interactions with other people, pay attention to what is happening between you and another person as mindfully as you can (know what you're experiencing while you're experiencing it). Pay attention to the "vibe," the facial expressions and body language, the tone and rhythm of your voices, as much as to the words of your conversation.

Notice your comfort or discomfort with how the nonverbal communication is going.

2. Attend to the rhythm of the exchange and how quickly and easily you take turns. Notice whether one of you seems to be doing most of the talking, the other most of the listening.

3. If necessary, use both your mindful empathy and your theory of mind to help you adjust the rhythm into a balanced back-and-forth exchange, each of you listening and being listened to openly and deeply by the other.

4. Depending on how comfortable you feel in the connection, you may guide the exchange with a cue like "I'd like to hear more about..." or "I'd like to tell you more about..." to make the conversation more balanced.

5. To deepen the closeness of the connection, you might want to share what it feels like to be conversing in this way, acknowledging the moment of meeting while it's happening.

Empathy deepens connection. The neural circuitry you use to pick up on what someone else is feeling is the same circuitry that allows you to feel those feelings yourself. (It can be helpful to check with the other person that you are perceiving and interpreting their feelings accurately.) A good rhythm of exchange acknowledges and fosters a healthy interdependence, the stable and flexible focus on self and others that builds relational resilience.

Level 2. Glitches and Heartaches, Sorrows and Struggles

Seeking connection with other people can feel much riskier when you're facing real hardship and doubting whether you're going to be able to cope well. Yet researchers have consistently found that connection helps.

You may seek that help from others in the form of refuge — a safe haven of family, friends, or community to hang out with until the worst of the storm has blown over. It might take the form of resourcing: asking people to aid you in practical, tangible ways that support your resilient coping. That might mean asking for a bowl of chicken soup when you're down with the flu or a warm, safe place to stay while your house is being restored after a flood or hurricane.

The data also demonstrate that when we offer help to others, we feel more resourced and resilient, too. These feelings come not from showing ourselves to be more competent or more altruistic than other people but out of a shared sense of humanity, recognizing and trusting our interdependence.

EXERCISE 5-4: Reaching Out for and Offering Help

This exercise is about rebalancing your own style of asking for and offering help. You may lean to the cut-off side, tending to say, "I'll do it myself" or "Why can't you do it yourself?" Independence and autonomy are good, but acknowledging our shared vulnerability as human beings and opening up to others is often even better. You can use the help you receive to invest your own energy in coping, rather than propping yourself up in isolation without enough energy left to cope.

Alternatively, if you don't trust or rely on your own capacities to cope, you may lean toward asking others for help all the time, driving your family, friends, and neighbors crazy. Being resilient means being both stable and flexible. You anchor in your inner secure base while you ask for and receive help from others.

1. Recall and reflect on five recent times when you legitimately needed some help — anything from being locked out of your house to being locked out of a promotion to being locked out of your daughter's life.

2. Notice whether, in those moments, you leaned toward asking other people for everything you needed, not relying on your own ability to respond, or whether you were inclined to rely totally on yourself, not wanting to bother anyone or have anyone think less of you for not being able to handle your distress on your own. Among the factors that may have influenced your leanings, notice whether trusting or mistrusting yourself, trusting or mistrusting others, and trusting or mistrusting the processes of relationship played a role in your decision.

3. Reflect for a moment on what conditioning, values, and beliefs might inform or block your choices about reaching out for help.

4. Reflect on whether your style of asking for help is reflected in your style of offering help as well; it could be.

5. As an experiment, the next time you are in difficulties, try leaning a little bit more in the other direction from your accustomed pattern. Notice whether you feel able to risk trusting yourself or trusting others more.

6. Notice any of the lessons you might be learning from this experiment. Notice whether those lessons influence your accustomed style in the future.

By rebalancing your inclination to depend too much on yourself or others, you are gently rewiring your brain for healthy interdependence.

In addition to learning to seek support from yourself and the people around you, you can create a portable, 24/7 circle of support in your imagination. This circle can include both real people you trust and feel supported by and imaginary people you would like to meet. Your circle may include a spiritual figure like Jesus or the Dalai Lama. It may include your own wiser self. Visualizing yourself as encircled by real or imaginary friends who have your back can greatly enhance your ease and resilience as you face an unknown or frightening situation.

EXERCISE 5-5: Circle of Support

1. Take a moment to identify two or three people (more if you wish) who give you a sense of safety and trust, connection and support when you think of them. These do not have to be people you already know, people you see every day, or even people you would necessarily go to for support. These are just people whose presence, real or imagined, calms your nervous system and makes you feel safe and protected.

2. Imagine these people gathered around you in a semicircle or walking beside you, lending you their faith and support as you face a difficult situation. Imagine them fully present, fully supportive. You are not alone.

3. If you wish, identify a specific situation for which you would like support, such as going to a supervisor to discuss a complaint or a raise, preparing for a tax audit, telling your brother and sister-in-law you won't be joining them for Thanksgiving this year, or confronting your teenage son about drug paraphernalia stashed in his bedroom closet. Rehearse walking into this situation with your circle of support staunchly with you. This rehearsal can *prewire* circuitry in the brain, making it much more likely that you will feel the support when you enter the actual situation.

4. Practice evoking this circle of support again and again until this circle be-
    comes a natural resource of your brain that you can call on anytime you
    need it. The people in your circle may change over time.

    Evoking your imaginary circle of support can feel as real to your brain as
    having these people physically present. The potential of using imagination to
    prewire your brain is vast. The next time you face an unexpected challenge
    or crisis, notice any increased sense of inner safety as you evoke your circle of
    support to help you act resiliently.

Sharing our glitches and heartaches, our sorrows and struggles with other people
can cause additional difficulties in relating skillfully with others. This exercise trains
both the speaker and the listener in responsible speaking and empathic listening, relating to themselves from their own inner secure base (I am who I am, and I love and
accept who I am) and relating to the other using their theory of mind (you are you,
different from me, and that's okay — I accept who you are). This practice requires
the speaker to take responsibility for their own feelings, especially their reactions to
another person's behavior, and it requires the other person to listen openly and receptively, without reacting defensively or trying to fix the situation.

EXERCISE 5-6: Communicating without Shame or Blame

1. Recruit a partner to practice this exercise with — a friend, colleague, or life
    partner. Decide who will speak first; then you may switch roles if you wish
    to. Allow at least fifteen minutes for each person to speak.

2. The speaker identifies a difficulty they are having with another person (but
    not the listener). They focus on the relational difficulty, not on casting the
    other person as difficult.

3. The speaker explores the difficulty in the form of "I" statements: "I notice
    I'm reacting to..." It's okay to describe the problematic behavior: "When I
    perceive Jack doing...," but the speaker should then refocus on their own
    response: "I'm reacting," or "I feel," or "I worry." Using the word *perceive*

means that you're taking responsibility for the perception: you're exploring your response to your perception, not shaming, blaming, or criticizing the other person for causing the perception. Keeping the statements brief makes it easier for the listener to remember and repeat them.

4. The listener listens and simply repeats what the speaker has said, word for word. "I heard you say..." It can be hard to simply listen and repeat, without reacting, advising, debating, or criticizing. After repeating each statement from the speaker, the listener asks, in a warm, neutral way, "Is there more?"

5. The speaker continues exploring their relational difficulty with the other person for as long as necessary. Interestingly, when the focus is on the speaker's own inner experience, this can take far less time than you might think — far less than complaining about the other person, which could go on forever.

6. The listener sums up everything they have heard. The speaker can agree or offer modifications to the listener's summary.

7. Both listener and speaker pause and reflect on what their role in the conversation was like for them. They do not offer an evaluation of how the other partner did!

There are two variations to this exercise that you might try.

Variation 1

The speaker identifies and explores a difficulty they are having with some aspect of their own behavior, perhaps in relation to another person, perhaps more general. The other person listens and repeats as before. The speaker and the listener debrief as before.

Variation 2

The speaker identifies a difficulty they are having with a behavior of the listener. As the speaker, you focus on yourself. As the listener, anchored in your secure base and theory of mind, you listen and repeat as before. The speaker and the listener debrief as before.

The effectiveness of this exercise depends on the absence of shaming or blaming and the practice of listening without fixing or defending, which create a sense of safety. Social engagement can reduce reactivity in the brain. The speaker gets to explore their own experience without having to worry about the reactions of the listener. The listener can listen without taking anything personally. The relational and communication skills developed here form the basis for conversations on negotiating changes in behavior, as addressed in exercise 5-10 below.

Level 3. Too Much

All this talk therapy is just an excuse to hang out long enough for the relationship to do the healing.
— KEYNOTE SPEAKER AT ATTACHMENT AND PSYCHOTHERAPY CONFERENCE

Presence and connection are healing. Even in the darkest of times, using your brain's tools of relational intelligence can provide both refuge and resource. You can create a sense of safety through the emotional resonance of the social engagement system, by accessing your inner secure base, and by activating the neural safety net of shared humanity. It may be hard to trust this process initially, but with practice, you can learn to trust and turn to other people when you feel you're about to go under.

EXERCISE 5-7: Getting the Most out of a Relationship Workshop or Support Group

Research shows us that brains learn best from interacting with other healthy brains. If you're seeking to develop more skills in relational intelligence, you'll learn most effectively by practicing relating to other people in a safe, trustworthy environment.

1. Look for a facilitator-led workshop or support group focused on developing skills in relating. Ask friends, colleagues, or spiritual advisers for recommendations. Consult listings of local mental health counselors and self-help organizations.

2. Interview the facilitator in depth, asking about their training and experience in addressing concerns and needs like yours. If you feel enough of a connection with the facilitator to try the workshop or group, you'll likely feel at ease with the participants as well.

3. Use all the tools you've practiced throughout this book as you first engage with the workshop or group: hand on heart, power posing, claiming your traits of resilience and your own lovable, whole self. Don't wait and see how the experience goes: be proactive in choosing how you want it to go.

4. As you participate, notice what you're experiencing while you're experiencing it. If you ever feel unsure or unsafe about what's happening, ask the facilitator for help. Ask privately if you're not comfortable doing that in the group — though in my experience, if someone voices a concern, it's likely something that other participants are experiencing as well.

5. Notice what you're learning. Notice what you need to learn that you never knew you needed. Practice cultivating positive emotions — recognizing moments of kindness, compassion, generosity, gratitude — to shift your brain out of any contraction and negativity and toward openness, receptivity, new perspectives, and optimism.

6. After the first session, review any positive shifts, noticing whether you feel any deepening of your response flexibility or any more comfort with the rhythm and dance of relationships.

Every block you may have developed about relating well to others has a chance to come up in a group setting devoted to learning about and removing those blocks. By consciously practicing relating with others in a safe setting, little and often, you prime the neuroplasticity in your brain to learn important skills and increase your response flexibility.

Besides learning new relational skills from others in a workshop or group, you can deepen your relational intelligence by providing that kind of support to others as well.

When you're called upon to be the compassionate companion for someone who is struggling to keep their head above water, focus on being with the person rather than fixing what's wrong. Be the refuge first, the resource second.

EXERCISE 5-8: Compassionate Companion

1. When you sense a person might need support, offer presence and companionship on their schedule, on their terms. Show up; be present; listen quietly. This person doesn't need to explain or defend anything; they simply need their story to be heard.

2. Offer a touch on the shoulder or a hug, but use your mindful empathy and your theory of mind to sense their degree of openness and receptivity to the companionship you are offering. Notice whether you need anything from this person yourself, like feeling good about yourself for being such a good helper, and try to let go of that expectation.

3. Convey your genuine trust in the person's capacities to cope, however long it might take them. Express your faith in their resilience and capacities to recover from the event or situation.

4. Be conscious of the timing as you shift to suggesting additional resources. A person who insists, "I'm fine!" is adopting one way of coping, and people can cope (or try to cope) that way for years. It doesn't work to hurry the person along. Nor does it work to try to hurry someone out of a need to feel better. "Don't worry. You'll be fine. Just get over it and move on" can feel completely misattuned, even insulting. Be patient. People need to be protected from being rushed through their process.

5. When you sense the person is ready to begin taking action on their own, offer the resources or links to resources that you sense will be helpful. Be sensitive about not making too many suggestions all at once. Give the person time and space to absorb what you are recommending.

Our resilience gets a tremendous boost when we feel the comfort of shared humanity, knowing that we're all in this together. By being present with someone when they are in distress and offering a comforting companionship, you can feel that shared humanity as well.

Out of a great need
We are all holding hands

And climbing
Not loving is a letting go
Listen, the terrain around here
Is far too dangerous for that.

— Hafiz

Reconditioning

As always with reconditioning, you juxtapose opposite experiences to cause neural networks in the brain to fall apart (deconsolidate) and rewire (reconsolidate) an instant later. With repetition, the new neural network grows stronger, and the new response becomes the habit. You can apply reconditioning to relationship dynamics by creating changes in behaviors that, over time, will change the neural circuitry underlying those behaviors, creating new and more resilient relational habits.

Level 1. Barely a Wobble

Through the exercises here, you can become increasingly comfortable with both closeness and distance, and more competent at negotiating change.

EXERCISE 5-9: Comfort with Closeness and Distance

In this exercise, you explore your levels of comfort with connection and disconnection by exploring variations in physical distance and closeness with another person.

1. Recruit a partner to do this exercise with you. You may notice different experiences of comfort or discomfort with different partners, depending on how well you know them.
2. Stand facing your partner, about twenty feet apart. Notice a baseline of comfort or discomfort at this distance.
3. Walk slowly toward your partner, noticing any shift in your comfort level as you're walking. Notice whether or when you cross a threshold from comfort to discomfort. You decide when to stop the approach: when your bodies are still beyond arm's length, almost touching, or touching. Return to the distance where you feel most comfortable and make a note of it.

4. Stand still while your partner walks slowly toward you, noticing any shift in your comfort level as they approach. Notice when your partner crosses your threshold of comfort or discomfort. You decide when your partner should stop their approach; say, "Stop, thank you," when you need to. Indicate where your partner can stand that makes you feel the most comfortable. Make a note of it.

5. You and your partner can switch roles at this point, so that your partner gets to choose when to stop the approach and reflect on that experience as well.

6. Start walking toward one another simultaneously and at about the same pace. Notice any shifts in your comfort level as you approach one another. Both you and your partner indicate the distance apart where you feel most comfortable (which may not be the same for both of you). Make a note of those distances.

7. Debrief with your partner.

Our autonomic nervous system is always processing its own perceptions of safety and danger in relationship to the environment and to others. Individuals vary in their comfort levels with physical distance and closeness, depending on the range of resilience of their own nervous system and on conditioning from their family of origin, other relationships, and their culture. This kind of exercise can be used for exploring comfort and discomfort in emotional connection and disconnection as well, as demonstrated in exercise 5-12.

EXERCISE 5-10: Negotiating Change

When something feels off in the dynamics of our relationship with another person, we may need to request a change in their behavior to help us feel safe in connection. To strengthen our response flexibility we must also take responsibility for changing our behavior in ways that will help us get our needs met.

This exercise builds on variation 2 in exercise 5-6 above.

1. The speaker, having explored their reactions to an aspect of the listener's behavior, now identifies and states:

    - A specific need they would like to have addressed — for example, to feel more connected, more respected, more appreciated.
    - Three things the listener could do that would enable the speaker to feel that their needs were being met, or at least addressed. These requests must be *positive* (the brain has a much easier time learning a new habit than undoing an old one). They must be *doable* (little and often!). They must be requests for changes in *behavior*, not in attitude or character. (Behavior is measurable; the listener knows what to do and knows when they have done it.) The new behavior must be done within a defined time frame (generally a week or two) without any nagging or reminding by the speaker. A wish that the listener be less angry could instead be articulated as "Say three things you appreciate about me in the coming week."
    - Three behaviors that the *speaker* is willing to do to meet his or her own needs. Again, the speaker takes responsibility for their own response flexibility. Again, the behaviors must be positive, doable, and done within a certain time frame.

2. Both the speaker and listener may negotiate and modify these requests. Each person chooses *one* behavior that they are willing to do in the agreed-on time frame.

3. At the end of the time frame, speaker and listener debrief. Did they do what they agreed on? If they did, kudos. If not, they can try to negotiate other behavior changes that are easier to achieve. Did the changes in behavior have the desired effect on the speaker, allowing them to feel that their needs were being met? If they did, kudos again. If not, the speaker takes responsibility for clarifying what behaviors either they or the listener could do that will better meet the identified need.

Neither compulsive self-reliance nor codependence can catalyze healthy changes in a relationship. Negotiating change is the dance of interdependence, a dynamic of give and take that strengthens the response flexibility in both partners and the resilience of the relationship. The little-and-often principle is important here. One change per week in each partner equals two changes per week for the relationship, which equals more than one hundred changes in the relationship dynamics in the course of a year. That's pretty resilient!

Level 2. Glitches and Heartaches, Sorrows and Struggles

Sometimes you may have to stop or correct negative dynamics and behaviors in a relationship if you want to continue to feel safe and connected. Exercises 5-11 and 5-12 address negative dynamics in interpersonal relationships. Exercise 5-13 helps us take responsibility for difficulties we create on a more global level.

EXERCISE 5-11: Setting Limits and Boundaries

Setting limits and boundaries is an essential skill of relational intelligence. You need to be able to trust that you can protect yourself from abuse or unfair treatment in a relationship, regardless of the other person's reactions or threats. Otherwise you risk becoming a doormat, too quickly acquiescing to the other person's needs even when they do not match your needs, staying connected at sometimes too high a cost. Or you can sacrifice the connection in order to stay safe, by cutting off, disengaging, or withdrawing emotionally and just going through the motions of a relationship. (These dynamics can go on in couples and families for years.) The vitality and growth necessary to a healthy relationship are lost.

1. Identify one person with whom you want to practice setting a limit and boundary. You may not want to work on your most challenging or most intimate relationship to start with. Practice on someone easier in order to give yourself — and your brain — a chance for success.

2. Identify one violation of a healthy limit or boundary you want to correct with this person — such as an unwanted intrusion into personal space, a disrespect of personal beliefs, or a disregard for personal welfare.

3. You may try requesting a positive behavior change, as you learned in exercise 5-10. If that doesn't satisfactorily resolve the situation for you, follow the next steps.

4. Identify a limit or boundary that would address your need. What do you need the person to stop doing in order for you to feel safe, respected, valued, or protected? Here you are asking someone to stop a negative behavior, which is probably harder for both you and the other person.

5. Identify at least three consequences if the other person continues to violate the limit or boundary you have articulated. These might include lost opportunities or privileges of connection, or a requirement to see a counselor to help resolve the problems in the dynamic. The other person may understand and agree to the consequences, but even if they don't, it's your decision to create a limit or boundary, identify consequences, and enforce them. Be clear that you will enforce the consequences if the limit or boundary continues to be violated. The last resort might be to end the relationship.

6. Identify how you would enforce the consequences. This is the hardest step of the exercise, particularly for women who have been socialized to be the connectors in relationships, to go along to get along. Knowing how you will enforce the consequences is essential for you to trust that you can. (This is why you are practicing with easy and little at first.)

In my workshops, when we explore the process of setting limits and boundaries, I give the example of my client Nancy, who was becoming more and more frustrated with her husband's going out drinking with his buddies. Nancy was clear that Jim's socializing with his buddies wasn't the issue: she was fine having a quiet time at home with the dog and a good book. The problem was that he would promise to come home by a certain time and then invariably come home at least two hours late, often without calling to let her know what was going on. Her frustration was with Jim's not calling to tell her about his change of plans, which left her feeling disrespected, not cared about, and unimportant.

Nancy tried talking to Jim about it. She was clear that she wasn't expecting him to call for permission to stay out later than expected, but she was also clear that she needed to be kept in the loop when his plans changed so that she wouldn't worry needlessly. Jim would dutifully promise to change his behavior but failed to do so several weekends in a row. Nancy was beginning to resent how powerless she felt to get Jim to change his behavior.

Nancy needed to specify a consequence for Jim's habit of forgetting to call. Rather than threatening to call the police or check with the local hospital, she told Jim that the next time he was more than thirty minutes late without calling, she would call his sister, who lived in the same town. Jim was very fond of this sister, almost revered her, and did not want to look bad in her eyes. Nancy never had to call the sister: she had created a limit with an enforceable consequence, and Jim's new habit of calling when he would be late started the very next weekend.

7. Enforce the consequence the very first time the limit and boundary is violated. This is essential not only for strengthening your response flexibility and that of the other person, but also for the flexibility of the relationship. Both of you acknowledge what has happened and what can be learned from what has happened, and you repeat the process until respecting the new limit and boundary is the new habit.

8. If the steps above don't resolve the unwanted behavior satisfactorily, try exercise 5-10 again to clarify what the issues are and what the resistance to the change is. And then try again.

Practicing the skills of setting limits and boundaries deepens your trust in yourself and in the process of relating. You can initiate communication in relationships and take risks that you might not otherwise believe to be safe. This strengthens your response flexibility and the resilience of the relationship itself.

EXERCISE 5-12: Repairing a Rupture

Even in "good enough" close relationships, we spend about one-third of the time in actual *relating* (attuned connection), about one-third in *rupture* (misattuned or disrupted connection), and one-third in *repair* (recovering the attuned connection.) Repair is the most important aspect of this pattern because it strengthens our capacities to respond flexibly to ruptures in connection and builds trust that we can. We are more willing to take risks and be vulnerable in our relationships with people when we trust that we can recover from any inadvertent misunderstandings. Learning to recover from a disconnection is also a powerful catalyst for choosing to rewire any problematic patterns of behavior. This exercise explores a process of acknowledging and repairing a rupture.

> *Out beyond ideas of wrongdoing and rightdoing, there is a field. I'll meet you there.*
>
> — Jalaluddin Rumi, "Out beyond Ideas"

1. Acknowledge to yourself and ask the other person to acknowledge that a rupture has occurred. The purpose here is not to assign shame or blame, but to avoid sweeping the pain of disconnection under the rug.

2. Choose to focus on repairing the connection; be careful not to get bogged down in trying to prove that you are right or the other person is wrong. Use the value you place on the relationship as the motivation to do the repair. Focus on sharing and understanding one another's experiences, not your opinions.

3. Use exercise 5-6 if you wish to identify any misunderstandings or misperceptions. Each person tries to use their own mindful empathy to understand and take responsibility for their part in the rupture. That acknowledgment of responsibility creates safety for the other person.

4. You can also use the format of exercise 5-6 to give each of you a turn expressing the felt sense of your experience and the behavior changes you would use to repair the relationship. Or you could have a back-and-forth conversation, noticing any slips from reciprocity.

5. Express understanding and mutual care and concern. These catalyze the neural resonance that restores safety to the relationship.

6. Use your now more-resonant relating to reengage in a healthy mutuality and interdependence. Discern whatever lessons can be learned. Move forward from here.

Besides repairing any specific rupture, success at repair deepens trust that you *can* repair. Each of you is more able to take healthy risks — to be open and vulnerable in the relationship—when you trust that you can repair and reengage as needed. The relationship strengthens its health and vitality, its resilience.

Relating resiliently to just one person at a time can be hard; negotiating relationships between groups of people can be even harder. Knowing who was kin and who was not, who was a member of the tribe and who was not, was essential for the survival of our human ancestors on the savannah. Our brains are evolutionarily hardwired to automatically distinguish between groups of "us" and "them" without conscious processing.

One of the heartaches of human civilization is how quickly and automatically our brains react reflexively to those differences. Theory of mind — the capacity to recognize and accept differences between people — can be distorted by layers of negative stereotypes and belief and behavioral systems that turn basic neurobiological responses into discrimination and oppression.

I experienced that heartache just recently: I was walking in my neighborhood, turning a corner, when I noticed someone dark-skinned walking toward me. I found myself wondering, "Hmm, are more Mexicans moving into the neighborhood?" *Instantly* I thought, "Linda! That's a racist thought!" And in the next instant I recognized the person as the computer guru I rely on every other week to resolve wobbles, glitches, and heartaches with my digital technology. That entire sequence of thoughts took less than ten seconds. The heartache and shame lasted much longer; and the rewiring, even little and often, will take longer still.

In *Deep Diversity: Overcoming Us vs. Them*, the racial diversity expert Shakil Choudhury tells of his own experience of "flunking" the Implicit Association Test, a psychological tool that is often used to detect unconscious biases. Then living in Toronto, Canada, Choudhury, who is of Pakistani descent, was chagrined to discover that the test indicated he had an unconscious preference for white people over black people. He developed his own practice to rectify (recondition) this bias. The exercise below is a modified version of this practice. You may choose to work with any group of people you identify as "other" toward whom you know you have a negative bias: men or women, elders or children, members of any minority group, people of a particular sexual orientation, football players, or CEOs.

EXERCISE 5-13: Us versus Them

1. Identify the category of "other" you are going to practice with.
2. Identify negative thoughts or assumptions that go through your mind when you encounter or imagine encountering someone in this group, especially perceptions of danger.
3. Identify several positive thoughts to use for the juxtaposition, especially thoughts or assumptions associated with safety: qualities such as being kind, generous, hardworking, and practical.
4. As you encounter (or imagine) a member of this group, repeat your positive thoughts. Keep repeating them until you notice a shift in your current perception of this person. Notice whether the original negative perceptions come up less frequently or begin to fade into the background.
5. Continue repeating this practice until these positive thoughts automatically come to mind when you encounter someone in this group. As you experience success with this tool, practice it with different groups, using different perceptions and messages.

When Choudhury took the Implicit Association Test again several years later, results indicated he had "broken the prejudice habit." His conscious practice of reconditioning had rewired his unconscious conditioned bias. This is a great example of deepening relational intelligence.

Level 3. Too Much

Sometimes you feel stuck in relationship dynamics that just won't budge. One of the most common relationship difficulties, which is also one of the most derailing of resilience, is the drama triangle of victim, persecutor, and rescuer. Forty years ago, transactional analysis identified many different games people play in their interactions with one another, even within their own psyches. This drama triangle, identified by Stephen Karpman, is particularly problematic and particularly enduring.

The victim embodies feeling wounded, abandoned, and betrayed by others, helpless, and at the mercy of others. Of course, in some situations identifying with a victim role may be a very realistic assessment of external injustice and oppression. Here, however, it refers to someone who adopts a "poor me" attitude, appearing unable to solve their own problems and powerless to effect change (roughly corresponding to the exiled, wounded inner child).

The persecutor embodies being critical, judgmental, powerful, authoritative, and dominant. To the persecutor, being flexible or exhibiting any weakness or human vulnerabilities is to be a failure. The persecutor (roughly corresponding to the inner critic) lords it over any potential victims, not allowing victims or rescuers to grow out of their roles.

The rescuer (roughly corresponding to a helicopter parent) adopts the role of savior of the victim: this requires the victim to stay in the helpless, victimized role. The rescuer depends on their mission to rescue the victim for their sense of self-worth, believing that they are not good enough on their own. They become a martyr rather than developing the theory of mind and self-responsibility that would release them from the triangle.

These are somewhat archetypal roles, easy to recognize and get caught in, but not easy to eliminate from our own minds or to stop playing with other people. To complicate things further, it's common for people in a relationship to exchange roles: it's also quite common for us to cycle through these roles in our own perception of ourselves. The dynamics of this drama triangle, whether it's played out inside our heads or with other people — or both — can tie us in knots, completely paralyzing our resilience.

The only relationally intelligent way to end the game is to get out of the triangle, reconditioning our neural circuitry by juxtaposing these toxic roles with our own mature, resilient authentic self and our mature theory of mind.

EXERCISE 5-14: Dismantling the Drama Triangle

Consider whether any of these roles — victim, persecutor, or rescuer — seems familiar to you. You may recognize them as parts of your own psyche, recognize them in someone else, or act them out with other people.

If you wish to rewire any of these roles within yourself:

1. Evoke an awareness of your resilient self *as* your true self. It may help to remember times when you actually have been strong and resilient to help you evoke this sense of yourself now. Strengthen this positive experience of yourself to be as present, vivid, and vital as possible.

2. Identify which of the three roles you wish to work with first. To begin with,

you may want to choose the one that is the least problematic for you in order to maximize your experience of success with this rewiring.

3. Remind yourself that every part of your inner psyche is there for a self-protective or self-enhancing reason. There's no shame or blame associated with any of these parts: they have emerged and coalesced as a result of evolutionary hardwiring, genetics, family of origin conditioning, and cultural expectations and reinforcement. Given the power of self-directed neuroplasticity, however, it is your responsibility to choose to heal what has become problematic and derailing of your resilience and well-being.

4. Imagine your resilient self inviting this first role in the triangle for a visit and a conversation. With as much acceptance and compassion as you can muster, allow this part simply to be. Tolerate its existence, and respect whatever gifts it has brought to your own survival and development.

5. As you toggle back and forth in your awareness of your resilient self and this part, identify with the resilient self as larger than any one of these parts and as representing who you truly are. From now on, you can recruit your prefrontal cortex to manage the comings and goings of this part, or any other part, without being hijacked by it or lost in it.

6. Let go of the sense of the part you have been working with. Rest your awareness in your resilient self. Notice how it feels to be your resilient self.

7. Repeat this visualization with the other two roles if that feels necessary and relevant to you. Repeat the exercise whenever you wish.

A similar process can help dismantle drama triangles in your relationships with other people. You may find yourself playing these roles, or find that another person is playing these roles with you. For example, someone acting as a rescuer may try to do your thinking for you rather than trust that you can think for yourself. They may protest if you resist, saying they "only want to help," and expect you to stay a dependent victim so that they can feel good about helping you. And you may find yourself responding to another person from one of these roles, even though that's not your intention or your common pattern.

If you wish to stop playing these roles with other people (or stop other people from playing these roles with you), the following steps can help:

1. Identify one of these patterns — victim, persecutor, rescuer — that seems to be played out in one particular relationship.

2. Anchor yourself in your own resilient self so that you stop acting the role you've been playing. (You can do this!)

3. The next time you experience this pattern being acted out or evoked by another person, anchor firmly in your theory of mind: you are you; you are not who they need you to be or expect you to be. Your inner self-assertion may feel dramatically different from the way you have experienced yourself with this person before; but remember, you don't need the other person's permission to shift.

4. Choose a different way to respond to this person, and notice your different response. This may evoke any manner of different response from the other person, because you're breaking the rules of the game.

5. When you choose to step out of the drama triangle, you create the opportunity for a shift in the dynamics of your relationship with the other person. You may choose to explore what's happening in this interaction, at this moment or later. Revisit exercises 5-10, 5-11, and 5-12 for help in renegotiating your relationship if you wish to. You may choose not to.

Reconditioning doesn't get rid of the parts of ourselves that play these roles. Our interactions with other people may evoke them again. But it does strengthen the experience and confidence that your resilient self is larger than any of these parts and that you can cease to identify with them. They are not who you are, and you no longer have to act them out.

And remember, choosing to shift your behavior with others, even unilaterally, can pop you out of the triangle. You don't need the other person's permission to shift; you don't need to try to persuade them of the validity of shifting. What's important is to notice the need to shift, to choose to shift, to deal with any consequences of the shift, and then to celebrate the freedom of shifting out of the triangle. Succeeding even once can encourage you to try it again with other people. You're launching yourself into a new world of relational intelligence.

Deconditioning

The focused attention of new conditioning and reconditioning allows you to use specific interactions with specific people to install or rewire specific patterns in your neural circuitry. Practices of deconditioning use the "play space" of the brain's default network to reopen the mind and heart to a sense of true belonging to the larger human community. The safety net of that belonging and interdependence in social communities is one of the most significant predictors of longevity and our long-term well-being.

Level 1. Barely a Wobble

By exercising your imagination, you can deepen your experience of shared humanity and reinforce the psychological safety net that this interconnection offers.

EXERCISE 5-15: Walk a Mile in Their Shoes

The time-tested practice of imagining yourself in someone else's shoes reliably strengthens a sense of shared humanity.

1. Identify someone you don't know — someone riding with you on the bus, standing in line with you in the grocery store, or sitting in the theater with you waiting for the movie to start.

2. Let your imagination play. What might their life be like? You can create an entire story about their background, their work, their family, and their ambitions for the future. Feel your way into what it might be like to be them, even for just a moment, facing their concerns and stressors.

3. Imagine how your lives might be similar, might interconnect; identify the shared concerns you might have navigating this challenging world.

4. Imagine how your life might have unfolded differently if you had been born into the same gender, race, class, and opportunities, or lack thereof, as this other person. How would these circumstances have shaped your resilience? What different strengths or vulnerabilities might you have, and how would you have learned to cope with them?

5. You can repeat this imagination exercise with many different people, noticing the common experience of coping with life's challenges that underlies seemingly huge differences in circumstances and life chances.

In this exercise, your brain is playing with a serious purpose, recognizing common threads between you and other people underlying the perceived or imagined differences.

EXERCISE 5-16: Just Like Me

This exercise helps cut through barriers that make you feel separate or different from others. It is a way you can actively sense your connection with other people, partly by focusing on shared human experiences.

1.   The next time you are talking with someone, in a meeting at work, looking at others in a café or on the street, or interacting with other parents at your children's school, reflect on these phrases:

Just like me, this person wants to be happy.
Just like me, this person wishes to be free of pain and stress.
Just like me, this person has a body subject to aches, pains, and aging.
Just like me, this person has had many joys and successes.
Just like me, this person has felt sadness, loss, and pain.
Just like me, this person desires to love and be loved.
Just like me, this person aspires to do their best in life.
Just like me, this person wants peace and happiness.

2.   As always, you can repeat this practice with many different people, coming to sense the shared humanity underneath the differences.

Saying these phrases to yourself is particularly useful when you are having a conflict or a challenging time with someone. The more you can sense the similarities between you and see that person as like you, the more likely you are to feel a sense of connection and find it easier to relate to them.

Level 2. Glitches and Heartaches, Sorrows and Struggles

Most of us experience injury, injustice, disappointment, or betrayal at some point in our lives. Staying caught in those experiences can block the development of our resilience and relational intelligence. Continuing to feel judgment, blame, resentment, bitterness, and hostility toward those who have caused us harm can bring us pain and suffering ourselves.

Sometimes, too, our interactions with other people have been less than benevolent; we have suffered harm or injury, or we have caused harm or injury.

Practicing forgiveness allows us to bring the brain out of the contracted states of anger, resentment, grudge, hostility, shutdown, and withdrawal and back to a state where it can take a broader perspective and recognize shared humanity. This openness is essential to our resilience. It also benefits us to practice forgiveness toward ourselves for harm we have caused others or ourselves. We want to rewire the behaviors of complaining, criticism, disgruntlement, and contentiousness we can so easily get stuck in and replace them with the understanding, compassion, grieving, and forgiveness that can move us into resilient coping and relational intelligence.

Forgiveness does not mean condoning, pardoning, forgetting, false reconciliation, appeasement, or sentimentality. It is a practice, daily and lifelong, of cultivating the inner secure base that allows us to see our pain as part of the universal pain of all human beings, to reset our moral compass, and to remain compassionate even in the face of injustice, betrayal, and harm.

We may even need to practice forgiveness of life itself, for the fact that we've been dealt the hand we've been dealt by life. Forgiveness practice is not the only skill needed for healing from hurt and betrayal, but it is an important one. The exercise in forgiveness below can help you recover your trust in yourself and in the process of relating to others.

Forgiveness is not an occasional act; it is a permanent attitude.
— MARTIN LUTHER KING JR.

EXERCISE 5-17: Forgiveness

1. Let yourself sit comfortably, allowing your eyes to close. Breathe naturally and easily. Let your body and mind relax. Breathe gently into the area of your heart, letting yourself feel all the barriers you have erected and the emotions you have carried because you have not forgiven yourself or others. Let yourself feel the pain of keeping your heart closed.

2. Breathing softly, move through each of the following possibilities for forgiveness. Begin reciting the suggested words, letting the healing images

and feelings that come up grow deeper as you repeat the phrases of forgiveness.

3. Seek forgiveness from others with the following words: *There are many ways that I have hurt and harmed others, have betrayed or abandoned them, caused them suffering, knowingly or unknowingly, out of my pain, fear, anger, and confusion.*

4. Let yourself remember and visualize the ways you have hurt others. See the pain you have caused out of your own fear and confusion. Feel your own sorrow and regret. Sense that finally you can release this burden and ask for forgiveness. Take as much time as you need to picture each memory that still burdens your heart. And then as each person comes to mind, gently say: *I ask for your forgiveness, I ask for your forgiveness.*

5. Seek forgiveness for yourself with the following words: *Just as I have caused suffering to others, there are many ways that I have hurt and harmed myself. I have betrayed or abandoned myself many times in thought, word, or deed, knowingly or unknowingly.*

   Feel your own precious body and life. Let yourself see the ways you have hurt or harmed yourself. Picture them, remember them. Feel the sorrow you have carried from this, and sense that you can release these burdens. Extend forgiveness for each act of harm, one by one. Repeat to yourself: *For the ways I have hurt myself through action or inaction, out of fear, pain, and confusion, I now extend a full and heartfelt forgiveness. I forgive myself, I forgive myself.*

6. Find forgiveness for those who have hurt or harmed you with the following words: *There are many ways I have been harmed by others, abused or abandoned, knowingly or unknowingly, in thought, word, or deed.*

   You have been betrayed. Let yourself picture and remember the many ways this is true. Feel the sorrow you have carried from this past. Now sense that you can release this burden of pain by gradually extending forgiveness as your heart is ready. Recite to yourself: *I remember the many ways others have hurt, wounded, or harmed me, out of fear, pain, confusion, and anger. I have carried this pain in my heart long enough. To the extent that I am ready, I offer you forgiveness. To those who have caused me harm, I offer my forgiveness, I forgive you.*

Gently repeat these three statements of forgiveness until you feel a release in your heart. For some great pains, you may not feel a release; instead, you may experience again the burden and the anguish or anger you have held. Touch this softly. Forgive yourself for not being ready to let go and move on. Forgiveness cannot be forced; it cannot be artificial. Simply continue the practice and let the words and the images work gradually in their own way. In time you can make the forgiveness meditation a regular part of your life, letting go of the past and opening your heart to each new moment with a wise loving-kindness.

Level 3. Too Much

Sometimes your perspective has to zoom out a very long way to hold the challenges of relating to other people with equanimity. Practicing this zooming out engages the play space of the brain and helps you learn to trust accessing that play space when facing new challenges.

EXERCISE 5-18: Honoring Shared Humanity

This exercise uses four ways of engaging with the experiences of other people — loving-kindness, compassion, sympathetic joy, and equanimity — considered in the Buddhist tradition to be part of the path to enlightenment. The exercise is a powerful way to experience the shared humanity we experience in our interdependent relationships.

> *Then it was as if I suddenly saw the secret beauty of their hearts, the depths of their hearts where neither sin nor desire nor self-knowledge can reach, the core of their reality, the person that each one is in the eyes of the Divine. If only they could all see themselves as they really are. If only we could see each other that way all the time. There would be no more war, no more hatred, no more cruelty, no more greed....I suppose the big problem would be that we would fall down and worship each other.*
>
> — Thomas Merton

Invite a friend to do this guided meditation with you. Sit across from each other so that you can easily maintain eye contact. Decide who will be partner A and who will be partner B. This exercise is done in silence.

1. Begin by simply gazing into each other's eyes, allowing yourself to see in your partner the nobility of their true nature, their innate goodness and radiance of their being, and their sincere wishes for peace, happiness, and well-being.

2. Partner A closes her eyes. Partner B begins to silently wish her well, sending her sincere expressions of loving-kindness: "May you know the deepest happiness; may you have ease of mind and heart." Partner A lets herself know that her partner is sending her expressions of loving-kindness; she allows herself to receive and take in the kindness being offered.

3. Partner B closes his eyes; both partners sit in silence, reflecting on the experience and giving and receiving wishes for loving-kindness, happiness, peace, and ease.

4. Partner A opens her eyes; Partner B keeps his eyes closed. Partner A sends Partner B sincere expressions of loving-kindness: "May you know the deepest happiness; may you have ease of mind and heart." Partner B lets himself know that his partner is sending him expressions of loving-kindness; he allows himself to receive and take in the kindness being offered.

5. Partner A closes her eyes; both partners sit in silence, reflecting on the experience and giving and receiving wishes for kindness and happiness, peace and ease.

6. Partner B opens his eyes; Partner A's eyes remain closed. Partner B begins to imagine what human sorrows Partner A might have experienced: what losses, what griefs, what pain of the human condition. Partner B silently begins to send Partner A expressions of compassion: "May your sorrows be held in loving awareness; may your sorrows ease; may your sorrows cease. May you be free of suffering, and all causes of suffering, and from causing any suffering." Partner A lets herself take in the care and compassion being offered.

7. Partner B closes his eyes; both partners sit in silence, reflecting on the experience of giving and receiving compassion and care for sorrows and suffering.

8. Partner A opens her eyes; Partner B's eyes remain closed. Partner A begins to imagine what human sorrows Partner B might have experienced: what

losses, what griefs, what pain of the human condition. Partner A silently begins to send Partner B expressions of compassion: "May your sorrows be held in loving awareness; may your sorrows ease; may your sorrows cease. May you be free of suffering, and all causes of suffering, and from causing any suffering." Partner B lets himself take in the care and compassion being offered.

9.   Partner A closes her eyes; both partners sit in silence, reflecting on the experience of giving and receiving compassion and care for sorrows and suffering.

10. Partner B opens his eyes; Partner A's eyes remain closed. Partner B begins to imagine what human joys Partner A may have experienced, what accomplishments and competencies she might have attained, what blessings of abundance and love she might have experienced. He silently sends her expressions of sympathetic joy, happiness for her happiness: "May you fully delight in your delight; may you feel your joy deeply." Partner A lets herself receive these sincere wishes.

11. Partner B closes his eyes; both partners sit in silence, reflecting on the experience of giving and receiving joy and delight.

12. Partner A opens her eyes; Partner B's eyes remain closed. Partner A begins to imagine what human joys Partner B may have experienced, what accomplishments and competencies he might have attained, what blessings of abundance and love he might have experienced. She silently sends him expressions of sympathetic joy, happiness for his happiness: "May you fully delight in your delight; may you feel your joy deeply." Partner B lets himself receive these sincere wishes.

13. Partner A closes her eyes; both partners sit in silence, reflecting on the experience of giving and receiving joy and delight.

14. Partner B opens his eyes; Partner A's eyes remain closed. Partner B begins to imagine what ups and downs Partner A might have experienced in her life, what twists and turns. He begins to send her wishes for equanimity, balance, and deep inner peace, wishing that she may remain calm and centered as she rides the waves of life. Partner A lets herself receive these wishes.

15. Partner B closes his eyes; both partners sit in silence, reflecting on the

experience of giving and receiving wishes for calm, equanimity, and deep inner peace.

16. Partner A opens her eyes; Partner B's eyes remain closed. Partner A begins to imagine what ups and downs Partner B might have experienced in his life, what twists and turns. She begins to send him wishes for equanimity, balance, and deep inner peace, wishing that he may remain calm and centered as he rides the waves of life. Partner B lets himself receive these wishes.

17. Partner A closes her eyes; both partners sit in silence, reflecting on the experience of giving and receiving wishes for calm, equanimity, and deep inner peace.

18. With eyes closed, both partners simply bring awareness to the experience of giving and receiving kindness, compassion, joy, and equanimity. They notice any changes in their sense of themselves and of one another.

19. Both partners open their eyes and simply gaze into one another's eyes. They exchange bows of thanks and gratitude for creating this experience together.

The phrases give some structure and focus to the exercise. Its main purpose, though, is to enable both people to experience the positive functioning of the default network mode of the brain, imagining the partner's experience and from deep in the heart wishing the partner well. This process deepens our capacities to honor the humanity we share with others, which in turn strengthens our trust of people as refuges and resources.

Because human beings are social beings, our networks of families and friends, the people in the places where we work and play, and our social, political, and spiritual communities can all be resources for our resilience. And because our brains learn best by interacting with other brains, resonant relating is key to experiencing and strengthening our resilience. This chapter has presented many tools to strengthen that relating — including honoring shared humanity, reaching out for help, communicating without shaming or blaming, negotiating change, setting limits and boundaries, repairing ruptures, and forgiveness and reflection practices that strengthen your resilience enough to deal with a lifetime of challenges.

The next chapter offers tools that will enable you to consciously reflect on — and shift — any long-term habits or practices that still threaten to derail your resilience.

CHAPTER SIX

Practices of Reflective Intelligence

Mindfulness, Seeing Clearly, Choosing Wisely, Equanimity

Through previous exercises in this book, you've already been learning the core practices of reflective intelligence, which supports your resilience: seeing clearly and choosing wisely, honing your perceptions and responses to any issue. And you've been strengthening your response flexibility — the ability to shift gears smoothly — which is the key to that clear seeing and wise choosing.

This chapter presents tools of mindfulness practice that allow you to uncover and examine complex patterns of "thinking" that can derail your resilience, and to rewire them if you wish to. You will learn to shift the functioning of your brain from a focused mode of processing — which allows you to bring into conscious awareness all the patterns your mind creates and that you want to rewire — to the defocused mode of processing, which allows you to be aware of the awareness that simply knows all of the mental patterns (all products of neural firing) without being stuck in or overwhelmed by any of them.

Anchoring in that awareness returns you to a baseline equanimity from which you can perceive clearly that events themselves are ever flowing and ever changing. The knowledge that "this, too, shall pass" is a form of response flexibility built into life itself. It applies even to the self. You shift, change, grow, and evolve all of your life. Grasping the truth of Buckminster Fuller's observation that "I seem to be a verb" allows you to completely reinvent yourself if necessary to respond to life's challenges.

With this equanimity, you can "take it all seriously and hold it all lightly," in the words of Andy Dreitcer, my friend and a Presbyterian minister. Informed by your own moral compass (another function of the prefrontal cortex), you can choose wisely. You get to "look out on life with quiet eyes" (a phrase of Howard Thurman's) and thrive.

Mindfulness

Many people think of mindfulness as a kind of thinking or cognition. That's not exactly it. Mindful awareness is about *being with* rather than *thinking about*: it entails knowing what you are experiencing while you are experiencing it. This awareness and reflection about experience (and your reactions to your experience) creates choice points in your brain. When you are aware of your choices, you can respond flexibly to whatever is happening, moment by moment.

Let's look at some of the steps of basic mindfulness as they apply to resilience.

1. Pause and Become Present

Whether they're responding from inexperience, defensiveness, or the upheaval of a crisis, too often people don't step back from a dilemma or disaster to reflect and discern options. Their reaction is often, "Don't just sit there! Do something!" And sometimes we do need to act quickly and save the reflection for later. But reflecting before reacting gives the brain time and space to do the job you are strengthening it for — functioning with response flexibility.

When you become present to what is happening, you step out of denial, out of distraction, out of dissociation. You show up, pay attention, and engage with your experience in the present moment.

2. Notice and Acknowledge

Becoming aware of your experience starts with simply noticing: "This...is...happening." Maybe you can't articulate what "this" is right away, nor your reactions: "I don't know what's happening! I am confused! And overwhelmed, and scared." Acknowledging and naming the experience — the confusion, the overwhelm, the fear — is the first step in being able to step back from it and observe it rather than *being* it. This step engages your prefrontal cortex to manage your reactivity so you can discern what is happening and choose how to respond to it.

3. Allow, Tolerate, Accept

You've been practicing this step throughout this book: *allowing* what is — the situation and your reactions; *tolerating* that experience, including your reactions to your

reactions, so that you can move beyond any hair-trigger reactivity; and *accepting* —
not necessarily liking or agreeing or condoning the experience or your reactions, but
making room for them, so that you can work skillfully and effectively with whatever
is happening.

> *Be willing to have it so. Acceptance of what has happened is the first step to over-*
> *coming the consequences of any misfortune.*
>
> — WILLIAM JAMES

4. Observe

Rather than staying caught in or identifying with the experience of the moment, try
to disentangle yourself from it and observe it, as though you're sitting high in the
stands watching it like a basketball game. You can observe what's happening — and
your reactions to what's happening — without believing that this is who you are or
that this is permanently true. Rather than identifying yourself as an angry person and
believing that you are angry all the time, you can observe, "I'm feeling very angry
right now," or even "The anger is pretty strong right now." This disentangling and
observation enable you to create choice points in the brain rather than simply acting
(or reacting) automatically as you have acted before.

5. Reflect on Increasingly Complex Objects of Awareness

You've already practiced bringing to your conscious awareness experiences of body
sensations, breath, touch, and movement; experiences of complex nuanced emotions,
even cascades of emotions; messages from inner parts that may support or derail your
resilience; and the interactive dynamics between you and another person that may do
the same.

In this chapter you will learn to work with "mental contents" — thoughts, beliefs, assumptions, values, points of view, identities — because these complex constructs of the mind can also support or derail your resilience. You'll become aware of
the processes of the mind that can create, get stuck in, and shift those mental contents.
You'll strengthen your response flexibility so you can shift and rewire even deeply
held beliefs, such as "But this is who I *am*!"

6. Discern Options

Response flexibility requires not only perceiving possible responses but also perceiving the possible consequences of those responses. In this step, you begin to integrate
the capacities of mindfulness to reflect on "what is" with the cognitive capacities of

the prefrontal cortex to reflect on what could be. These capacities of executive functioning are what enable you to analyze, plan, make judgments, make decisions. Integrating them with mindfulness allows you to "monitor and modify" your responses to your experience, not just in the moment but for the long haul.

7. Choose Wisely

Resilient choices are guided by your own values and inner moral compass. Every tribe and society, every philosophical and spiritual tradition that has ever pondered resilience has also had to ponder and teach the values and virtues it believes can best guide individuals in meeting life's challenges and foster well-being for themselves and others, so the values that guide your decisions may have been previously conditioned by lessons learned in your family and culture.

Defining your personal code of morality is beyond the scope of this book (though morality is a function of the prefrontal cortex). But living out of alignment with your chosen values and virtues will quickly and powerfully derail your resilience. You can't move forward when you are disastrously off balance within.

Even here, you don't want to get bogged down in categorical definitions of right and wrong, or good and bad. You allow, tolerate, and accept in order to be flexible, to discern skillful from unskillful, wholesome from unwholesome. Your mindfulness allows you to notice and reflect on any choice that might put you out of alignment with your core values.

Awareness

As you learn to shift from the focused mode of processing, which can bring any content into conscious awareness, to the defocused mode, which can contain and play with any content, you'll begin to notice (using your reflective intelligence) that all of these perceptions — or contents or apparent truths — can shift on their own. And they do.

I remember attending a long meditation retreat years ago. A week into it, my awareness was pretty steady. One lunch period, standing in line, I noticed that the dining hall had run out of broccoli. And then I noticed that I was in a snit because there was no more broccoli. Becoming aware of my snit, I practiced letting that negative state go.

Later that afternoon, I was sitting outside on a low stone wall surrounding the courtyard, overlooking gentle hills and valleys rolling away into the distance. I took in the golden grasses, clear blue sky, warm breezes, the simple quiet contentment of a California summer day. After a time, my attention focused on a single ginkgo leaf fluttering in the breeze on a tree about twenty feet away. I began to imagine myself being that leaf gently resting on the wind.

My awareness spontaneously zoomed out from being that leaf quietly floating on the air to being the tree that anchored it, strongly rooted in the earth (with no problem supporting the hundreds of leaves in my branches), being the breeze that fluttered the leaves, being the full earth and the open sky that held me, being the awareness that held me as tree, as breeze, as earth, as sky. I dissolved into a state of bliss, a sense of oneness with everything — and with just enough awareness to notice, "Oh! This is pleasant!"

I hung out there for the better part of an hour. When the bell rang to return inside, I realized that this experience, too, was only a pattern — perhaps a pattern brand-new to me, and a delightful one to boot, but still only a mental pattern that would come and go, as all patterns of mental firing do.

Then came the awareness that *all* experiences are fleeting: they come and go. All patterns are only patterns: they too come and go — unpleasant, pleasant, or neutral. I could choose to let go of any pattern and simply rest in the larger awareness that is aware of all the comings and goings. This awareness allows us to abide in a deep equanimity from which we can make wise choices, no matter what is coming or going. The awareness of the possibility — the certainty — of shift gives us permission to create shifts on our own as we need to, You will learn how to start doing that in this chapter, without having to spend a week in retreat.

Equanimity

Mindfulness is simply being aware of what is happening right now without wishing it were different; enjoying the pleasant without holding on when it changes (which it will); being with the unpleasant without fearing it will always be this way (which it won't).

— James Baraz

Accepting the reality that underlies all reality — that everything changes, nothing is fixed or permanent — helps you let go of how things have been or need to be. You can tolerate how things are and trust your capacities of response flexibility to change them if need be. That neuroception of safety primes the neuroplasticity of the brain to discern new choices and find the courage to choose among them.

New Conditioning

By strengthening the pathways that stabilize and steady the brain's attention, you can learn to simply be with what is and consciously reflect on the truth of the experience before choosing to change it or to shift your responses to it.

Level 1. Barely a Wobble

The following exercises illustrate the basic steps of steadying your awareness through mindfulness practice. They develop your capacity for present-moment awareness, seeing clearly what you are experiencing while you are experiencing it, so that you can return to a home base of clarity and equanimity.

EXERCISE 6-1: Steadying Awareness

1. Focus on the breath, flowing in, flowing out. Focus on sounds, coming into awareness, fading away. Focus on an ache in the knee, now sensing it, now not sensing it.

2. Train your attention and steady your awareness by mindfully attending to simple activities of daily living. When you wash the dishes, pay attention to your experience moment by moment: your hands moving through soapy water, the weight of the plates as you move them from sink to drainer. Notice when your attention wanders off into planning the next meal. You're observing the dance between your brain's focused and defocused modes of attention. When you notice that your attention has wandered, strengthen your brain's capacity for focused attention by refocusing it on the experience of doing the dishes. You can train the brain in the same way by paying attention to your experience of taking a shower, combing your hair, opening or closing windows, getting dressed or undressed.

3. Notice the awareness that is allowing you to notice your experience. Know that you are tying your shoelaces and know that you know. (This awareness of awareness becomes a refuge when the experience you are paying attention to is something difficult or distressing.)

4. Notice any opinions or judgments that come into your mind about how well you are doing this exercise. That mental content becomes an object

of your awareness, too, and you can let it go and continue to focus your attention on tying your shoes.

The object of your awareness — the breath, the dishes, the getting dressed — is in the foreground. The awareness that knows you are doing what you are doing is in the background, but you can learn to make that awareness itself part of the foreground. This is essential when what you meet and pay attention to is more challenging.

EXERCISE 6-2: Noticing Going Into and Out of Awareness

Human beings go into and out of steady awareness all the time. That's not "wrong:" it's how the human brain works. When you're not deliberately focusing your attention on something, your mind will naturally wander into the default network mode of processing.

You can strengthen the circuits of your brain's attention by noticing when you're paying attention to present-moment experience and noticing when you're not. This exercise sounds simple, but it's a workout! Research shows that this kind of practice brings measurable results: longtime meditators have increased the volume of brain cells in the structures of the brain that are used to pay attention.

1. Focus your awareness on your breathing, breath flowing in, breath flowing out.

2. Count each inhalation-exhalation cycle as one breath. Count ten breaths. When you complete ten breaths without losing focus, start over at one. Count another ten breaths.

3. When you notice your mind has wandered at breath 5 or 7, refocus your attention on your breathing and start over at one. The first time you try this, it's hard to get past three breaths: our minds wander all the time. There's no shame or blame, no judgment or evaluation attached to this wandering. Simply start over and continue the practice.

In this exercise, becoming an expert breath counter is not what's important. It's the process — tracking attention and steadying awareness — that's invaluable in strengthening our ability to stay grounded in the face of harder and harder life challenges.

EXERCISE 6-3: Tracking Shifts in Experience

As your awareness steadies, you can notice more easily how objects of that awareness shift on their own over time.

1. Choose a single object of awareness to track for a week, a day, the next two hours, or the next two minutes. What you choose to track could be very simple, like the color blue or the shape of a circle.
2. As you track the object, also track the shifts in the object or in your perception of it and your reactions to it.
3. Also note the background process that is the steady awareness, regardless of any shifts in the content.
4. As you become more skilled in steady awareness, you may want to choose a more complex object of your awareness, like feelings of resentment or dread. Notice when they are present; notice when they are not. Notice the voice of any inner part, coming and going. Notice if it comes and takes up residence, not departing as a messenger should. Notice any shift in the dynamics between you and another person, in your moods or theirs.

As you become more adept at paying attention, you begin to focus as much on the shifts of the content as you do on their presence. You become more aware, more comfortable with the idea that all things come and go. And if you are focusing attention on feelings that get stuck, you can shift to noticing the background awareness that isn't stuck, that is simply aware.

As my meditation teacher James Baraz teaches, "That which is aware of fear is not itself afraid." Developing your awareness is good groundwork for increasing resilience.

Level 2. Glitches and Heartaches, Sorrows and Struggles

Sometimes your thoughts can drive you crazy, blocking clear thinking and impeding response flexibility. Sometimes your thoughts trigger further thoughts, evaluations, judgments, and condemnations that reduce your resilience. These thought patterns are ways of filtering reality that can be counterproductive.

You can learn to work mindfully with your thoughts, and with all the amazing, creative, dazzling constructs of your default network mode, especially when those constructs turn dark or constricting, so that you can also experience their coming and going. Even your deeply held beliefs about the truth of the way things are can shift. And you can come to understand the processes of your brain that create, install, and defend those constructs to the death.

> *The problem is not that there are problems. The problem is expecting otherwise, and thinking that having problems is a problem.*
>
> — THEODORE RUBIN

Here's a list of common thought processes that human beings use to filter their experience.

1. *Assumptions*: We learn from past experience, and based on that experience we sometimes think we know more than we know. We filter our perceptions of reality through those assumptions rather than seeing clearly what is actually true or needed now.

2. *Projections*: We assume that what we have learned is true for ourselves is true for other people as well. We project our assumptions onto them, usually without their knowledge or permission, abandoning theory of mind.

3. *Objectification*: We lose the sense of ourselves or another person as an active agent of changing experience. Instead we see ourselves (and others) as an object, a thing, an "It" at the mercy of external events and other people's choices, powerless to change our experience (or our responses to it).

4. *Mind reading*: We presume we know what another person is thinking, feeling, or needing without empathically checking with them. Or we may presume that the other person already knows what we think or need without bothering to tell them directly: "If you loved me, you would know how I feel."

5. *Discounting the positive*: We fail to register positive traits in ourselves or in others, belittling ourselves, devaluing others, and deflecting or neglecting appreciation in either direction.

6. *Overgeneralizing*: We may exaggerate attributes of an experience, perceiving things as global and pervasive, applying to everything and everybody; we see things as "always" or "never." We may take things personally whether or not that's true or relevant, seeing things as permanent and unchanging. (This overgeneralizing is known as the three Ps: pervasive, personal, permanent.)

7. *Catastrophizing*: We may immediately assume the worst: if we sneeze, we assume we're catching a cold, which means missing work for three weeks, which means losing the job, which means losing our home — from sniffle to disaster in less than three seconds.

8. *Black-and-white thinking*: We see everything in categorical terms, with no shades of gray, few options, and no possibilities of compromise. This rigidity in thinking, which can lead to a serious derailing of response flexibility, is also known as neural cement.

9. *Inability to disconfirm*: We are so rigid in our opinions that no new information can change them.

You may recognize similar patterns in your thinking.

EXERCISE 6-4: Identifying Thought Processes That Derail Resilience

1. Review the list above. Identify any of these patterns you recognize as operational in you or in people you know, without attaching any shame or blame. You'll learn to rewire any of these patterns in exercise 6-12 below. For now, simply acknowledge any patterns you identify that you might want to rewire later.

2. Pick one pattern relevant to you that you're willing to investigate; it need not be the one that is most difficult for you.

3. Track this pattern in your thinking for a week. Notice when this pattern is operating in your thinking; notice when it's not.

Becoming aware of your common patterns of perceiving and responding, and acknowledging them in your conscious awareness, is essential if you want to rewire them. Steadying your awareness with more and more difficult objects of awareness is reflective resilience.

Mental constructs can be very stable and long-lasting, more like the climate you live in than the weather that changes from day to day. Emotions that might flit through your awareness in a matter of minutes or half a day (weather) can settle into a longer-lasting mood (climate). The moods we deem negative — depression, discouragement, despair — are the ones we're more likely to notice and want to shift than the lighter-hearted moods of joy or contentment.

As human beings, we adopt roles, preferences, priorities, and goals that filter our perceptions and shape our responses over long periods of time. We prioritize family over work, or work over family, based on deeply held values and convictions. We construct entire philosophies of living, belief systems, and identities that filter our perceptions and response to reality. Formulating values to live by is part of resilience: they are part of a moral compass that guides our life choices. But locking ourselves into values that cannot be changed in response to new experiences is not resilient.

At this stage of new conditioning, you're simply training your awareness to realize that any thought is a product of the processes of your brain, and thus any thought can change. Entire patterns of thought, no matter how complex, can change. Roles, preference, priorities, and even entire belief systems can change over time — and they do.

EXERCISE 6-5: Climate Change

1. Identify a pattern of thinking, a mood, a belief system, or an identity that is part of the climate you live in. You may see yourself as a resourceful manager or a clueless parent, and that lens filters how you see things and shapes your responses day by day. It's like the air you breathe or the water a fish swims in, so fundamental to your existence that it is invisible to you.

2. Bring this pattern or system to your conscious awareness and reflect on it. How long has it been present in your life? Was there a time when it wasn't present in your life? Has it changed or evolved over time?

3. Continue this reflection for as many patterns as you can bring to conscious awareness. Notice whether reflecting on these patterns evokes any pride or regret, but mostly explore them with interest and curiosity.

Bringing a long-held mental pattern or construct to awareness creates the possibility for it to shift. Bringing what has become routine to the "plane of open possibilities" primes the brain for learning and change, for response flexibility.

Level 3. Too Much

Drifting out of your role as mindful observer of your experience, losing your awareness of what's happening and becoming mindless of your reactions to what's happening, may not lead directly to tragedy, but in times of trouble, you can get yourself in deeper trouble if you're not paying attention to what's happening, how you're responding, and how you need to respond.

It's not always possible to pay attention at every single second during a crisis. You need a break; you need to seek refuge sometimes. But the purpose of a break or a refuge is to help you come into presence and awareness again, to see clearly, so that you can choose wisely how to show up and whether you need to change course.

EXERCISE 6-6: Checking In

1. Create a practice of checking in with yourself very regularly as you go through your day — as often as every five minutes at first if you wish, and eventually every few hours — becoming aware of any felt sense in your body as you ask yourself:

    -   Am I experiencing anything positive in this moment?
    -   Am I experiencing any confusion or suffering?
    -   Am I experiencing any excitement, anxiety, loneliness, or other feeling?

    No shame or blame attaches to your answers. There's no need to change or fix anything immediately. You're simply noticing what's going on, being aware of it, being with it, and then deciding consciously if you want to shift a thought, a mood, or a behavior.

2. If you do feel that something needs shifting, take a moment to reflect. How are you relating to what's happening? What different response might be more skillful, more effective?

    By cultivating a habit of checking in with yourself frequently, you are prioritizing seeing clearly, choosing wisely, and strengthening the neural pathways of response flexibility, little and often.

EXERCISE 6-7: What Story Am I Believing Now?

In addition to tracking the felt sense of your experience moment by moment, it's useful to notice any thought loops you might be stuck in. A running joke in meditation circles is that once you start paying attention to your thoughts, you notice that you have a Top Ten playlist that you hear over and over. If you can notice those loops, you can shift them, too.

1. Check in with yourself at regular intervals throughout the day. What am I thinking about right now? More importantly, how am I thinking about it? Lightly and freely? Ruminating and worried? Stuck in a loop?

2. Record your observations in a journal for a week. Again, there's no shame or blame; you're just seeing clearly.

3. At the end of the week, see if you can identify your five most often-repeated thoughts or your five most often-repeated patterns of thinking. (Refer to the list on p. 175 if that's helpful.)

4. Choose one single repetitive thought to practice with. Practice noticing and letting it go, noticing it and letting it go. You want to receive the messages, but you don't want to be stuck in an endless loop. Once the thought catalyzes some constructive action, some skillful behavior, you can let it go.

Letting go of a thought or story can be a novel experience. You want to make sense of your experience, using the tremendous power of your prefrontal cortex. But when you can let go of one possible explanation and open your mind to the possibility that there might be others, you strengthen your response flexibility. "That's my story and I'm sticking to it" is sometimes the right stance. But when it's not, letting go can allow you to be open to other, more resilient choices.

Reconditioning

You can begin to discern the content of a thought, or a process of thinking, as something that could change. You can begin to notice how the ideas and processes do shift, very often, on their own, and from there you can begin to discern how you can shift them yourself through your own wise choices.

Level 1. Barely a Wobble

By strengthening the circuits of mindful awareness, you learn to perceive, and create shifts, in both thought processes and the contents of those processes that may limit your response flexibility.

EXERCISE 6-8: Creating Shifts

1. Notice moments where you do already create shifts in your experience, maybe even without bringing that shift to conscious processing. Here are a couple of examples:

   - You're working at your desk. Without paying much attention to your thought process, you notice that you stood up and walked outside for some fresh air. Then you notice that you had been stuck in your thinking, and that taking a break and moving your body got your thoughts moving again in a productive way.
   - You're feeling anxious. You call a friend, pet the dog, go for a walk, make a cup of tea, or eat some chocolate to shift your mood, or at least shift your experience of your mood.

2. Make a list of five examples of these shifts you already routinely make even without conscious reflection.

3. Create a list of circumstances where you would like to make a shift, and decide the shift you would like to make. For example:

   - You feel dread every time you have to call your long-winded brother-in-law. You might make a shift by calling at a time when you already have another appointment to go to, or you might think about a positive experience you can look forward to after you've made the call.
   - You wake up in the morning already anxious about the day's to-do list. You shift your mood by committing to a five-minute gratitude practice before you get out of bed, or reading a poem or encouraging quote before you sit down to plow through your list.

4. Practice making these shifts for a week, and then reflect on any shifts in your experience as a result of your practice.

Little and often is fine. When you empower yourself to create a shift, you deepen your trust that you can. Then you can apply that response flexibility to increasingly difficult shifts.

EXERCISE 6-9: Recognizing Past Shifts

When we consciously notice that many patterns in our lives have already changed, either spontaneously or through our conscious choice, it's easier to open up to the possibilities of more change and to embrace such changes as a necessary part of our resilience.

1. Identify and write down five beliefs or habits you were taught when growing up, but which you no longer adhere to.

2. For each item, reflect on what prompted the shift. What role did your own reflection or choice play in the shift? How much did these shifts simply happen on their own over time?

This exercise helps loosen the power of the idea that whatever has been true in the past must still be true, which limits our ability to change.

EXERCISE 6-10: Change Every *Should* to *Could*

We all have unconscious patterns in our language that filter how we perceive our experiences and thus shape how we respond to them. *Should* is one of them. *I have to* is another. Because *should* and *have to* imply obligation, duty, even judgments of right or wrong, the mind contracts. Changing every *should* to *could* opens up possibilities and choice, and thus strengthens response flexibility. Shifting *I have to* to *I get to* similarly shifts your thinking from burden to privilege and strengthens your resilience.

1. Without making this exercise another *should*, remind yourself fairly regularly that *could* is a possibility. Whenever you hear yourself *shoulding* on

yourself, repeat the phrase "Change every *should* to a *could*" and notice any shifts in your own thinking.

2.   Likewise, whenever you hear yourself say, "I have to" (which may be often!), practice saying, "I get to" instead. This shift helps us experience gratitude for the privilege of being alive and having the opportunity. Notice any shifts in your responses to what's happening and your reactions to it.

3.   Even if there are still shades of obligation lingering, ask yourself if there is anything positive in the moment. Let the recognition of that positive re-open your brain to optimism and learning. "I *could* finish the taxes by this weekend." "I *get* to take the kids to school every morning this week."

Should creates an unconscious expectation and sets us up for criticism if we "fail" to perform. *Could* creates an unconscious perception of possibility and sets us up for pride in our learning and growth. Noticing how you talk to yourself, and choosing to change how you talk to yourself, shifts how you relate to yourself and can create wise changes in your behavior. This one practice of modifying your self-talk can have some of the biggest effects on your resilience.

Level 2. Glitches and Heartaches, Sorrows and Struggles

A central practice of mindfulness-based cognitive therapy is to identify automatic negative thoughts (ANTs) that derail your resilience, and create positive automatic thoughts (PATs) as antidotes to the habitual negative self-talk. You use reconditioning to rewire limiting beliefs, patterns of mental process, and entire mindsets that can block your resilience. Even though these tools use thoughts to rewire other thoughts, you still draw on all the tools you have learned so far — somatic, emotional, and relational — to help rewire the brain. The more neural networks you can light up, the more thorough the rewiring.

EXERCISE 6-11: Changing ANTs to PATs

1.   Identify and write down five habitual messages you hear from various parts of yourself that devalue you and make you feel inadequate or inferior. Here are some examples:

- You're so lazy!
- You've never succeeded at this before, so what makes you think you can do it now?
- Really? You think they'll be interested in that idea?

2. For each of these ANTs, think of and write down at least one PAT as an antidote:

   - I'm motivated about things I'm truly interested in.
   - I've been studying and watching people do this; I'm ready to try.
   - I like this idea! I want to try it out. I'll find the people who agree with me.

3. A PAT will rewire an ANT most effectively if it feels realistic and doable. First practice saying the PATs to yourself many times a day, until they become fairly automatic and you don't have to "think" to say them.

4. Then pair an ANT with its PAT and say them both out loud many times a day.

5. Gradually reduce the number of times you repeat the ANT and repeat only the PAT many times.

6. The next time you hear the ANT in your mind, notice if the PAT comes into your awareness, too. If it does, great! You're rewiring. If not, keep practicing until it does.

This exercise is reconditioning at its finest. Conscious choices lead to conscious rewiring. Your growing sense of competence may catalyze further rewiring of your sense of self and strengthening of your resilience.

EXERCISE 6-12: Rewiring Complete Thought Processes

Becoming aware of not just individual thoughts but also the mental processes by which your mind generates those thoughts enables you to begin rewiring those mental processes. Note the distinction between mindfulness and thinking. Your mindful awareness of your experience — the experience of having a thought — allows you to monitor and modify your thinking — both the content of the thought and the process that generates it.

This is Olympic-level brain training here. Give yourself plenty of time and self-encouragement to learn this tool.

1. Identify one of the common thought processes listed on page 175 or another habitual thought process you have noticed. Here we'll use three of the most common as examples:

    -   Discounting the positive
    -   Overgeneralizing
    -   Catastrophizing

2. Practice looking for clues that you are engaging in this particular thought process.

    -   Discounting the positive: "Wait a minute. Did I just miss a positive moment here? Did I not take in something that could have been a compliment? Was I so focused on nearly tripping over the tricycle in the driveway that I missed my daughter running to give me a hug?"
    -   Overgeneralizing: "I just heard myself say 'never' for the third time in five minutes." Or "I notice I'm taking things personally, feeling singled out, losing the big picture."
    -   Catastrophizing: "Geez, as soon as I noticed another 'senior moment,' forgetting what I walked into the kitchen for, I went right to wondering if I'm getting Alzheimer's already."

3. Identify an antidote to this pattern of thinking.

    -   Discounting the positive: "Let me notice five positives in this moment or in memory. One, I'm alive in my body. Whatever I'm dealing with, I *get* to deal with it. Two, I can take in the love of my family and their good intentions toward me right now. Three, I can stop and notice the sun, the clouds, the trees, the birdsong. Four, I can remember positives — oh yeah, Shirley said I looked good in this shirt, and I didn't even register that. Five, actually I was enjoying my own good thoughts just earlier this morning."
    -   Overgeneralizing: "Let me check the three Ps right now. Did I see things as pervasive? Yup, I went global. Not everybody in the world is

rude just because that customer service rep was. As personal? Yes, he may have been rude to other people besides me this morning. As permanent? Well, that call is over, and the problem got solved. I'll probably get a different rep the next time I call."

- Catastrophizing: "Whoa! Back up! Let me focus on what's actually happening. I forgot what I walked into the kitchen for because I was thinking about something else. When I walked back into the kitchen again, I remembered. And I'm making the lifestyle choices that will help me prevent the onset of Alzheimer's. I can relax and trust I'm okay."

4. Write down these antidotes to use any time you notice the pattern arising in your thinking. Notice if these antidotes help you catch and stop the pattern more quickly.

Acknowledge your efforts in noticing and rewiring habitual mental thought processes. You strengthen your response flexibility by both practicing it and noticing it. Noticing that you are rewiring your thought process may itself be a new process. It is still reconditioning your brain.

As always, use the little-and-often approach to give your brain the best chance of success at this rewiring. Rewiring the mental processes that generate negative thoughts is a huge task. It could take many repetitions over a long period to rewire the most deeply encoded processes.

Reframe any *should* about this practice, or how long it might take, into a *could*. Add the great helper of strengthening response flexibility — "I haven't mastered this — *yet*." And persevere. Just knowing that this tool is available to you and that it works can give a great boost to your resilience.

A ship is safe in harbor, but that's not what ships are for.
— REAR ADMIRAL GRACE HOPPER, US Navy

In her book *Mindset*, the psychologist Carol Dweck describes two opposite mindsets that greatly predict the likelihood of our accomplishing our goals: a fixed mindset and a growth mindset. In a fixed mindset, we are likely to believe that our success is predetermined: if we're smart or talented, we'll succeed easily, and if not, it isn't worth trying because we'll never succeed. A fixed mindset makes it difficult to take in any feedback about how we might do better. When we experience a failure or a setback, we're likely to give up and not bother. We may even blame others or circumstances for our lack of success. This fixed mindset leads to avoiding challenges rather than risking failure.

In a growth mindset, we are likely to believe that success depends more on effort than on talent or intelligence. If we keep trying and work hard, we'll learn, improve through practice, and eventually succeed. People with a growth mindset don't blame anyone else when they encounter a setback. They seek out feedback; they are more likely to seek out new challenges and less likely to give up when things get hard or go wrong. As you can imagine, the growth mindset fosters response flexibility and resilience; the fixed mindset derails them.

EXERCISE 6-13: Shifting Mindsets

To practice identifying and shifting your own mindset, follow these steps:

1. Reflect on situations where you faced a challenge or simply encountered something unfamiliar. Reflect on your own thought process and your own behaviors. Recall times when you did operate from a fixed mindset, hanging back, hesitating, or refusing to attempt something you perceived to be a bit beyond your capacities. Recall times also when you approached a challenge with a growth mindset, with interest, curiosity, and some confidence, or at least a willingness to give it a go. Most of us have had both kinds of experiences.

2. For one of the times when you acted from a growth mindset, reflect on what made possible your decision to try and your perseverance in trying. Identify both internal and external resources.

3. For one of the times when you were caught in a fixed mindset, imagine how you could have behaved differently, finding inner courage and encouragement from others to go ahead and try, engage, and persevere until you experienced some success, or at least a healthy pride in your effort.

4. Identify a situation now where you could try acting from a growth mindset rather than a fixed mindset. Choose a situation where you might realistically have a chance of success. Focus on shifting your mindset from fixed

to growth. You can use tools you have learned, like changing every *should* to a *could*, remembering your traits of resilience, or reviewing genuine expressions of appreciation from others. Reflect on any difference this choice makes on your behavior.

When you choose to shift mindsets, you are choosing to strengthen your response flexibility in a major way. You'll experience new confidence in your resilience.

Level 3. Too Much

It's possible to re-condition our relationships to even the most difficult events of our lives. Reframing is a process of conscious reflection that allows you to "rewrite" a glitch, a mistake, even a dreadful disaster as an AFGO — another frickin' growth opportunity. By "turning a regrettable moment into a teachable moment," as the neuroscience writer Jonah Lehrer puts it, you can somewhat redeem the outcome of the experience by salvaging a sense of your own resilience in relationship to the event.

This process is sometimes called finding the silver lining, or finding the gift in the mistake. By finding lessons in your response to the event, even possibilities that you can see more clearly in retrospect, you can strengthen your response flexibility for future similar events.

EXERCISE 6-14: Finding the Gift in the Mistake

Failure isn't fatal, but failure to change might be.

— John Wooden

1. Begin small. Remember a single, not too overwhelming occasion when things went wrong and you were still able to discover something right in the situation: in your response, in other people's responses, in an outcome you never could have predicted. This may be something as simple as realizing, "If I hadn't missed my flight, I wouldn't have run into an old college friend at the airport." Or "If I hadn't been looking for my lost wallet, I wouldn't

have discovered Timmy's old teddy bear under the bed." The gift or the right doesn't have to be as large in scale as the mistake or the wrong — just a small, previously unrecognized beneficial outcome or lesson learned. Sometimes the learning is that there can be gifts even in disasters.

2. Recall another time when things went wrong and you honestly didn't think any good came out of it at all. Even from this situation, look for lessons you could learn now, and think about what a different response might have been then. Could more response flexibility have changed the outcome or your feelings about the situation? Find the learning in the AFGO, and gain confidence that you *can* learn.

You can now reframe past events to see more response flexibility in them. Even if you can't change what happened, you can shift your relationship to what happened, and that change in your response can enable you to see yourself differently, more resiliently, now.

People are always telling themselves stories; it is how we make sense of the significance of what has happened to us. In the wake of trauma, people are often telling themselves stories of mental defeat and hopelessness. And they need to be in a position to begin reframing their story, as one that looks to the future and begins to view things in a beneficial way.

— Stephen Joseph

Sometimes you do have to integrate a deeply traumatizing event into the story of your life — the death of a child, the loss of your home in a flood or fire.

Researchers have found that journaling can be a powerful tool in coming to terms with a traumatizing event, because the brain processes an event differently when you're writing about it than when you're thinking or talking about it. Writing puts you in more of an observer's role, holding the event in a larger awareness. You can begin to see that what happened is part of your story, but not the whole story. There was a time before, then something happened, and there is an after, even if your life after the event is very different from what it was before. What happened is still included in your larger life story — not forgotten or denied or glossed over as though it never happened — but it does not determine the entire story. Whatever happened has its place in your life, but it doesn't have to determine the rest of your life.

EXERCISE 6-15: Creating a Coherent Narrative

Allow at least thirty minutes to do this written reflection, even if you are working with a small, manageable event. Taking the time to reflect creates space in your brain's processing to generate insights you might not have expected.

1. Identify a single event you want to practice with. Choose an event that you did manage to cope with, one that you processed successfully and learned from. You want to stay in your range of resilience in this exercise and not risk being retriggered or retraumatized. (With practice, however, this tool can help you process anything that has ever happened.)

2. Write your reflections for each of these prompts, and take as much time as you need.

    •   Describe what happened; describe the consequences. Use your tools of mindfulness and self-compassion to come to the awareness and acceptance of a compassionate observer's perspective. Try to relate to the event somewhat objectively.

    •   Describe the resources, practices, tools, and coping strategies you used at the time. Recall these clearly, with honesty and pride, no shame or blame. It's important to recover the strengths and resources you already had at the time.

    •   Describe the resources and strategies you would use now if you could do this over. You have probably grown and learned since the event occurred. This step integrates that learning.

    •   Describe the lessons you learned, the growth you experienced, the positive meanings you found. Take all the time you need; this step is the turning point of the exercise.

    •   List the things you appreciate now because of the event. Resilience involves more than coping. It's finding the new lessons, the new possibilities, the new opportunities, the new sense of meaning and purpose and life direction because of the event, not just in spite of it.

3. When you have finished this written reflection, set it aside for two or three days. When you reread it, notice whether you've had any additional insights to add to what you have already written.

4. Reread this reflection again a month or a year later, and notice how your relationship to the event has continued to shift.

5. Create a coherent narrative for as many challenging events in your life as you wish. Eventually your brain will learn to generalize this process: you can reframe events more quickly and more easily.

This exercise helps you let go of any stories about yourself that are not helpful to you now and to reflect on and claim any resilience you have already developed. It can also help you trust that you will be resilient in the face of whatever might happen in the future.

The response flexibility that results from using tools of reflective intelligence in the focused modes of new conditioning and reconditioning is expressed in the poem "Autobiography in Five Short Chapters" by Portia Nelson:

I
I walk down the street.
    There is a deep hole in the sidewalk.
    I fall in.
    I am lost...I am helpless.
        It isn't my fault.
It takes me forever to find a way out.

II
I walk down the same street.
    There is a deep hole in the sidewalk.
    I pretend I don't see it.
    I fall in again.
I can't believe I'm in the same place.
        But, it isn't my fault.
It still takes a long time to get out.

III
I walk down the same street.
There is a deep hole in the sidewalk.

I see it is there.
  I still fall in…it's a habit…but,
    My eyes are open.
    I know where I am.
It is *my* fault.
I get out immediately.

IV
I walk down the same street.
  There is a deep hole in the sidewalk.
  I walk around it.

V
I walk down another street.

Deconditioning

Mindfulness practice allows you to develop a steady awareness, focusing your attention on specific aspects of your experience, or of yourself, that are shifting or that you want to shift. This conscious reflection allows you to see how your mind is operating and evolving, sometimes seeing clearly and choosing wisely, sometimes not. Engaging in this process of conscious reflection strengthens the prefrontal cortex and associated structures in the brain, creating an upward spiral of response flexibility.

With deconditioning, you temporarily suspend the guardianship of the prefrontal cortex, not focusing on a specific thought pattern or aspect of yourself. This letting go drops you into the default network mode of the brain, giving rise to a different kind of reflection that you may experience as a daydream or reverie, as the mental play space that gives rise to intuition and insight, or as the vast spaciousness of awareness itself. You are aware of the knowing and of yourself as the knower, containing all of that knowing.

Mindfulness teachers sometimes liken awareness to a vast sky that can hold all the clouds and storms moving through it. We usually pay more attention to the shape of the clouds and the drama of the storms than to the sky that contains them. As the Zen teaching tells us, when our attention is focused, it's like looking at the sky through a pipe. With the spaciousness of awareness, we become adept at putting down the pipe and looking at the whole sky again.

Level 1. Barely a Wobble

Letting go is not the same as dissociating or blanking out or becoming unaware. It's simply becoming aware of any experience arising in your consciousness — you just sneezed, you're fantasizing about a trip to Hawaii, you're worried there won't be enough money to buy a new car if your current car conks out — and letting it go. You anchor first in that larger sense of awareness that can truly hold anything at all, and then you practice letting go as an aid to disentangling from thoughts, worries, complaints, resentments that could derail your response flexibility, or at least don't help you move forward. The letting go releases you from spinning your wheels and frees up the mental bandwidth you need to see clearly, discern options, and choose wisely. Letting go allows you to take whatever is happening less personally. You don't have to shore up a personal sense of self (hopefully, the practices of chapter 4 have helped you develop a secure inner base, not easily derailed even by drastic shifts in circumstances). You can use your energy to deal with whatever needs to be dealt with.

EXERCISE 6-16: Letting Go of Thought Patterns

1. Sit comfortably in a place where you won't be interrupted for thirty minutes. Let yourself come into a sense of presence, being aware of being in your body, in this moment, in this place.

2. Focus your awareness on your breathing. When your mind begins to wander into the thoughts you are practicing letting go of, you can always refocus on your breath and start again.

3. As you focus your awareness on your breathing, notice the awareness that allows you to know that you are breathing. Notice your awareness of that awareness, more open, more spacious, of the knowing (awareness) of what is known (your breathing).

4. As you rest your mind in awareness, notice specific contents of thoughts as they arise. "Oh, taking things personally — here I go again." "Oh, I went all the way down the rabbit hole to the full catastrophe, yup, I did." "Hmm, I assumed, and that assumption wasn't correct. Back up and try again." Simply notice, let them go, and return your awareness to awareness.

5. Repeat as you need to. "Simply" noticing and letting go can be a lifelong practice, and one that becomes easier over time. You persevere with

noticing your thought patterns over and over again until you can relate to them as thought patterns, not as who you are.

There are no worries as you hang out in this larger awareness, simply noticing all thoughts coming, then letting them all go. Your nervous system is still on duty, unconsciously scanning the environment for impending danger. If it needs to, your prefrontal cortex will resume its guardianship of your attention literally in a heartbeat, allowing you to refocus your attention whenever necessary.

Even when your thought patterns are repetitive, stubborn, or stuck, your larger awareness allows you to relate to them in a friendly way — "Oh, fear of disapproval, I know you well" — without identifying these patterns as who you are. You strengthen your resilience as you shift from being what's known to being the knower who can see clearly and choose wisely.

Level 2. Glitches and Heartaches, Sorrows and Struggles

The response flexibility essential to your resilience is supported by your brain's maturely functioning prefrontal cortex. Many tools in this book are designed to strengthen that functioning. Effective functioning of the prefrontal cortex also allows you to cohere a stable, authentic sense of personal self. As a psychotherapist who has been helping people recover and strengthen their resilience for twenty-five years, I know well the value of developing a healthy, strong, well-functioning personal self. People can be truly resilient; they can truly thrive.

As a mindfulness practitioner and teacher for twenty years, I also know the value of "letting go" of that self. Not taking things personally — letting the self "dissolve" into the larger awareness that can know but not be entangled in all the comings and goings — brings relief from suffering.

Letting go of the self can trigger an alarm in the nervous system — "What? Not exist?" The exercise below is a very benign, safe way to experience the liberation of letting go of the self.

EXERCISE 6-17: Letting Go of the Self — Breathing into Infinity

1.   Sit comfortably. Allow your eyes to gently close. Focus your awareness on your breathing, gently in and out. As you follow your breathing, notice

your own awareness of your breathing, the awareness that allows you to know that you are breathing.

2. When that awareness of your breathing is steady, begin to notice the breathing of any people around you, or people you imagine being around you. There's no need to do anything; just notice or imagine other people breathing as you are breathing, and notice your awareness of that. Notice what you are aware of in your own being as you rest in this awareness.

3. Staying anchored in an awareness of your own breathing, expand your awareness of breathing to include the breathing of more people you know, who are not necessarily physically near you. Notice your awareness of your awareness of everyone breathing. Notice your awareness of your own being as you remain aware.

4. Still anchored in an awareness of your own breathing, expand your awareness further to include people you don't know, outside the building you are in, perhaps elsewhere in the neighborhood, throughout the city, across the region. Become aware of all of them breathing together. Notice your awareness of your awareness: you are simply being, and being aware.

5. Continue to expand your awareness to include people breathing all over the country, all over the planet. Expand your awareness to include all living creatures breathing in the parks, the forests, underground, in the lakes and rivers, in the oceans, the sky, of all sentient beings breathing together. Notice your awareness of your awareness of existence, and your awareness of simply being.

6. Expand your awareness to include all forms of existence, some breathing, some not — the air, the water, the rocks. And notice your awareness of your awareness of the breathing, and your awareness of simply being.

7. Expand your awareness beyond our planet to other planets, other stars, other galaxies, and the space between the planets and stars and galaxies, as far as you can possibly imagine; notice your awareness of your awareness expanding. Rest comfortably, safely, in this vast spacious awareness, in this vast simply being, for as long as you choose. Take your time.

8. Gently bring your awareness back to your awareness of sitting in the room you are in, in this moment, breathing. Focus your awareness on simply

breathing. Take a moment to shift gears and reflect on your experience of simply being. You may experience a lightness, a spaciousness, or an openness in your being.

On reflection after this exercise, you may realize that at some point your sense of self dropped away. You can come back to that sense of self in a heartbeat anytime you need to. But you did not need a sense of self to experience the vastness of awareness accessible in this defocused mode.

Level 3. Too Much

Praise and blame, gain and loss, pleasure and sorrow come and go like the wind. To be happy, rest like a great tree in the midst of them all.
— JACK KORNFIELD, *Buddha's Little Instruction Book*

"Resting like a great tree" in the midst of loss and sorrow can seem an elusive state indeed when life events dump you out of your boat and you fear you are about to go under. The exercise below helps you hang on to your intentions to see clearly and choose wisely even as you let go of control over how things will turn out.

Letting go of control may be as much of a challenge as letting go of thought patterns (exercise 6-16) or letting go of a sense of self (exercise 6-17). Throughout this book I have encouraged you to discern options and make wise choices, to act in the face of anxiety or fear. Letting go of control doesn't mean letting go of the capacity to think, choose, and act: it means letting go of trying to control the outcome. Life is bigger than we are, and we can't always see or understand the larger forces at play. Letting go of control is about finding the courage to persevere, to be as resilient as you can be, moment by moment, when you don't have control of what's going to happen next.

EXERCISE 6-18: Letting Go of Control — Hanging On to Your Intentions

This exercise uses the practice of inclining the mind, using the intentional phrasing *May I* without adding the pressure or expectation of *I will* or *I must*. *May I* might seem overly gentle, inadequate for facing a challenge or crisis. But researchers have found that intentions phrased with *May I*, giving permission but not compelling, are more effective in motivating people to persevere.

1. Identify a challenging situation in your life right now where you can't control the outcome, though you can hope to influence it and to manage your reactions to it. Here are some examples:

    - Your insurance company has denied your claim in an auto accident.
    - Your father was just diagnosed with prostate cancer.
    - The company where you have worked for seven years was just acquired in a hostile takeover, and your future there is uncertain.

2. Identify your intentions for coping with this situation, including your intentions to influence it and to manage your reactions to it.

    - May I quickly find someone in the insurance company open to hearing my side of things; may I remember to breathe and stay grounded in my body when I talk with them.
    - May I help my father find the resources he needs to cope with his treatment; may I be compassionate and caring toward my father and toward myself in the coming months.
    - May I quickly find out how my job will be affected; may I be aware of, accept, and manage my own reactivity (including anger, fear, or shame).

3. Bring your intentions to mind first thing every morning for the next week. As you move through your day, notice whether you are acting on your intentions. ("May I act on my intentions" may become another intention; "May I have compassion for myself when I forget" may be another.)

4. As the situation evolves, reset or revise your intentions as you need to. Little and often is fine here. The perseverance is strengthening your resilience.

Setting an intention, and then noticing yourself carrying out that intention, deepens your trust in yourself and in life, even in the darkest of times.

Faith is taking the first step, even when you don't see the whole staircase.
— Martin Luther King Jr.

You hang in there, you show up, you stay engaged, you manage your responses. Because you are doing your part, no matter how things turn out, you rest in a deeper equanimity in the midst of it all. That deeper equanimity allows you to "look out on life with quiet eyes."

In this chapter, you have practiced tools of mindful awareness to help you see clearly what is happening and your reactions to what is happening, to rewire any habitual mental patterns that might block your adaptive responses now to whatever is happening, to reframe mistakes and even disasters as opportunities to find the silver lining and grow, and to cultivate the equanimity that can "hold" whatever is happening, strengthening your capacities to discern options and make wise choices. These tools of conscious reflection play an essential role in any of the intelligences in this book.

The next chapter focuses on learning to integrate all your multiple intelligences, radically strengthening the response flexibility in your brain to cope with anything, anything at all.

CHAPTER SEVEN

Full-On Resilience

Coping with Anything, Anything at All

The art of living lies less in eliminating our troubles than in growing with them.
— **BERNARD M. BARUCH**

In this book, you have been learning to grow by strengthening your response flexibility — rewiring your brain step by step, little and often, practicing using a variety of tools to meet challenges to your resilience that range from barely a wobble to just too much.

In the preceding chapters, I have dealt with specific intelligences — somatic, emotional, relational (both intra- and interpersonal), and reflective — as though they were separate and distinct. In truth, of course, each intelligence works with all of the others. The prefrontal cortex, which you have been learning to strengthen, integrates the functioning of all of these intelligences. And when your intelligences are working well together and integrated in their functioning, you function well, too.

This chapter offers tools for integrating all of your intelligences so that your base of resilience becomes increasingly steady and reliable. You will be able to deal with increasingly challenging difficulties more quickly and effectively.

Here's a story of my own to illustrate what I mean by integration. I relearned these lessons about resilience just a few weeks before I sat down to write this chapter.

I had traveled to the Bahamas to teach some workshops at the Sivananda Ashram Yoga Retreat Center. It was already nighttime and dark when I arrived, and I was tired. While stepping from the dock into the boat that would take me across the bay to the ashram, I misstepped and plunged right into the water. My first reaction as I popped up to the surface and grabbed the edge of the boat was, "I'm alive! I'm alive."

Within a second, however, I realized that my computer was in my backpack, and my backpack was still on my back. I knew there was no chance of modern electronics surviving even a brief dunking in ocean water. My computer was fritzed — and my cell phone, too.

Just one second later — yes, it really did happen that fast — I found myself thinking about the wildfires that had recently devastated a wide area just forty miles north of where I live — resulting in a hundred thousand people evacuated and five thousand homes and businesses burned to the ground. "Put this in perspective, Linda — this is a computer and your data. You're alive; you get to deal."

By the time the Sivananda staff pulled me back into the boat and we headed to the ashram, we were all laughing. I joked that it was so hot in the Bahamas, I just couldn't wait to get into the water!

Sivananda is a spiritual community dedicated to service, peace, and love — a community of shared humanity reminding me of my community of friends back home who would have been supportive, too, if they had known. As soon as we arrived at the ashram, residents were offering me replacement computers and phones. But instead I chose to stay unplugged. For the four days of my visit, I stayed off the digital devices and focused instead on working with the practices I've been sharing here, to muster my resilience and capacity to cope.

Though I later noted a lot of practical lessons for next time (watch your step getting into any boat, put all the luggage in the boat before you get in; wrap everything electronic in watertight plastic; store computer and cell phone in separate places, much as parents of young children sometimes choose to fly on separate flights in case one plane crashes), in those first few moments of adjusting to what had happened, I very deliberately chose to focus on self-compassion and gratitude rather than shame or blame. I was alive; I was *getting* to deal with the problem. And I noticed that I was making that wise choice.

Twenty minutes after my dunking, eating dinner in dry clothes on dry land with the staff who had pulled me into the boat, I experienced a moment of awe. Of course at some level I knew that the resilience training I'd been teaching all of these years was valuable. I had experienced its benefits myself many times; I had seen how it helped many of my clients and workshop participants. But now I experienced a heightened awareness that, indeed, resilience can be strengthened. "I'm not reacting in the ways I would have many years ago. I'm doing way better than I even would have expected, and it's because I've practiced — self-compassion, not shaming or blaming, gratitude, not catastrophizing. I'm living my resilience right now."

Still, I'm human, and I felt a fair amount of anxiety about how I would manage my busy life when I returned home the following week. How would I finish the last two chapters of this book, or triage and respond to the two hundred emails a day that

I'd missed? How long would it take to order a new computer and get it up and running? Did I really have all my files on my back-up drive at home? Could my email contacts and internet passwords be reconstructed?

What to do with all those worries? I made an elaborate, step-by-step list of everything I could do starting at 7:30 the morning after I got home. And then I parked all of my worries there. I chose not to focus any longer on what I couldn't yet do anything about.

I slept well that first night. And when the anxiety resurfaced, I parked it again in the list of tasks I had mentally rehearsed (prewired) for the following week. For the next three days, I focused on teaching my four workshops: Resilience, Mindfulness and Self-Compassion, Brain Care as Self-Care, and Post-traumatic Growth. How synchronous. It was a skillful distraction, and I knew it. I had wanted to unplug while at the ashram anyway, and frankly, no one missed the PowerPoint slides. At breakfast one morning, the head swami remarked, "Life made this decision to unplug for you."

Yes. I could choose to deepen into experiences of just being, recognize my overall well-being, and use that baseline equanimity to help me cope.

Because the weather forecast had been for pretty solid rain, I had brought several work projects with me in case I was indoors a lot. (In fact, it was delightfully sunny.) Without my computer, I took a work bypass, too, giving my mind something to focus on other than my computer disaster. I read three books by fellow clinicians. When do I ever take the time to read three books? I also continued writing — in longhand! Being creative in these ways was both grounding and comforting. I also found teaching and connecting with so many earnest seekers on the path very reassuring. And I had the chance to savor my friend Doug von Koss's *Gratitude Goulash: Poems and Stuff* — the best medicine possible.

Eventually the bruises from my stumble emerged and I came down with a cold, but I also swam in the Caribbean and had wonderful conversations with the swamis at dinner.

I arrived home late on a Monday evening. At 7:30 on Tuesday morning, I was at North Bay Computers, a company with which I have a wonderful working relationship, intentionally nurtured over ten years. Within three hours — the time it took to do laundry and retrieve the cats from the vet — they had loaded my email and Microsoft Word onto a loaner computer; they confirmed that my book files were on my flash drive (also dunked in the Caribbean but wrapped in plastic) and uploaded them onto the loaner; and confirmed that my backup drive, which had been safe at home, did indeed have the latest data and would be uploaded to the new computer.

From all of this I learned again, in a deeply visceral way, that resilience is learnable and recoverable. It was the integration of many different practices over time that allowed me to have as much response flexibility as I did. These practices included:

- My own mindful awareness — knowing what I was experiencing and tracking shifts in those experiences, both outer and inner, moment by moment
- Prioritizing calming my nervous system (through exercises like hand on the heart, feeling the soles of my feet) so that I could function and discern options
- Choosing to acknowledge and shift my inner reactions as skillfully as I could by:
  - consciously practicing my self-compassion phrases over and over to avoid sinking into feeling badly, pitying myself, or devaluing myself for my mistake
  - focusing on everything there was to still be grateful for — and there was more than enough
  - refusing to catastrophize (that was a minor miracle)
  - dealing with my anxiety about the future by parking it in the future and practicing trusting that future
  - opening to a sense of vast being and the benevolence of the universe (residing in a spiritual community for four days certainly encouraged that)
- Claiming my own resilience (which became a source of resilience itself: "I'm okay; I'm doing okay; things will work out eventually")
- Reaching out to people for help — and by accepting the help that was so generously given, I did not feel alone in my coping. The support evoked a deep sense of safety no matter how things might turn out.
- Learning that I was learning: figuring out what to do differently next time and what to do differently right now

My mini-catastrophe was by no means the worst-case scenario. The struggles and heartache of losing a loved one, losing one's health, losing one's job or home, or losing a sense of direction or purpose are far more challenging to our resilience. My point here is that the integration of the tools offered in this book *can* prepare you to meet and recover even from those catastrophes.

Practices that Lead to Post-Traumatic Growth

Researchers in the emerging field of post-traumatic growth suggest five practices that foster that integration and that predict a person's success at *bouncing forward*: dealing with, healing from, and moving beyond any potentially traumatizing event into new strengths for coping, new learning, new possibilities for discovery and growth, deeper connections with people and community, and a deeper sense of meaning and purpose for living.

You have already been learning tools to engage in these practices.

1. Accepting Reality

Whatever has happened, it's not fair. It never should have happened, but it did. The first step, of accepting what happened, draws on all the practices of mindful awareness and compassionate self-acceptance, both of the event and of our perceptions and reactions to the event. "I'm alive! I *get* to deal with this."

2. Turning to Other People

When you feel vulnerable, other people — in person, in memory, in imagination — can provide safe havens where you don't have to keep it together or take care of anyone else. This gives you a respite until you can deploy the tools you have practiced using to return to your inner equilibrium and begin healing and dealing.

People can also be resources, providing support in the form of encouragement, practical help, and safety nets. People can help you work around and work through whatever difficulty you're facing for however long it takes.

3. Drawing On the Positive and Seeing Possibilities

The direct, measurable outcome of practicing gratitude, kindness, compassion, love, joy, tranquility, and contentment is resilience: openness to the big picture and optimism about the future. The direct, measurable outcome of choosing to approach life's challenges from a growth mindset — seeking to learn and trusting that you can learn — is resilience. "Maintain a positive outlook" and "See the glass half full rather than half empty" are not clichés. They are commonsense wisdom backed by science.

4. Learning the Lessons

As soon as you begin to "turn a regrettable moment into a teachable moment," as Jonah Lehrer says, the brain begins to shift how it is perceiving and responding to the event. Finding the silver lining, finding the gift in the mistake, is considered to be the turning point in the process of post-traumatic growth. Learning the lessons in the event is fundamentally useful, not just for coping better in the future but for coping better right now.

5. Creating a Coherent Narrative of the Event

You practiced using this tool in exercise 6-15. By placing a previously or potentially traumatizing event in the larger context of your life, you create a more vivid sense of past, present, and *future*. (The sense of continuity of self over time is one of the integrative functions of the prefrontal cortex.) You can begin to find a deeper sense of meaning and purpose for your life, not just in spite of the event but often because of the event. Your resilience begins to generate a genuine sense of thriving and flourishing.

When you can pull the practices in this book together — mindfully practicing gratitude while walking in nature with a friend, calling on your compassionate friend to soothe the distress of any inner part — your resilience becomes almost unshakeable. You will be equipped to cope with anything and everything, and to trust that you can cope.

New Conditioning

You are integrating circuits of response flexibility, the brain's base of your resilience, so that the resilience is ready when you need it, for *any* level of challenge.

Level 1. Barely a Wobble

You're creating "recipes" for practices that draw on your multiple intelligences simultaneously, creating the conditions that enable them to create more integrated circuitry in your brain.

EXERCISE 7-1: Recipes for Integration

To encourage the integration, the examples here are presented as one flow of experience rather than set out step by step:

1. Walk with a friend in some beautiful natural landscape. Notice the calming of your nervous system from being in nature — the sensations of walking on earth or grass, the smells of the fresh air, the sounds of trees rustling in the wind or dogs barking as you pass. Savor the resonance and synchrony of connecting with your friend — sharing ideas, feelings, energy. Take five minutes each to share what you are grateful for in your lives. Include

any moments of appreciation for the ease of connection between you, any moments of awe inspired by the landscape you are walking through, any moments of opening to a larger view of your lives. Take a few minutes to reflect on your entire experience, including the richness of your experience when all your intelligences work together. This "recipe" becomes an inner resource. Trust that you can create these moments of integration in your brain many times over.

2. When you notice that you're feeling out of alignment or off balance in some way, try to identify what inner part might need attention, soothing, and reassurance. Acknowledge this inner part and the legitimacy of its distress or discomfort. In your imagination, invite this inner part to visit with your compassionate friend (in your safe place, if you wish). Let a dialogue unfold between your distressed inner part and your compassionate friend, who listens receptively and empathically. Ask your inner part to reflect on its experience. Writing as your inner part, journal about the experience, noticing any insights or "aha!" moments that emerge.

3. Plan your own recipes for integration, using tools that draw on at least three different intelligences. Try out your recipes. Let them evolve based on your experience.

As you practice integrating many tools into a recipe, you're creating and strengthening circuitry in your brain to do that integration. You're engaging with and responding to experience in more complex ways. Becoming comfortable with that complexity becomes part of your base of resilience.

Level 2. Glitches and Heartaches, Sorrows and Struggles

Jon Kabat-Zinn, the developer of mindfulness-based stress reduction, describes the need to strengthen our resilience this way:

We all accept that no one controls the weather. Good sailors learn to read it carefully and respect its power. They will avoid storms if possible, but when caught in one, they know when to take down the sails, batten down the hatches, drop anchor and ride things out, controlling what is controllable and letting go the rest. Training, practice, and a lot of firsthand experience in all sorts of weather are required to develop such skills so that they work for you when you need them. Developing skill in facing and effectively handling the various "weather conditions" in your life is what we mean by the art of conscious living.

EXERCISE 7-2: Expect the Unexpected

You can train for the unexpected so that your skills of resilience are there when you need them. This entails not just making a checklist for what to do but practicing ahead of time. The drill wires the behavior into your neural circuitry and installs the procedural learning of what to do into your body memory. You don't have to think to remember. You can act quickly, automatically, following the patterns you have installed. You can train the integrative circuits of your intelligences in the same way.

1. Identify one scenario where you might have to act quickly in response to a potential catastrophe. Start small. The car won't start and you have to drop the kids off at school, meet a client, or pick your sister up at the train station in fifteen minutes. Do you have jumper cables in the trunk? A taxicab phone number stored in your phone? A friendly relationship with a retired neighbor whose car you can borrow? Again, this is not just a checklist. You rehearse the skills ahead of time and prepare your safety nets and resources. Practice using the jumper cables, overcoming any anxiety about that. Look up the cab company number. Rehearse asking your neighbor if you can borrow the car. Once you rehearse the behaviors, you can see yourself doing them when you need to, and you can remember how to act without having to think about it.

2. Identify a more challenging scenario. Say your spouse falls over on a toy left on the stairs. You hear something crack. You rehearse ahead of time your practices to calm your nervous system. You rehearse what you'll say when you call the ambulance, your neighbor, the network of resources you have cultivated ahead of time. You rehearse remembering your wallet or purse and any ID you need for a trip to the emergency room.

    Again, you can't control everything. If an accident occurs, there will still be much uncertainty, but preparing to the extent that you can becomes part of your resilience.

3. Identify another more difficult situation: a sudden workplace downsizing, a more serious medical emergency, a natural disaster. It's not morbid; it's prudent to anticipate what you can, to see yourself acting competently so that you can trust your resilience.

Creating external safety nets of resources — logistical, financial, relational — is part of strengthening your resilience. Preparing a safety net in the brain, in your procedural memory, is just as essential. Rehearsing for the many "weather conditions" of life is skillful resilience building.

Level 3. Too Much

When you feel like you're in a full-blown hurricane, you can still find ways to respond resiliently, drawing on all your intelligences to keep your head above water.

EXERCISE 7-3: At Least I Can Still...

1. Identify one movement your body can still do — wake up, get up, walk, eat, pee and poop (no joke — these are signs of essential basic functioning), see, hear, distinguish warm from cold, remember how to make a pot of coffee. Little and slow, maybe, but at least you *can*.

2. Then add capacities from your emotional intelligence. If you get annoyed at your neighbor's child crying in the middle of the night and know that you're annoyed, it's a sign that you're alive. If you can remember that the child has an ear infection and is probably more miserable than you are, you're stretching your muscles of mindful empathy. That's a sign that you are more than alive — you are engaged. If you can evoke compassion for everyone around who's losing sleep tonight, you're activating your coping skills, opening to another point of view.

3. Then add capacities from your relational intelligence, both within yourself and with others. You could continue with the example above. The

compassion evoked by your neighbor's sick child at least reminds you of your shared humanity. You're not the only person on the planet losing sleep tonight for one reason or another; you're not alone in that suffering. There might be other examples, too: at least you're not beating yourself up for feeling annoyed; at least you find a smidgen of forgiveness for the child who's annoying you.

4. Add even reflective intelligence to this recipe by noticing any effect that this practice is having on your coping. If you can say "at least," it may be a sign to you that you *are* coping, at some level. Give yourself some credit for at least this much coping.

By reflecting on the small ways in which you're coping, you're keeping your head above water. You're not engaging in extravagant heroics, not even valiantly treading water — just staying afloat, and knowing that you *can*.

Reconditioning

In exercise 6-14, you learned to recondition the experience of a mistake or even disaster by reframing the event as an AFGO — another frickin' growth opportunity — and by finding the gift in the mistake, the silver lining in a disaster. Let's take that a few steps further.

Level 1. Barely a Wobble

In these exercises, you expand this practice of asking, "What's right with this wrong?" by integrating elements from other intelligences, expanding the possibilities of acting more resiliently in the future.

EXERCISE 7-4: "What's Right with This Wrong?"

1. Ask three or four trustworthy friends to do this exercise with you. Explain the purpose of the exercise, which is to help all of you develop the capacity to find the silver lining in a problematic event, to find the learning that might redeem a regrettable moment.

2. Set the ground rules for discussion at the beginning of the meeting: it can include sharing, listening, and brainstorming, but no criticism, no "fixing." These guidelines allow members of the group to feel safe in acknowledging their vulnerability *and* in claiming their strengths.

3. Each person takes about ten minutes to share some mistake they made or some major bump in the road that challenged or even derailed, their resilience, at least temporarily. Each person also shares how they coped, what lessons they learned in the process of recovering their resilience, what they would do differently now. Other group members listen empathically, but without offering a lot of comment.

4. As each person shares, everyone pays mindful attention to their own experience, in sharing their own story, in hearing other people share their stories. They notice not just what they are learning from reflecting, but what they are experiencing in this moment of experiencing.

5. After each person has shared their experiences, the group members begin to explore together what they are learning and what new insights into their own experience they have gained from hearing other people's stories.

6. Each person reflects on and takes in the support they feel from other group members. This step (which could be in the form of written journaling) allows each person to reflect on what they have learned about resilience from this exercise.

Social engagement with trustworthy people creates the neuroception of safety that primes the brain for learning and growth. The mindful attention to the process and to the experience creates a safe space in which each person can experience and acknowledge both their own vulnerability and their own strengths. Hearing other people's stories evokes the mental play space of the default network mode in the brain, where new understandings and insights can emerge.

Level 2. Glitches and Heartaches, Sorrows and Struggles

In exercise 3-20, you learned the tool of visualizing a wished-for outcome, which can rewire a moment of shame, when an interaction between you and another person went awry, by imagining a new, more satisfactory resolution to the situation and juxtaposing it with the original negative experience. You can use the same practice to rewire any negative emotional memory, including any moment of regret, as long as the new wished-for ending evokes strong positive emotions in you.

EXERCISE 7-5: Rewiring Regret about Lack of Resilience

1. Find a safe space in real life to do this exercise, or visit your imagined safe place. You may also ask a friend to simply sit with you while you do this visualization on your own; nothing more is needed than presence and caring.

2. Anchor your awareness in your own mindful self-compassion, being aware and accepting of your experience and yourself as the experiencer.

3. Recall a moment when some disappointment, difficulty, or even disaster happened and you responded less resiliently than you would have liked — something you've been carrying regret about ever since.

4. As you recall the event, "light up" the networks holding that memory — the feelings of regret, where you feel that regret in your body now, any negative thoughts you have about yourself now because of what happened — or didn't. Take care not to be overwhelmed by evoking this memory, but recall the details of your experience as vividly as you can.

5. Let go of this negative memory temporarily. Begin to create the positive resource to juxtapose with it by imagining a different ending to this scenario. Imagine how you could have responded differently and coped more resiliently, even if that never could have happened at the time.

6. Let this new ending evolve in your imagination until it feels satisfactory to you. Notice how this wished-for outcome makes you feel and where you feel those feelings in your body. Notice any thoughts you have about yourself now as you imagine yourself coping more skillfully and being more resilient. Make the experience of your feelings, sensations, and thoughts as vivid as you can.

7. Bring the original negative experience to mind again. Toggle back and forth between the old negative and the new positive several times, always refreshing the positive so that it's strong and vivid, always touching the negative lightly and letting it go again.

8. Let go of the negative completely and just rest your awareness in the experience of the positive.

9. Reflect on your entire experience, noticing any shifts in your sense of yourself as a resilient person.

10. If you have asked a friend to sit with you during this exercise, you may choose to share the results of the exercise with them. You may also choose to write your experiences in a journal to reread a day or two later. Notice whether any new insights emerge.

Few exercises are more helpful than rewiring any regret you have now about not being as resilient as you wish you had been then. There may still be lessons to learn and consequences to clean up. But as you shift your focus to *now*, and choices you can make about how you view yourself now, those perceptions become the platform for responding more resiliently in the future.

Level 3. Too Much

In exercise 6-15, you practiced creating a coherent narrative of a traumatizing event. You placed that single event in the larger context of your life. You created a more vivid sense of past, present, and future. Here you'll work with timelines again.

Creating a timeline of all the events of your life that have ever derailed your resilience, and your notes about how you coped with each of those events, gives you a very large overview of how your resilience has developed over time (or not — and perhaps that's why you're reading this book).

Part of strengthening your resilience is *trusting* that you are resilient. The exercise below helps you see that you are.

EXERCISE 7-6: Creating a Timeline of Resilience

1. You'll be creating an overview of your resilience throughout your entire life. Use a roll of butcher paper or several good-sized pieces of paper taped together to give yourself plenty of room to record key events. Gather a variety of colored pens or pencils or highlighters.

2. Create a timeline on the paper from the day you were born (or even before then, if there was medical trauma in utero) up through many years beyond

today (envisioning your future). Mark blocks of time for every year or every five years.

3. Begin noting down events that disrupted your resilience. Categorize them as level 1 (the least disruptive to your resilience), level 2, or level 3 (the most disruptive). You may choose to focus first on level 3 events; however, including level 1 and level 2 events gives you a fuller and more encouraging view of your resilience. Use different colors, sizes, and shapes to indicate the significance or severity of each event. Take as much time as you need for your default network mode to bring memories to awareness. You can return to this timeline over the next few days (or weeks) to add events as they come to mind.

4. On this timeline or in a separate journal, record how you coped with each event. What skills did you already know how to use well, and what skills could you have improved? You may have used tools similar to the tools in this book, or completely different tools. Notice whether there were any patterns to your coping. Record also your sense of how *well* you coped with each event. Did your practices return you to a baseline physiological equilibrium, emotional well-being, an inner sense of secure self, connections with people as resources, or the clarity you needed to discern options and choose wisely? Do your best to reflect on your responses given the intelligences you could draw on at the time.

5. Review this timeline again in a month. Notice any shifts in your view of yourself as resilient.

6. You may wish to share this timeline with a trustworthy friend; if you do, take in the good of their feedback to you about your resilience.

Granted, this is a large undertaking. You're recognizing where you already were resilient, seeing clearly with compassion where you weren't, and reflecting on these times with openness and curiosity — how could things have gone differently?

Use your timeline as a learning tool: rather than falling into judgment about yourself, discern what worked and what didn't. What skills did you already know how to use well, and what skills could you have improved? Let the learning help you bounce forward into the next new challenge to your resilience.

Deconditioning

There may be nothing more challenging to our resilience than facing our own mortality, especially if we've grown up in a family or culture that avoids talking about or planning for the end of life. Yet when we can face that eventuality with some equanimity, we are far better equipped to deal with anything disruptive along the way.

Level 1. Barely a Wobble

EXERCISE 7-7: Morning (Mourning) Pages

Many years ago, Julia Cameron, the author of *The Artist's Way*, developed the tool of morning pages to help people unblock their creativity. It's a form of stream-of-consciousness journaling that's effective in clearing out mental and emotional debris and priming the pump to let the creative imagination flow again.

You can apply free-flowing, stream-of-consciousness journaling to *any* topic — should I marry? Should I divorce? Do I follow my heart and choose a course that offers no money but lots of adventure? Should I confront my brother about his drinking? Accessing the defocused mode of the default network allows your brain to play, even with very serious topics, and generate ideas and insights you didn't know you had and might not have found any other way.

In this exercise, you focus your attention lightly on the topic of your own death and dying, open to your own intuitive wisdom, and see what insights emerge.

Cameron suggests writing morning pages first thing in the morning, when you have better access to the defocused mode of processing in the brain because the mind hasn't yet focused on the tasks of the day. You can even keep a journal and pen by your bedside so that you can start writing before you even get out of bed. If you choose to write your pages later in the day, that's fine, too. Try to write at about the same time every day: the routine creates a cue to your unconscious to settle into the flow.

1. Write free-form, nonstop for three minutes. Don't plan or think or censor or stop. Just let your mind play. After three minutes, close the journal and set it aside. Don't reread what you've written.

2. Write your morning pages for three minutes every day for two weeks. Ever so gently, plant a seed of intention each day: "Hmm. Life and death, living and dying. I wonder what I think about that?" And then don't think: let the intention subside into your unconscious and just continue the free-form writing. The writing may make no sense at first. (That's why you don't derail the process by rereading what you've written.) It doesn't need to make sense yet. You're simply clearing the pipes for clearer writing to emerge as you go along.

    At some point, however, you will begin to notice that your ideas are making a lot of sense, even though you couldn't have known or planned that ahead of time, and even though you haven't reread the pages you've already written. The clarity emerges from the process.

3. After two weeks or longer, write about your reflections on the process. Notice any shift in your view of your own mortality. You may or may not have brought to awareness any insights about living and dying, but most likely you did. Notice any insights you have received about anything important to your living.

You are practicing a valuable tool for accessing your own deeper intuitive wisdom about *anything*. That can strengthen your response flexibility and wire your resilience for any level of challenge.

Level 2. Glitches and Heartaches, Sorrows and Struggles

Wisdom tells me I am nothing.
Love tells me I am everything.
Between the two, my life flows.

— SRI NISARGADATTA, *I Am That*

EXERCISE 7-8: I'm Here; I'm Not Here

Imagining your own nonexistence paradoxically helps you feel more alive now and deepens your gratitude for being alive. Your priorities can shift when you are aware that the time you have on this planet is finite and that the possibilities for your life during that time are more than enough. If you have read Stephen Levine's *A Year to Live*, you will already be familiar with this exercise; it's a practice you can do anywhere, anytime.

1. Focus your attention on your own embodiment of yourself — knowing you are in your body, walking, standing, or sitting.

2. Notice your physical surroundings: a room in your home, walking through your neighborhood, in a store.

3. Imagine everything in your surroundings still existing exactly as it is now — without you there. It still exists; you don't.

4. Return your awareness to yourself existing in your own body right now. You *do* still exist — whew!

5. Play with imagining that you exist, you don't, you do, while the landscape remains unchanged.

Playing around with being and nonbeing, developing an equanimity in the skillful flow between the two, and anchoring your resilience in that equanimity vitally strengthens your ability to cope with anything, anything at all. You experience yourself as simply one particular amazing form of that consciousness that can — does — hold everything that has ever been or will be.

Level 3. Too Much

I've suggested from the beginning of this book that how you respond to the issue *is* the issue. And I've also suggested that it's the response flexibility innate in the prefrontal cortex of your brain that allows you to manage, shift, and rewire those responses.

Those various responses may be activated by the revving up, calming down, or shutting down of your nervous system, by emotions calling your attention to something important, by various inner parts that have their own strong habitual responses, by the resources available to you through other people, and from the clarity of your mindful reflection, through which you can discern options and make wise choices. The prefrontal cortex integrates all these different sources of input into skillful, coherent, resilient responses to whatever is happening, anything and everything. Here's one last exercise to strengthen the flexibility of that integration.

EXERCISE 7-9: Nesting Dolls

This exercise is based on an image of the Russian wooden nesting dolls my grandmother kept on the mantelpiece. One tiny doll is nested inside a slightly larger one, which is nested inside another doll. Here, we imagine a set of three dolls as a metaphor for the multiple, complex layers of the whole self "nesting" inside one another, with the prefrontal cortex navigating among them from the inside out.

Inner child. This is the layer of early patterns of being, behaving, and coping that are encoded in our neural circuitry as parts, facets, aspects, and states of ourselves. Some of these early parts we now admire and are proud of; some we may not like or may even loathe; some we may be too ashamed of to identify with; some, whether they were resilient or not, may have been lost or forgotten.

Adult. This is our grown-up personal manager, navigating the world as best it can with what it has learned about how the world works, how people work, and who the personal self is. This adult self chooses how to use the strengthened prefrontal cortex to rewire those patterns of the inner child; to the extent that it is stable yet flexible, it can harness the neuroplasticity of the brain to strengthen its resilience. It can also call on the resources of the wiser self to inform and guide its actions.

Wiser self. This is the imagined resource of our strongest, most loving, most compassionate, most generous, most resilient self, our own personal flavor of the innate goodness and well-being of universal true nature. It guides the choices of the adult self with wise, intuitive knowing.

(My own schema also includes the realm of higher consciousness that infuses all of these layers of self because it is embodied in all of existence. That works for me. In this exercise you'll focus on just three layers: inner child, adult, and wiser self.)

1. Identify moments when you have experienced each of these layers of self. You might recall the elation of your inner child when you hit a baseball out of the park or its pissy grief at having the measles and missing out on a class field trip to the beach. You might remember the pride of your adult self on completing a marathon or making a successful career move,

or its worry when the paycheck couldn't cover all of the bills. You may have experienced the patience of your wiser self navigating a decision about whether to have another child or to retire early. Even if you find yourself spending more time in one layer than the others, try to identify moments of experience in each layer to recover a felt sense of these different layers of experience and different capacities in different phases of your life.

2. Notice moments of shifting from one layer to another. (Your adult self noticed some reactivity by some part of your inner child, identified it as not so helpful, and chose another course of action, perhaps guided by the deeper wisdom of your wise self; or your wiser self noticed that your adult self had gone offline, that you were reacting only from survival responses, and brought that to the attention of your adult self.) Notice the fluidity of these shifts.

3. Bring to mind a specific issue of concern for you right now. Notice how you might perceive this issue differently from each of these layers. For example, maybe your adult self has noticed an abrupt downturn in your widowed father's health and is debating whether to move him to live with you and your family, move him to an assisted living facility or nursing home, or adopt a wait-and-see attitude while he remains in his own home.

    Besides your dad and other members of your family who have opinions on the matter, your layers of self will have opinions, too. Your inner child may remember playing chess with your dad growing up and feel excited about playing chess with him again if he moves in with you. But another inner child part remembers that years ago, your dad became so busy he couldn't even come to your high school graduation; it still harbors resentment about that and would rather bar the door. One adult part of you anticipates more decline in your father's health down the road and would like him to move to assisted living now, to avoid more upheaval later; another adult part feels loyal to the part of your dad that treasures his independence and wants to support that. Your wiser self weighs in, offering patience with the process, trust in the process, and compassionate acceptance of all of the parts and all of the inner messages.

    The practice of intentionally shifting from the perspective of one layer to the others helps you know which parts of you are responding in which ways. Knowing who is responding to the issue could *be* the issue.

4. Take a moment to reflect on your entire experience of this exercise, especially on the role that the major player in this exercise — your prefrontal cortex — plays in managing the shifting.

This practice of shifting and attending to the needs, worries, and concerns of all of the layers may not bring you to a resolution of the issue. There may be other people and external factors to consider. It is your prefrontal cortex that will integrate the perspectives of all of these facets of yourself into a final or evolving decision. Decision-making is one of the major functions of the prefrontal cortex, and by attending to all of these perspectives of many parts of yourself, you are strengthening the response flexibility and resilience that allow you to make the wisest possible choices.

Throughout this book I've emphasized using the individual tools of brain change *little and often* to give your brain a chance to succeed. The confidence you gain with these small successes reinforces the recovery and strengthening of your resilience.

You can apply the same principle when creating recipes for integration: they can consist of small practices woven together, repeated many times. Even when reviewing all the times your resilience has been derailed (and then recovered) in your lifetime, or facing the inevitability of the end of your life, you can still experience success by practicing little and often, giving your brain's neuroplasticity a chance to integrate its learning and strengthen its response flexibility to cope with anything, anything at all.

The complexity of this process of integration underlies learning something new — one of the seven lifestyle choices presented in the next chapter to help you care for the physical brain that does all of this magnificent rewiring and healing. You will experience success here, too, little and often.

CHAPTER EIGHT

Caring for and Nourishing Your Amazing Brain

Lifestyle Choices That Support Resilience

The human brain is the most dazzlingly complex entity in the entire known universe: eighty billion brain cells, with additional neural cells throughout the body. Each neuron connects across synaptic gaps to thousands of other neurons, resulting in trillions of connections responsible for all of the brain's internal communications and processing and all of our external behaviors and creations. Neuroscientists are beginning to map those connections, drawing the brain's neural "connectome," much as molecular biologists have mapped the human genome. There are as many neuronal connections in a single cubic centimeter of brain tissue as there are stars in the Milky Way galaxy. All this in what my friend Rick Hanson calls "3½ pounds of tofu in the coconut." Contemplating the brain boggles the mind.

Protecting and nurturing the functioning of your brain is important for your long-term health and well-being. You can make lifestyle choices that protect, exercise, and strengthen the physical brain, which in turn supports the complexity of all of your emotional, relational, and cognitive functioning, which supports your resilience.

This chapter differs from the preceding ones, presenting seven lifestyle choices you can make that support the health and functioning of your physical brain:

exercise and movement
sleep and rest
nutrition

learning something new
laughter and play
hanging out with healthy brains
digital vacations

All of the exercises are still organized by the processes of brain change you use to get the most benefit for your brain — new conditioning, reconditioning, deconditioning — at any level of challenge to your resilience. Begin "little and often," enjoy the process, and savor the way your brain's increased flexibility and vitality support your resilience.

Exercise and Movement

Research in the last ten years has made it abundantly clear — we need to move our bodies not just for the health of our heart, lungs, muscles, and joints, but also for the health of our brain. One of the best things you can do for your physical brain is to break a sweat with aerobic exercise.

Vigorous exercise makes your brain release brain-derived neurotropic factor (BDNF). This is the hormonal growth factor that causes your brain to grow new neurons, particularly in the hippocampus, the structure of the brain that consolidates learning from new experiences into long-term memory. BDNF also stimulates those new neurons to increase the length, density, and complexity of their dendrites (the extensions of the neurons that receive input from other neurons), creating "thicker," more complex networks in the brain. In addition, BDNF speeds the maturation of new neurons into fully functioning brain cells. This protects related structures, like the prefrontal cortex, from brain atrophy and cognitive decline. Exercise makes you smarter. It can help you think more clearly well into old age. Exercise can even help reverse memory decline as you age.

The adult brain weighs only about three pounds, but it uses 20 percent of all of the oxygen consumed by the body. Regular exercise also stimulates the heart to pump more blood to the brain, increasing the flow of oxygen and glucose in the brain that fuels *all* of the brain's activity. Furthermore, exercise causes the release of essential neurotransmitters like serotonin, dopamine, and norepinephrine that stimulate various types of brain activity; endorphins that make you feel better (the source of the "runner's high" or "athlete's flow" that some people experience); and acetylcholine, which increases alertness. Because of these effects, exercise has been shown to be as effective an antidepressant as Prozac in head-to-head clinical trials.

Exercise regenerates our telomeres, the protective protein sheaths at the ends of our chromosomes, likened to the plastic caps on the ends of our shoelaces that keep our shoelaces from unraveling. Because telomeres keep our chromosomes from unraveling as they replicate, protecting our telomeres prevents copying errors in our DNA and extends our span of healthy life. Exercise also extends our span of healthy life because it acts as an anti-inflammatory, reducing the underlying causes of many systemic diseases and delaying the onset of degenerative diseases.

The body needs to move for about thirty minutes for the brain to release feel-good endorphins. Three times a week is good enough. Five times a week is great. Little and often applies here, too: moderate exercise over several days is more effective (and safer) than a big workout once a week.

Activities like running, vigorous walking, bicycling, swimming, and using the stair climber at the gym are bilateral movements (moving the two sides of the body alternately, thus stimulating the two hemispheres of your brain alternately) and have an especially calming effect on your nervous system while nourishing your brain. Exercising with others — dancing, tennis, basketball, and volleyball — activates your social engagement system, creating a sense of safety in the brain and priming its neuroplasticity. Activities like these also engage the dopamine pathway of pleasure and reward in the lower brain that keeps you motivated. Mix it up to keep your exercise routine interesting. Recruit a buddy or join a good gym to expand your options and enhance your motivation.

If aerobic exercise is reaching beyond your body's physical capacities, see exercise 8-2 for gentler exercises that help you move your body and nourish your brain.

New Conditioning

It's a lot easier for your brain to create a new habit than to override or eliminate an old one. Using tools of new conditioning, you can create new, healthy habits, knowing that you are choosing to work out and protect your precious brain every day.

EXERCISE 8-1: Four-Minute Brain and Body Workout

When there's simply not enough time in the day to work out at the gym, or go for a swim, hike, or bike ride, try these simple four-minute exercise routines to stimulate growth and health in your brain. You can repeat them several times a day if you wish.

1. Walk up and down flights of stairs to your favorite upbeat song for four minutes.

2. Do a combination of desk push-ups and squats at work. Invite a friend or coworker to do this exercise with you.

3. While you are brushing your teeth, do a set of deep leg squats and side bends. Face the mirror and slowly lean your torso to the right and to the left, stretching out the ribs on the side opposite to the direction you are leaning.

4. Play a four-minute game of tag with your kids, or borrow a friend's kids to play tag with. Be a kid again yourself by spinning a hula hoop for four minutes. It's an amazing aerobic workout for your abdominal and core muscles.

5. Set a timer for four minutes, and clean up as much of your home or office as you can as fast as you can. Try cleaning the bathtub or do some speed vacuuming or mopping; that can really work up a sweat, and the chore will be over in four minutes!

Though you may not trigger a runner's high in four minutes of exercise, your brain is getting many of the other benefits of vigorous exercise, including protecting its long-term functioning.

EXERCISE 8-2: Life Is a Gym: Exercising through Daily Activities

There is a poster in my doctor's office at Kaiser Permanente showing a woman carrying two bags of groceries walking down a sidewalk with the caption "Life Is a Gym." Whatever your lifestyle, you need to move your body every sixty to ninety minutes to refresh your brain. Incorporating frequent movement into your daily routine is essential for maintaining brain health and it's easy to do.

1. If you work at a desk, get off the computer, get up, and walk down the hall or around the block. You can get hyperfocused or feel the stress of a deadline and forget, but taking regular breaks helps your brain refresh and reset itself; you avoid brain fog or brain fatigue.

2. Walk to work. Park a few blocks away from work and walk from there.

Walk up the stairs. Walk at lunch. When you move your body, you nourish your brain.

3. Do your chores mindfully: pay attention to your movements when you make the bed, do the dishes, fold the laundry, pick up the kids' toys, take out the garbage, weed the garden, mow the lawn, or wash the car. Notice the stretching, the bending, the flexing. Notice the changes in sensation, in balance, in energy. These tasks may not be aerobic, and they may not last thirty minutes, but they can all count. Study after study has shown that mindful movement brings extra benefit to the brain: the focused attention keeps the brain awake and engaged, giving it a workout, too.

4. A wonderful way to pay attention to movement is forest bathing (exercise 2-14). Walk through nature, noticing the feel of the air or sun on your body, hearing birdsong, smelling a flower or a pine needle, touching a stone or a leaf or the bark of a tree, seeing the changes in colors and shape, light and shadows. A walk of ten to sixty minutes is healing to the brain.

5. If your mobility is more limited, practice yoga, chi gong, or tai chi at home. This is mindful movement par excellence. The regular practices of gentle movements integrated with breath awareness benefit the brain more than exercise without awareness, or meditation practice without movement.

Keeping your body flexible and limber helps keep your brain flexible and agile, too, ready to meet the ever-changing challenges of life.

Reconditioning

Reconditioning uses a positive experience in one direction to rewire or reverse a negative experience from the opposite direction. Anat Baniel has developed neuromovement exercises based on the Feldenkrais Method, which uses very small movements in the body to reprogram the brain, helping it create new pathways from new experiences.

Our brains are organized through movement....As we introduce new patterns of movement, combined with attention, our brains begin making thousands, millions, and even billions of new connections. These changes quickly translate into thinking that is clearer, movement that is easier...and action that is more successful.

— ANAT BANIEL, *Move into Life: The Nine Essentials for Lifelong Vitality*

EXERCISE 8-3: Neuromovement

1. Sit on the edge of a chair with both feet flat on the floor, a comfortable distance apart — approximately hip width. Rest your hands, palms down, on the tops of your thighs. Call this your neutral position. Turn your head to look to the right. Do so easily, always within your comfort range, without forcing anything. Notice how far you can turn your head comfortably. You might want to note a visual reference point you can use to measure changes as you go along. Now turn your head to the left and find a similar reference point.

2. Still sitting on the edge of the chair, place your right hand a few inches behind you on the seat of the chair and lean back on it so it's bearing some of your weight. Turn your head to the right and then turn your head back to look straight ahead of you. Making sure you stay within your comfortable range of motion, notice how far to the right you can see. Repeat this movement two or three times. Then come back to the middle, placing both your hands back on your thighs, and rest for a moment.

3. Again, sit on the edge of your chair and place your right hand behind you and lean on it as before. Now lift your left arm, bend your elbow, and rest your chin on the back of your hand. Gently turn your head and your arm together, as one unit, to the right, and then come back to center. As you turn, make sure that your chin is in contact with the back of your left hand all the time. Do this movement three or four times. Stop, come back to your neutral position, and rest for a moment. Notice if there are any changes in the way you are sitting or feeling.

4. Using the same position as above, with your chin on the back of your left hand, turn to the right as far as is comfortable for you and hold that position. Now gently move only your eyes to the right and to the left. Repeat the movement three or four times, then stop and rest in your neutral position.

5. In the same position as step 4, turn as far as you comfortably can to the right and stay there. Now lift your left buttock off the chair an inch or so and put it back down three or four times. Feel how your ribs move on your left side, coming closer together and then moving farther apart as you

lift and lower your left buttock. Stop, come back to neutral, and notice whether you are sitting differently on your right buttock than on the left.

6. Once again, lean on your right hand behind you and turn your head to the right. Notice whether your neck moves more easily and whether you can see farther behind you than before.

7. Now return to your neutral position, with both hands, palms down, on the tops of your thighs. Gently turn your head to the right, then to the left, and notice whether you turn your head more easily to the right than to the left. You have just experienced the power of movement with attention to stimulate the brain to reorganize its circuitry and learn new patterns.

8. Wait thirty to sixty minutes so that the improvement of the neuromovement on the right side of the body really installs in the brain. Then repeat the entire exercise for the left side of the body.

While we think of the motor cortex of the brain as directing the movements of the body from the top down, you can also use these micro movements to communicate new information to the brain, to "reverse engineer" new circuitry in the brain, creating pathways that make any movement easier and easier for the brain to direct.

Deconditioning

When your body moves playfully, your brain gets to play, too. You refresh your brain, allowing you to see yourself and events in your life from a new perspective.

EXERCISE 8-4: Dancing Your Brain to Health

To dance is to be out of yourself. Larger, more beautiful, more powerful.
— Agnes de Mille

Dance of any kind is good for the brain. Free-form dance is spontaneous movement that allows the brain to play. Whether you're dancing to music, dancing with others, or dancing on your own to music in your head, the joy and delight evoked is as good as a coffee break to reset the brain.

1. You can dance anywhere — in your living room, in a ballroom, in a parking lot, on a playground, even lying on your couch. You can begin to dance spontaneously as the mood in your body moves you. Expressing grief or angst through movement is a powerful way to shift the bodily felt sense of those emotions.

2. Over time, you can build a playlist of music that helps you express or process various moods (light, heavy, open, closed) and various states (agitated, flowing, peaceful). Give yourself permission to dance through difficulties, even disasters. Playful movement is not a luxury; it's an essential cultivator of response flexibility and a key component of our resilience.

Music and dance are older than spoken language. For millennia, human beings have expressed and communicated their innermost truths and met their most challenging struggles through music and dance. Tap into your body's energy: dancing creates some breathing space in your brain to reset and restore.

Sleep and Rest

Enough sleep, and deep sleep, is essential to brain and body health. Many of us routinely don't get enough sleep; our lives are too busy, too stressed. Young people especially don't get enough sleep. Teenagers may get five to six hours of sleep a night at a stage of development when their brains need eight or nine hours to finish growing. Lack of sleep affects your metabolism, immune system, and genetic health — and especially brain health. If you get only five to six hours of sleep every night for a week, you likely have the same level of cognitive impairment as if you were legally drunk.

While you are sleeping, doing "nothing," the brain is doing vital tasks:

1. Consolidating learning and memories from the day and storing that learning in long-term memory. Sleep optimizes cognitive functioning, restoring your ability to process information and retrieve information quickly when you are awake.

2. Restoring the equilibrium of the nervous system. Sleep absorbs the stress hormone cortisol. REM sleep is the only time the brain is clear of norepinephrine (adrenalin), processing memories of the day but without emotional charge. There's less anxiety in the morning.

3. Regular housekeeping, cleaning out dead and atrophied neurons.

4. Allowing the prefrontal cortex to rest from its executive functioning and from controlling your impulses, making it better able to function again the next day. You have probably noticed that your judgment and impulse control are impaired when you are tired.

New Conditioning

EXERCISE 8-5: How to Get Enough Good Sleep

The stress hormone cortisol binds to BDNF in the hippocampus, killing newly forming brain cells. When you're stressed, you have less brain power available to manage emotions and cope with challenges. Loss of brain cells leads to depression; lack of sleep can double recovery time from depression.

Many of the exercises in chapter 2 are designed to help you manage the stress that can derail your resilience anytime in your life. You can further enhance your resilience by destressing at night. In *Why Zebras Don't Get Ulcers*, Robert Sapolsky points out that the brain is not like the engine of a car that you turn on and off with a switch: it's more like a jet plane that needs a long runway to take off and to slow down on landing. Similarly, the brain needs time to land in a good night's sleep. Here are some ways to improve sleep.

1. Stop daily activities one hour before bedtime. Destressing may mean not watching the evening news; watch a movie instead. Turn off the computer and your phone — the content is too stimulating, and the blue light of an LCD screen (like daylight) inhibits the release of melatonin, the hormone that tells your brain it's time to sleep.

2. Develop a bedtime routine. Putter around, talk with family members, read a book, do your bathroom routine. Let the brain settle down and relax and begin to rest.

3. Before going to sleep, try practices that will counter negativity bias or anxiety in your brain. You can do progressive muscle relaxation (exercise 2-11). You can do a gratitude practice for the blessings of the day (exercise 3-8). You can take in the good (exercise 3-10) or the sweet resonance of a moment of meeting (exercise 5-2). You can place your hand on your heart and remember a moment of feeling safe, loved, and cherished (exercise

2-6). Use these practices to intentionally let go of any worries from the day. Whatever problem you need to resolve will still be there in the morning. (Though sometimes the default mode network will resolve an issue for you while you're asleep.) You can take a fresh look at the problem tomorrow, when you're rested.

4. Cuddle with a partner or a pet if possible. Warm, safe touch releases oxytocin, the brain's direct and immediate antidote to the stress hormone cortisol. (It really helps when the relationship feels safe at the moment, not strained or anxious.)

5. Go to bed at the same time every night and get up at the same time every morning, even on weekends. This trains the brain to know when it's time to go to sleep and when it's time to get up. Plan for enough time to get seven to eight hours of sleep.

6. Sleep in a cool, dark, quiet room. Reduce noise: install double-paned windows, decorate with heavy curtains and rugs, use earplugs. Use your bed only for sleeping and making love.

7. Monitor your intake of coffee (a stimulant) and alcohol (a depressant), trying to avoid both after 6 PM. If you habitually use over-the-counter or prescription sleep medications, experiment with not taking them. Instead, try taking a melatonin supplement to trigger the sleep response or gamma-aminobutyric acid (GABA) to calm down the stress response. Both are available at health food stores.

8. Above all, don't worry too much if you have an occasional bad night; don't worry if you think you haven't slept well. In *The Secret Life of Sleep*, Kat Duff tells the story of a sleep science researcher who woke up one morning ready to complain to his wife about how poorly he had slept, but then he noticed that his chest was covered with chunks of plaster. There had been an earthquake in the middle of the night, causing part of the ceiling to fall in, and he had slept through it.

Cultivating new behavioral habits creates the neural circuitry in the brain to support them. Notice how a good night's sleep becomes easier over time.

Reconditioning

Sleep researchers have long known about the brain's two main forms of normal sleep. REM (rapid eye movement) sleep is a slight activation of the sympathetic nervous system. We dream during REM sleep (nightmares result from too much activation). Slow-wave sleep is a deeper, nondream sleep, an activation of the parasympathetic nervous system. Through imaging technologies used in sleep study labs, scientists have discovered that the brain has a third form of sleep. If your brain gets overtired during the day, it will shut itself down for a fraction of a second — a break so short you don't notice it — and then turns itself back on so that you keep functioning.

EXERCISE 8-6: Give Your Brain a Mini-Break

You can give your brain deliberate little breaks as you go through your day.

1. Any time you need to, take a ten-breath mini-break. Inhale fully and deeply to activate the sympathetic nervous system and wake up your brain. Exhale fully to relax your brain, pushing every last bit of breath out of your lungs to make room for fresh oxygen.

2. Stop what you're doing and do something else with your brain for five minutes. Just switch the channel. Think about something else: plan a dinner, or daydream. Get up and do something else: wash the dishes, take a bathroom break, do a quick crossword puzzle. Talk to someone else during a coffee break. Play with your pet if you're at home. Go for a walk, in nature if possible. (Researchers at the University of Michigan found that walking for ten minutes in a park led to better cognitive functioning than walking for ten minutes downtown or in a shopping mall.)

3. Take a twenty-minute nap sometime between 2 PM and 4 PM. This is long enough to revitalize your brain, and it's timed so that it doesn't interfere with a good night's sleep.

Even a mini-break can reset your brain, making you feel fresher and sharper when you return to your task.

Deconditioning

As much as your dreams are interesting to your psyche, and probably do help process unresolved experiences from the day or from the past, slow-wave sleep is what is restorative to the brain, bringing the deep peace of equanimity.

EXERCISE 8-7: Deep, Deeper, Deepest Sleep

1. To maximize your chances of experiencing deep, slow-wave sleep, use the new-conditioning tools of exercise 8-5 to destress your brain as you are falling asleep. At first, keep your focus on falling asleep, not anything else, then gradually let go of any focus at all, trusting the process of letting go.
2. If you wake up in the middle of the night, intentionally let go of any worry or anxiety about that. To help yourself do this, focus on the positive through a gratitude practice, savoring, or placing your hand on your heart. Trust that you will get all the sleep you need to function the next day.
3. Savor the refreshment when you wake up from deep sleep in the morning. Let that savoring reinforce the benefit of these practices.

As you begin to trust your skills in creating the conditions for a good night's sleep, you'll have less and less anxiety about not sleeping (insomnia). You will have actually rewired your brain to get the good sleep it needs.

Nutrition

You truly are what you eat. Everything that nourishes the body and the brain comes from the food you eat and drink. The bottom line about a diet good for the brain comes from Michael Pollan, author of *In Defense of Food*: "Eat food. Not too much. Mostly plants."

New Conditioning

Researchers have identified foods that promote good brain health. The MIND diet (standing for Mediterranean Intervention for Neurodegenerative Delay) is a good example, recommended to help prevent, reduce, and reverse cognitive impairment from aging and dementia. It includes lots of vegetables, dark leafy greens, nuts, berries, beans, whole grains, fish, poultry, and olive oil. The omega-3 fatty acids found in fish and some nuts and seeds are particularly important nutrients for the brain.

EXERCISE 8-8: Choosing Healthy Foods for a Healthy Brain

1. If you're already eating healthy foods in healthy amounts, consciously acknowledge that to yourself. Reinforce your good habits.

2. If you know your eating habits or patterns of thinking about eating aren't so great, don't panic, and don't try to radically change your diet overnight. Your body won't like that, and your brain may even resist the changes. Introduce new healthy foods to your taste buds and your digestive system little and often, repeated many times. Start with what appeals to you the most — more salads, more nuts, more fresh wild-caught fish. Let the new foods become your new automatic choices.

3. Reinforce good eating habits by combining these practices with other lifestyle choices recommended in this chapter:

    *   Enjoy the good company of other healthy eaters. Be creative and playful in trying new recipes. Try hosting a potluck dinner sharing your dishes, enjoying good conversation as well as good food.
    *   Eat a healthy snack as part of giving your brain a mini-break during the day or to reenergize your body and brain after a vigorous walk in nature or a workout.
    *   Practice gratitude for the abundance of healthy food you get to eat, and perhaps even a little awe at the biological processes that allow food to become the energy that nourishes everything you think and do.

    As you become more conscious of what you eat, you can make better choices about what you eat. Seeing ourselves as having choices and choosing wisely is part of strengthening resilience.

Reconditioning

Here, reconditioning is not about losing weight, though many people could benefit by becoming aware of the costs to their physical energy and mental sharpness of eating too much sugar and too much processed (junk) food. Instead, it's about reconditioning our taste buds, learning to prefer the brain-healthy foods that bring energy to the body and sharpness to the mind.

EXERCISE 8-9: Choosing More Juice, Less Junk

1. Begin eating more healthy foods such as those recommended in the MIND diet.

2. Give up an item on the not-so-healthy list for a week — donuts, processed lunch meat, soda pop. Couple that renunciation with the awareness that giving up this item is beneficial to your physical health and mental functioning.

3. As an experiment, reinstate the item after one week or longer. Notice whether your taste buds, digestive system, or energy levels register any change. Try giving up the same item for another week or two, or longer, gradually getting out of the habit of eating this item, especially if you have been in the habit of eating it somewhat mindlessly.

4. Gradually try giving up additional less-healthy items as you continue to add healthy foods to your regular diet. Little and often could make quite a difference in your brain and in your functioning.

By cultivating practices that promote the health and functioning of your physical brain, you're also creating habits of wise choice and self-discipline. Seeing yourself as someone who can do that strengthens your response flexibility and resilience.

Deconditioning

As with exercise, your body-brain gets more benefit from eating food when you bring mindful awareness to eating by slowing down, paying attention, and savoring every mouthful. You get to enjoy nourishing your body and brain.

EXERCISE 8-10: Savor a Raisin Meditation

This exercise is taught in meditation centers worldwide to help practitioners come into a sense of presence and mindful awareness. You can apply the exercise to mindful eating of *anything*. Here we start small, with one raisin.

1. Hold one raisin in the palm of your hand. (You can also practice with one grape, one peanut, or one cherry tomato if you don't like raisins.)

2. Focus your attention on the raisin. Bring your curiosity to this exercise. Notice the raisin's size, shape, and color; feel the weight of it in your hand. Roll it around in your hand with your finger. Notice your own reactions to the raisin. Are you experiencing any desire or anticipation of eating it? Any disgust?

3. Put the raisin in your mouth, but don't bite it yet. Roll the raisin around in your mouth with your tongue. Notice its presence in your mouth; notice any hint of flavor.

4. Now bite into the raisin; notice the burst of flavor. Chew the raisin slowly, noticing the ability of your teeth to chew.

5. When you're ready, swallow the raisin. Notice its absence in your mouth. Notice your own reactions to its absence. Do you feel desire for another raisin? Relief that the exercise is over?

6. Notice your noticing — any shift in your relationship to your food that comes from focusing your attention on it.

Eating more mindfully helps you enjoy your food. It also nourishes the brain with the awareness of the nourishing. To bring even more mindful awareness to eating, another helpful practice is to eat one meal a day without doing anything else, simply savoring the food that is nourishing your body and brain. Try that awareness practice for one meal a week, at least, and notice whether you enjoy your meals more.

Learning Something New

The brain learns and rewires itself from experience all the time. The more complex the experience or the learning, the more integrated the functioning of the brain, because more of our senses and regions of our brain are engaged in taking in the new information and processing it. That work of integration and complexity, which harnesses the brain's neuroplasticity, is a protection against brain atrophy — losing brain cells as we age. It's called *building cognitive reserve*. You did that when you were younger by going to college or mastering a craft. By keeping your brain active, you have more brain cells in the bank, so to speak, to buffer the loss of brain cells that comes naturally with aging.

New Conditioning

To create a surplus of gray matter, try:

learning to play a musical instrument
learning to speak a foreign language
learning to play a complex game like chess or go
learning your way around a new city
learning your way around a new relationship
learning your way around a new service activity in the community

All of these examples involve procedural learning: the brain is learning how to do something and processing that experience, not just memorizing new facts. The more complicated the learning, the better. The first two examples, learning to play a musical instrument and learning to speak a foreign language, can reduce the risk of Alzheimer's by 50 percent (because you build a reserve of healthy brain cells). According to the neuroscientist Tracey Shors of Rutgers University, "A colossal number of brain cells, hundreds to thousands, are born each day, but most die within weeks unless the brain is forced to learn something new. Learning rescues these new cells from death. Then more neurons revive and sprout connections to their brethren. The harder the task, the more survivors."

EXERCISE 8-11: Give Your Brain a Workout

1. Choose one option from the list above, or identify your own new focus of procedural learning — knitting, woodworking, making pottery — as long as your choice is something challenging for you and complex for your brain, and something you will enjoy learning over an extended period.
2. Begin little, repeat often, and extend your practice for a significant length of time. If you devote ten hours a week for one full year to mastering the game of chess, you can achieve a fully satisfying level of competence at the game, and you will greatly build your cognitive reserve. (You may have already devoted this much time to mastering a skill or craft.)
3. Pursue your learning with a partner or small group of people if you wish.

The social engagement can be powerfully motivating, encouraging, and rewarding.

You already know that if you don't move your body, your muscles can weaken and atrophy. The same "use it or lose it" principle applies to the brain. You create new neural circuitry by learning something new. You lose that circuitry if you don't repeat the firing of those neurons. These practices, which my friend Ron Siegel calls "dementia prophylaxis," not only preserve neurons needed for new learning but also build a cognitive reserve so that extra neurons are available for other cognitive tasks: paying bills, doing your taxes, choosing new colors to repaint the house.

Reconditioning

It is not hard to learn more. What is hard is to unlearn when you discover yourself wrong.

— MARTIN FISHER

Throughout this book, we have used reconditioning to rewire negative emotional experiences, memories, thoughts, and beliefs by juxtaposing them with stronger, more positive experiences. That process catalyzes the deconsolidation of the old neural networks and reconsolidates them into new neural networks more supportive of your resilience. It's also often important to leave the previous neural network deconsolidated, dissolved, faded — to let your brain "unlearn" that pathway. When you're sleep-deprived, tired, or stressed, the brain can still default to those old pathways if they are still accessible.

You can help your brain unlearn or lose its previous learning by intentionally not going there when an old negative memory first comes into consciousness again. You don't try to deny it: you simply choose not to reinforce it. You can counter the memory with something positive, as you learned to do in exercise 6-11, or simply be aware of it, acknowledge it, and let it go, as you learned to do in exercise 6-16.

When we don't feed unskillful patterns of response by reusing and reinforcing the neural pathways that sustain them, they can fade away and be unlearned. In the following exercise, you're making a conscious choice to lose a pattern you no longer wish to use.

EXERCISE 8-12: Unlearning

1. Identify a mental habit you would like to unlearn simply by letting it fade away, by not going there. As always, choose something little and not very triggering to begin with, something just present enough to allow you to notice it and work with it successfully. Maybe you want to let go of associating a rainstorm today with a bad storm you were caught in ten years ago, let go of a grudge triggered by your neighbor's car blocking your driveway a year ago, or let go of assuming someone doesn't like you if they don't respond to your email for three days.

2. Identify a positive thought or antidote to juxtapose with this habit. It can be a generic thought like "I'm learning to do it differently now" or "Yup — there's that sensation/feeling/thought again. Don't need to do that anymore."

3. Practice pairing the new positive with the old negative, gradually focusing more on the positive and letting the negative fade.

4. Notice the fading. This can be a little bit like watching yourself fall asleep, but the focus on the fading keeps you from focusing on the content of the thought. Someday you may even notice that the old habit of thought is completely gone.

You're doing your own mental housekeeping here. Less time spent on old unneeded mental activity creates more bandwidth for the new.

Deconditioning

The psychologist Mihaly Csikszentmihalyi suggests that *flow* is the sweet spot of mental activity between too much anxiety or stress and too much boredom. Flow happens in the default network mode of brain processing, the source of the brain's creativity. And creativity is a special form of procedural learning, exploring what's not yet known, not yet manifested. Any creative endeavor — stream-of-consciousness journaling, process painting, mixing ingredients together without a recipe, making up a new game with your children — pushes the functioning of the brain into new territory and puts the brain in a state of flow. That puts new brain cells to good use. Curiosity can be an important part of creativity — following one idea, one turn in the road after another, with open-minded interest and without preconceptions or judgment.

Curiosity is a great spur to creativity. Children tend to approach their world with uninhibited curiosity and wonder at the most ordinary rainstorm or bug.

When I look at a patch of dandelions, I see a bunch of weeds that are going to take over my yard. My kids see flowers for Mom and blowing white fluff you can wish on.

When I feel wind on my face, I brace myself against it. I feel it messing up my hair and pulling me back when I walk. My kids close their eyes, spread their arms and fly with it until they fall to the ground laughing.

When I see a mud puddle I step around it. I see muddy shoes and dirty carpets. My kids sit in it. They see dams to build, rivers to cross, and worms to play with.

— ANONYMOUS

EXERCISE 8-13: Exercise Your Curiosity

1. You can cultivate curiosity about *anything* — the ant crawling across the page as you read this book; the sudden dimming of the lights in a power blip; why you tripped on a crack in the sidewalk (or flubbed a presentation in a meeting) but didn't fall or fail. Pursuing any new source of wonder will benefit your brain.

2. Focus your curiosity on your brain itself. When are you most alert during the day? When an automatic negative belief came to consciousness or a startle response arose in your nervous system, how did you respond this time? Was that different from other times today, last month, or last year?

3. Commit to practicing any tool in this book for thirty days, with the intention of noticing any difference in the functioning of your brain at the end of that period.

Both curiosity and creativity have been shown to extend a person's longevity by up to four years. They can certainly amplify the enjoyment of the miraculousness of our brain minute by minute.

Laughter and Play

A person without a sense of humor is like a wagon without springs — jolted by every pebble in the road.

— HENRY WARD BEECHER

Many people think of laughter as an emotion, or something akin to one. Not so. Laughter is a physiological mechanism that reduces stress in the body and the brain. Laughter releases catecholamines, dopamine, and norepinephrine — neurotransmitters that make the brain feel sharper and brighter. Laughter is often a good way of breaking the ice and bonding with people, and bonding with people is super good for the brain.

Play — encountering or creating new situations, dropping into the default mode network in the brain, making up new rules, new characters, or new worlds — gives the brain a good workout. Play often also engenders laughter, a sense of connection with other people or things in our world, and a sense of relaxation and ease. All of those are good for the brain, too.

> *Those who play rarely become brittle in the face of stress or lose the healing capacity for humor.*
>
> — STUART BROWN, *Play: How It Shapes the Brain,*
> *Opens the Imagination, and Invigorates the Soul*

We can be so busy and pressured that we forget to laugh and play, and then we forget how to. If you experienced a lot of trauma in your early life, you may never have learned how to safely laugh and play. This capacity is fully recoverable with practice.

New Conditioning

EXERCISE 8-14: Relearning How to Play

1. There are many "little and often" ways to recover laughter and play:

    *   Watch little kids, puppies, or kittens play.
    *   Play with kids or pets yourself; borrow your relatives or neighbors' kids and pets to play with to give yourself more options.
    *   Watch some of the endearing videos on YouTube of babies singing or animals taking care of each other across species: dog and horse, cat and ducklings, tortoise and hippopotamus.
    *   Play with your food — be curious! Notice when you are surprised by something and a little "Ha ha!" comes out.

2. Schedule a play date with yourself, with a partner or friend, or with your children. Spend two hours deliberately being goofy or watching a goofy movie.

3. Join a laughing yoga class — thirty minutes of facilitated movement and laughter. The positive effects of resetting your nervous system have been known to last for up to five hours.

You have permission to have fun while you're retraining your brain to be more flexible. Joy and laughter create an upward spiral supportive of resilience.

Reconditioning

This book has suggested many ways to juxtapose positive and negative experiences to shift out of or rewire negative thought patterns or emotions. It may seem counterintuitive to experience moments of laughter or play even in times of deep grief or intense fear. But giving yourself permission to notice and savor glimmers of humor and joy even in the midst of truly difficult times can provide a healing respite. And it's common to experience a moment of ironic humor, or even a fit of the giggles, in the midst of troubling times.

EXERCISE 8-15: Savoring Joy, Even in Grief

When you're going through something difficult, try these suggestions for giving yourself a break and experiencing some joy.

1. Watch a lighthearted comedy or romance with an empathic friend who can help you hold both the lightness of the movie and the darkness of whatever you're facing simultaneously.

2. Play games that have brought you delight and laughter in the past: wiffle ball or your children's favorite card game. Both the memories and the interaction with other people now can bring a little lift to your spirit.

3. Play with a puppy, a kitten, or a toddler, as in exercise 8-14. Their joy in their own play is emotionally contagious: you may laugh out loud in spite of the heaviness you're carrying. And these young beings, so full of life and energy, remind you that life continues, life changes; your life can, too.

Trying to play or find joy in hard times can seem like work, but it *is* the work of resilience to be flexible, to shift gears, to see things from a different perspective. Play helps strengthen your response flexibility, sometimes even when that's the farthest thing from your mind.

Deconditioning

Creating fantasy worlds and imaginary roles for ourselves is not used as a way to avoid dealing with the real world and its challenges. But using the mental play space of deconditioning to envision new roles and new futures can be a form of unpressured rehearsal of responses that creates new circuitry and response flexibility in your brain that you can use later.

EXERCISE 8-16: Future Fantasies

1. Imagine at least three different future versions of yourself, five, ten, or fifteen years from now. To begin with, these future selves can be anchored in reality, natural extensions of who you are and what you are interested in now.

2. Begin to imagine two more future selves with a little more playfulness or whimsy in them — futures that would be quite a stretch for your present self.

3. Imagine two more futures for yourself that could never happen, like winning an Olympic gold medal in downhill skiing or discovering a cure for breast cancer (unless that vision belongs in the lives you've imagined in step 1 or 2). The point is to let your imagination run wild and lift your mood, shifting the functioning of your brain as it does so.

Giving your brain permission to play gives your unconscious brain permission to surprise you with new possibilities, new insights, new "aha!" moments. You're accessing the intuition that might reveal the germ of a new direction in life and serve as a tool in discerning wise choices.

Hanging Out with Healthy Brains

You've been learning to hang out with healthy brains throughout this book — through social engagement in chapter 2, mindful empathy in chapter 3, finding a true other to your true self in chapter 4, creating healthy relationship dynamics with other people in chapter 5, and exploring the skillful, playful spaciousness in your own brain in chapter 6, which allows you to see others spaciously as well.

Here we focus on the power of social interactions with people, casual as well as intimate, to foster brain health and psychological health.

> *This is what our brains were wired for: reaching out to and interacting with others. These are design features, not flaws. From an evolutionary perspective, perhaps the smartest among us are actually those with the best social skills. These social adaptations are central to making us the most successful species on earth. And . . . increasing the social connections in our lives is probably the single easiest way to enhance our well-being.*
> — MATTHEW LIEBERMAN, *Social: Why Our Brains Are Wired to Connect*

New Conditioning

You may already participate in social groups — book clubs, choirs, bowling leagues, volunteer organizations, or political campaigns. What may be new to you is discerning who among the like-minded people in these groups has also developed their skills of relational intelligence and can engage in resonant conversations with you from their own secure interdependence. This isn't true of everyone you encounter all the time, of course, but such people are well worth seeking out.

EXERCISE 8-17: Breaking the Ice

If you find it difficult to strike up conversations with people you don't know well, try these approaches.

1. I learned this practice from a client who told me he uses it when attending an out-of-town conference. Simply say to someone, "Hi, I don't know anyone here. Would you be willing to talk to me?" (Use your mindful empathy, of course, to discern the other person's receptivity to your approach; you want to create safety in this moment of meeting.) This easy experiment

often has surprisingly successful results. It's useful on occasions where there are likely to be like-minded people — standing in line at a film festival or book signing, getting your annual flu shot, eating in a family-style restaurant while traveling, or volunteering at a soup kitchen.

2. As a variation, still among like-minded people, try "I'm not sure where to find [a person or place] or where to return [an object]. . . . Could you help me?" Most people want to feel helpful, useful, and needed and to experience a moment of shared humanity.

Nourishing social connections helps keep our spirits — and our brains — healthy as we get older. Even when, as Ron Siegel says, "it takes a village to complete the end of the sentence," we thrive when we belong to supportive social communities.

Reconditioning

To exist is to change; to change is to mature; to mature is to go on creating one's self endlessly.

— HENRI BERGSON

We continue to evolve as we mature and move through life in new ways. Sometimes we coevolve with others, and marriages, friendships, business partnerships, social groups stay intact and flourish. Sometimes shared interests and life paths diverge, and we find ourselves drifting out of touch with people who were once close and significant to us. Sometimes in our own maturing and healing we are no longer as tolerant as we once were of hanging out with unhealthy brains.

EXERCISE 8-18: Taking Stock of Healthy Social Connections

There's a poignancy to doing a periodic inventory of where you want to allocate your time, energy, and relational skills to people in your life. You use your own mindful empathy and self-compassion to consciously choose to nourish, prune, or set new boundaries in relationships.

1. Make a list of all of your current relationships, no matter how close or distant, chosen or obligatory, in person or on social media. This organizational process could be an exercise in itself. You may naturally organize these names into categories:

    -   family and friends
    -   neighbors and acquaintances
    -   colleagues and coworkers
    -   business and service providers

2. Recategorize all of these people by:

    -   the joy and delight that you experience from interactions with them, however frequent, however brief, however rare
    -   the meaning that you derive from the interactions or from giving or receiving care
    -   the loyalty involved in the relationship: its history, ties of obligation, and memories
    -   the benefits of the relationship to you and to the other person

3. Draw a mind map on a large piece of paper; you can use different colored pens or pencils if you wish. Draw a bubble representing yourself in the center and then let your brain freely draw bubbles representing the other people in this inventory. You're not judging them or the relationships, just playing. Use different sizes, shapes, and colors of bubbles for different people. Take ten to fifteen minutes to do this exercise, giving your default mode network time to play.

4. When you finish, step back and reflect. Notice the size of bubbles for various people, their proximity or distance from your bubble, and whether the bubbles are bright or muted colors. Let this map of current connections soak into your unconscious.

5. Let the insights from this map guide you in consciously choosing which relationships you want to nourish, set limits around, or let gently fade into memory.

Just as the brain regularly clears out atrophied neurons to make room for new healthy neurons, just as we clean out our closets or the garage to make room for new things, just as we temporarily clear our calendars to travel and experience something beyond our daily routine, so, too, it is useful to consciously prune the relationships we have accumulated over time, letting go of those that no longer nourish us or support our resilience. Just as gardeners prune trees, shrubs, and flowers to make room for a new season's growth, we honor what has been, choose what to continue, and make room for the new.

Deconditioning

The brain's neuroception of safety primes its neuroplasticity for learning. Hanging out with healthy brains (at least like-minded folks) in silence can be a wonderful resource for both resting and nourishing the brain.

EXERCISE 8-19: Communities of Silence

1. Join a meditation group, yoga class, tai chi, or chi gong class where you can practice nourishing your brain in the safety of a mostly silent community.

2. Enjoy the social atmosphere of sitting in a theater, concert hall, or movie theater, knowing that the performance has attracted like-minded people. Even without conversation, there's a resonance that is nourishing to the brain.

3. Spend time in nature, especially in quiet, open spaces. When you spend that time with a friend or two, designate some of that time to be silent together, sharing a deepening awe and appreciation for the beauty and mystery you are experiencing together.

It's essential to know how to "use your words" to relate to other people skillfully and efficiently. It is also essential to cultivate and trust the brain's social engagement system, which reassures you nonverbally that you are safe when you are with safe others. Spending silent time with others restores that capacity, which is essential to your resilience.

Digital Vacations

I can pull the fire alarm here.

On average, American adults now spend 40 percent of their waking time on their digital devices, checking their cell phones every 6.5 minutes. On average, American teenagers spend 50 percent of their waking time on devices, and 25 percent of teenagers are using a device within five minutes of waking up. Spending that much time on digital devices, though widely accepted as normal, has serious consequences for brain function and person-to-person relating. Our brains are not computers, and interacting with people through computers and phones is not a substitute for face-to-face interactions.

Researchers are documenting our rapidly escalating overuse of digital devices and identifying the increasingly serious effects on our brains, our relationships, and our resilience — especially the effects on young, still-developing brains.

In a world where your brain is constantly bombarded with emails, texts, tweets, and posts, one of the best things you can do for it is to let it rest. Take a break from long periods of energy-consuming focused attention and the overstimulation of incessant incoming messages that can negatively affect several essential capacities of your brain.

Attention, the Foundation of Reflective Intelligence

No matter how fond or proud you are of your capacities for multitasking, over time juggling many tasks at once is costly to the brain's functioning and efficiency. The truth is, the brain does only one thing at a time. It can shift focus from one thing to another very quickly, but it is not evolutionarily adapted for rapid and sustained shifting of attention. Every shift takes metabolic energy. As you switch from a job-related task to sending a tweet to answering a question from your child to responding to a friend's email, over time your focused attention gets scattered and fragmented. After sixty to ninety minutes in multitasking mode, your brain's performance suffers, and you make more mistakes. As your brain goes into fatigue or brain fog, the CEO of resilience, the prefrontal cortex, can't function as clearly or creatively anymore; it begins to have trouble focusing for three to four minutes on a project, let alone three to four hours.

Reputable scientists are taking this decrease in functioning very seriously. Some suggest that the reduction in the capacity to concentrate may be permanent. At a minimum, the brain that is constantly bombarded by stimulation goes into another kind of overload: it loses the capacity to distinguish the relevant from the irrelevant. You start out looking something up on the internet that you need for work, and forty-five minutes later you're lost in something else — interesting, but not relevant to the task at hand.

Resonant Relationships, Preserving Our Relational Intelligence with Others

We all have our preferences for how we want to connect and communicate with others, but the situation of having a thousand friends on Facebook but no real-life close friends is becoming true for more and more people. This is a particularly disturbing trend among young people, who feel more lonely and isolated than ever before and often feel bad about themselves when they compare themselves to other people's posts on Facebook, carefully crafted and polished for public consumption. Young people don't see the doubts and angst of other people like them; it all looks like MTV.

Sherry Turkle, a professor of psychology at MIT and an early observer of the impact of digital technology on relationships, reports that the style of people relating to each other now is much more superficial, what she calls "pancake" style, rather than the "cathedral" style of perhaps fewer but deeper conversations with people. She calls this "the illusion of companionship without the demands of friendship."

Research does show that teenagers can use social media to maintain a social network when they already have friends. But young people trying to build a social network from scratch through social media generally fare worse. Resonant relationships are essential for harnessing the brain's neuroplasticity. Without them, resilience erodes; young people feel lonely, isolated, and depressed, and they become vulnerable to shame and cyberbullying.

Mindful Empathy, the Foundation of Emotional Intelligence

Spending less time in resonant person-to-person relating can lead to a reduced capacity for empathy. Turkle and other researchers have observed that people have reduced tolerance for messy emotions and less interest in and compassion for other people's feelings. People are choosing the protection of distance over closeness and vulnerability. When we spend too much time on devices, we lose the capacity to get in touch with our feelings, to tolerate and accept and learn how to manage difficult feelings, to learn to use our brains and pick up the emotional signals of others accurately, or to assess safety and comfort or danger and toxicity in relationships. Young people may not even know what these capacities are or that they lack them.

Self-Awareness, the Foundation of Relational Intelligence within Oneself

Unfortunately, the ability even to be aware of what capacities might be diminishing is also diminishing. People are becoming less comfortable with solitude, less tolerant of boredom, less able to simply reflect, introspect, or daydream, more superficial in relationships with themselves as well as with others. With so much stimulation, there's hardly any time left for the brain to consolidate all the learning of the day into long-term memory.

The brain releases dopamine, the neurotransmitter of anticipation, pleasure, and reward, whenever it hears the ping of an incoming email, phone call, or text. There's a rush of pleasure along the mesolimbic dopamine pathway in the lower brain, the neural pathway underlying any and all addictions: "I'm connected! I'm wanted! I'm loved!" That's not just psychological; that's neurological. As people spend more time communicating through emojis and less time connecting with people's emotions in satisfying and nourishing ways, we actually lose our capacities to find that nourishment in deep connection. When relationships are difficult, we have less willingness to hang in there through the messy emotions and painful ruptures to repair them and find our resonance again.

> *Technology can be our best friend, and technology can also be our biggest party pooper. It interrupts our own story, interrupts our ability to have a thought or a daydream, to imagine something wonderful because we're too busy bridging the walk from the cafeteria back to the office on our cell phone.*
>
> — STEVEN SPIELBERG

New Conditioning

EXERCISE 8-20: Practice Your Practices

The practices you've learned throughout this book give your brain substantial protection against the ravages of digital overuse. What's important is to keep practicing them. Let your brain do what it loves to do when you're not glued to a screen.

1. *Mindfulness*, staying present and knowing what you're experiencing while you're experiencing it, can help keep you grounded in your body and tracking the shifts in your emotions and thoughts. You're less distracted even while you're texting or emailing.

2. *Mindful empathy* can help you monitor your interactions with people, maintain your tolerance of challenging moments in those relationships, and even strengthen your interest in communicating directly in real time, person to person, heart to heart.

3. *Positive emotions* help you ride the waves of disappointment when people aren't instantly available or responsive, shifting your perspective back out to the larger picture.

4. *Resonant relating*, person to person, in real time, maintains the brain's social engagement system, which regulates our nervous system. Even when engaging with people directly feels riskier than communicating through the buffer of a device, maintaining our interpersonal resonance and relational resilience is more fulfilling in the long run.

Human brains have evolved over tens of thousands of years to process information and communicate well with fellow human beings. They have not had enough time to evolve or rewire sufficiently to cope with the level of stimulation bombarding them from the digital revolution of the last twenty years. These practices help keep your brain functioning well as you navigate these new demands.

Reconditioning

EXERCISE 8-21: Digital Detox

The idea here is simply to counteract all the time that you, and children you may be responsible for, spend on your devices with some intentional, protected time away from your devices, finding it anywhere you can.

1. Consider designating device-free zones and times in your household and family activities: the dining room table, the kitchen, short trips in the car, attending children's soccer games or piano recitals. In these zones, people can talk to each other directly, sharing the highlights and the low points of the day. Researchers have found that time spent talking at the dinner table every evening is a more significant contributor to children's academic

success than the amount of time spent in school, on homework, on sports, or at religious services.

2. Designate device-free times on the calendar: no devices before breakfast; no devices in the hour before bedtime (a practice that also helps prepare the brain for a good night's sleep); a regular device-free Saturday afternoon or Sunday morning. It's most effective to leave devices turned off and in another room.

3. Mute the alerts for incoming messages on your computer and phone. Interact with your device when you choose to, not every time it seems to demand your attention.

The prefrontal cortex is the structure in the brain foundational to our response flexibility. It is also the structure that manages our impulses, that maintains discipline and choice, that says no. Choosing to unplug from our devices regularly creates a buffer in the brain that helps us pause and avoid mindlessly sliding into one more hour surfing the net or just three more emails before turning our attention to the living person in front of us. For children, whose prefrontal cortex is not fully mature and who can't always manage their impulses well, having someone else say no for them, in a way they can tolerate, helps strengthen the impulse control circuits in the developing brain so that they can learn to say no for themselves. And there are practical payoffs to a digital detox: you remember how to write in longhand, read a map or a newspaper, feel the heft of a book in your hands, make choices about what movie to see in a way that isn't driven by an algorithm on a social media platform.

Deconditioning

Just as we take a vacation to replenish our well-being in general, we can take a digital vacation to let the brain play and restore itself. With deconditioning, you let the brain "empty" itself in the spacious, daydreaming mode of the default network. Unplug from all devices, all digital input, for a minimum of half a day or longer whenever possible. Just simply let your brain take a vacation, and then spend that vacation time doing what brains used to do and still love to do.

EXERCISE 8-22: Digital Vacation

1. Immerse yourself in nature. Hike in the woods, walk through a rose garden, play on the beach. Let your brain space out as you watch a butterfly or a sunset. The longer you linger in nature, the more your brain relaxes and resets. (One study found that a three-day immersion in a wilderness setting boosted people's creativity by 50 percent.)

2. Play with your kids; play with your friends. Even fifteen minutes of tossing a football around in the backyard or bicycling through the neighborhood together helps your brain reset. In longer periods of physical play, your brain gets to play, too, opening up to curiosity, imagination, and fantasy and often coming up with new insights, new perspectives out of the blue.

3. Allow yourself to daydream, fall into reverie, reminisce about pleasurable or meaningful moments in the past, and fantasize about pleasurable or meaningful moments in the future. Let the brain meander as it wishes. When you take a vacation from being productive, from demands and expectations, rich insights very often emerge.

These digital vacations restore your brain's abilities to focus and concentrate, do the deep thinking that both creativity and productivity require, interrupt any possible addictive tendencies, and help you celebrate that your life is already full of "abundant enoughness," resonant connections, meaning and purpose, laughter and well-being.

This chapter has presented many tools that nourish and strengthen your physical brain, supporting all its capacities, including neuroplasticity and response flexibility. Even though I have consistently recommended practicing exercises little and often, by the time you add up all the practices in this entire book, you will have completed a marathon of learning and rewiring.

A few more thoughts as you take a breath and reflect on your wise and very persevering effort:

Resilience is part of your human birthright, innate in your brain, innate in your being. Anyone can learn to be more resilient — more flexible, more open to new perspectives, growth, and change. You have chosen to do that learning.

I hope you will continue to practice the tools offered here, strengthening your capacities to respond to any adversity with skill and courage. There are no *shoulds* here. The tools in this book are meant to help you cope better with any challenges to your well-being. As you experience their effectiveness in helping you bounce back from any level of disruption to your resilience, your brain will learn from that success. It will reinforce the neural wiring of your response flexibility in how you respond to any issue. You deepen your trust in yourself as someone who can learn, who can be flexible, who can be resilient.

> *It is not the strongest of the species that survives, nor the most intelligent that survives. It is the one that is the most adaptable to change.*
> — attributed to CHARLES DARWIN

You will do more than survive. You will thrive.

Acknowledgments

Resilience contains over 130 exercises. The vast majority were originally developed for my two books, for my workshops, or for my monthly e-newsletters and weekly posts.

Where exercises have been adapted from the work of my colleagues, credit is given below and in the notes, and permission has been granted to include the exercises in this book.

It has been a true blessing, privilege, and joy to learn my deepest lessons about resilience — showing up and saying yes in the face of adversity — from the hundreds of clients, workshop participants, and students I have worked with over the years. Although they are not named here individually, to have listened to and observed, to have sometimes guided and sometimes helped shape their learning and their choices, has been a treasured opportunity for me to learn and grow myself. And all of that learning and wisdom has improved and refined the practices that are now presented in *Resilience*.

I have been blessed all of my professional life to have been taught by mentors, teachers, and colleagues who themselves embody the core strengths of resilience — calm, compassionate connection, clarity, and courage.

The list here is long: these names represent living, nurturing people and the many hours of reading, study, presence, guidance, conversations, and moral compass that have taught me what they know, taught me what I know, and taught me that I know it.

My deepest bows to:

Bonnie Badenoch, Anat Baniel, James Baraz, Jane Baraz, Judi Bell, Natalie Bell, Teja Bell, James Bennett-Levy, Sylvia Boorstein, Tara Brach, Ashley Davis Bush, Christine Carter, Debra Chamberlain-Taylor, Ann Weiser Cornell, Deb

Dana, Tim Desmond, Michelle Gale, Daniel Ellenberg, Lisa Ferentz, Janina Fisher, Diana Fosha, Ron Frederick, Birgit Genz, Chris Germer, Paul Gilbert, Elisha Goldstein, Susan Kaiser Greenland, Michaela Haas, Rick Hanson, Dacher Keltner, Jack Kornfield, Jerry Lamagna, Ben Lipton, Ada Lusardi, Kelly McGonigal, Richard Miller, Kristin Neff, Pat Ogden, Frank Ostaseski, Jonah Paquette, Laurel Parnell, Stephen Porges, Natasha Prenn, David Richo, Richard Schwartz, Dan Siegel, Ron Siegel, Rich Simon, Tami Simon, George Taylor, Sherry Turkle, Bessel van der Kolk, Barbara Voiner, David Wallin, and Chris Willard.

More deep bows to the very good folks who have sponsored my teachings at venues where people come to learn, grow, and transform their lives. Here again is a list, with cherished memories of deeply resonant, rewarding moments and deepening friendships with the people who open the doors:

1440 Multiversity, Arbor-Seminare, Cape Cod Institute, Esalen Institute, FACES, Focus on Kids, Hollyhock, Insight LA, Institute of Noetic Sciences, International Congress on Pastoral Care and Counseling, Island Institute for Trauma Recovery, K Events, Kripalu Center for Yoga and Health, Leading Edge Seminars, Learning and the Brain, Marina Counseling Center, Mindful Awareness Research Center, Momentous Institute, National Institute for the Clinical Application of Behavioral Medicine, Omega Institute, Open Center, PESI, Psychotherapy Networker Symposium, Sivananda Ashram Yoga Center, Sounds True, Spirit Rock Meditation Center, U.S. Journal Training, and Utah School Counselors Association.

Then there's the matter of translating lived knowledge and wisdom into a book and into online resources:

Deep thanks again to Caroline Pincus, publishing midwife extraordinaire, for her wise guidance and skillful editing, sometimes knowing better what I wanted to say than I knew myself, shaping this book into a program of practices that flows.

Deep thanks again, too, to Jason Gardner, executive editor at New World Library, for once again believing that recovering and strengthening resilience would be interesting and relevant to people in these always challenging times. And thanks to Erika Büky, copy editor extraordinaire. The readability and accessibility of this book owe a great deal to her skillful eye and conscientious revisions.

And deep bows to my beloved technical team — Ryan Barba, Stacey Harris, and Brandy Lawson — whose stellar support literally rescued this manuscript, my computer, my website, and my sanity more than once, with a faith and a lightheartedness that is deeply treasured.

And deep bows for the steady friendships that time and time again provided nourishment and encouragement for all of the above. Whether hiking a splendid wilderness trail, diving deep into soul-to-soul conversations about the true meanings and purposes of our lives, or experiencing the joy and tears of sharing poetry, thank you all for the blessings: Paul Basker, Marilynne Chophel, Kathryn Collier, Margaret Deedy, Terri Hughes, Bonnie Jonsson, Phyllis Kirson, Cariadne MacKenzie-Hooson, Lynn Robinson, Eve Siegel, Marianne Stefancic, Stan Stefancic, Mark Stefanski, Beverly Stevens, William Strawn, and Dina Zvenko.

And final bows to you, the reader, for finding the courage and perseverance to do the work, learn to use the tools, and practice the practices in challenging moments large and small. May your life be full of hope and wise choices.

Permission Acknowledgments

Mindful Self-Compassion Exercises (page 32, Exercise 2-2 — Affectionate Breathing; page 33, Exercise 2-3 — Focusing on the Soles of the Feet; page 51, Exercise 2-20 — Soften, Soothe, Allow; page 76, Exercise 3-11 — Meeting Your Compassionate Friend; page 84, Exercise 3-17 — Cultivating Compassion with Equanimity; and page 118, Exercise 4-14 — Writing a Compassionate Letter to Retire the Inner Critic): Adapted from Christopher Germer and Kristin Neff, *Mindful Self-Compassion Teacher Guide* (San Diego: Center for Mindful Self-Compassion, 2016). Used with permission of the authors.

Page 53, Exercise 2-21 — Focusing: Adapted from and used with permission of Ann Weiser Cornell, internationally known author and psychology educator who has been teaching and refining the Focusing process since she learned it from Eugene Gendlin in 1972.

Page 84: "Compassion" by Miller Williams, from *The Ways We Touch: Poems* (Champaign-Urbana: University of Illinois Press, 1997), *American Journal of Psychology*. Copyright © 1952–1997 by Miller Williams. Used with permission of the University of Illinois Press.

Page 122: "The Guest House" by Jalaluddin Rumi, from *The Essential Rumi*, translated by Coleman Barks (New York: HarperCollins, 1995). Used with permission of Coleman Barks.

Page 146: "Out of a Great Need" from *The Gift: Poems by Hafiz, the Great Sufi Master*, translated by Daniel Ladinsky (New York: Penguin Putnam, 1999). Used with permission of Daniel Ladinsky.

Page 160, Exercise 5-16 — Just Like Me: Adapted from *Make Peace with Your Mind: How Mindfulness and Compassion Can Free You from Your Inner Critic* by Mark Coleman (Novato, CA: New World Library, 2016). Used with permission.

Page 161, Exercise 5-17 — Forgiveness: From *The Art of Forgiveness, Lovingkindness, and Peace* by Jack Kornfield (New York: Bantam, 2002; London: Rider, 2002). Used with permission of the publishers.

Page 224, Exercise 8-3 — Neuromovement: Adapted from chapter 2, "The Learning Switch — Bring in the New," of *Move into Life: The Nine Essentials for Lifelong Vitality* by Anat Baniel (New York: Harmony, 2009), copyright © 2009 by Anat Baniel. Used by permission of Harmony Books, an imprint of the Crown Publishing Group, a division of Penguin Random House LLC. All rights reserved.

List of Exercises

Endnotes

Introduction

2 *We now also know*: Daniel Siegel, *The Mindful Brain: Reflection and Attunement in the Cultivation of Well-Being* (New York: W. W. Norton, 2007), 42–44.

4 *the brain learns best through the repetition of experiences*: Paul Gilbert, "The Practice of Learning and Change," Mindfulness and Compassion conference, Greater Good Science Center, University of California, Berkeley, September 2015.

Chapter One: The Basics of Strengthening Resilience

8 *In trying to sort out*: Mihaly Csikszentmihalyi, *Flow: The Psychology of Optimal Experience* (New York: HarperCollins, 1991), 8–10.

10 *A mature adult brain*: Jeffrey M. Schwartz and Sharon Begley, *The Mind and the Brain: Neuroplasticity and the Power of Mental Force* (New York: HarperCollins, 2002), 21–53.

10 *Neuroplasticity means*: Daniel Siegel, *The Mindful Brain: Reflection and Attunement in the Cultivation of Well-Being* (New York: W. W. Norton, 2007), 30–32.

10 *Self-directed neuroplasticity requires the engagement*: Siegel, *The Mindful Brain*, 42–44.

11 *The brain is shaped by experience*: Richard Davidson, "Project Happiness," *Common Ground*, August 2012.

11 *Because our earliest experiences*: Louis Cozolino, *The Neuroscience of Human Relationships: Attachment and the Developing Social Brain* (New York: W. W. Norton, 2006), 146–48.

11 *our brains are entrained to function*: Diana Fosha, *The Transforming Power of Affect: A Model for Accelerated Change* (New York: Basic Books, 2000).

12 *"neural cement"*: Bonnie Badenoch, *Being a Brain Wise Therapist: A Practical Guide to Interpersonal Neurobiology* (New York: W. W. Norton, 2008), 52–75.

13 *Too many adverse childhood experiences*: Bessel van der Kolk, *The Body Keeps the Score: Brain, Mind, and Body in the Healing of Trauma* (New York: Penguin, 2015), 107–24.

13 *75 percent of all Americans*: Joseph Stephen, *What Doesn't Kill Us: The New Psychology of Post-traumatic Growth* (New York: Basic Books, 2011).

13   *trauma is a fact of life*: Peter Levine, Trauma Therapist Project, www.thetraumatherapist project.com, accessed October 12, 2017.

14   *fight-flight-freeze-fold*: Pat Ogden, Kekuni Minton, and Clare Pain, *Trauma and the Body: A Sensorimotor Approach to Psychotherapy* (New York: W. W. Norton, 2006), 29–36.

14   *Negativity bias*: Rick Hanson, *Hardwiring Happiness: The New Brain Science of Contentment, Calm, and Confidence* (New York: Harmony Press, 2013), 17–31.

14   *Our brain unconsciously filters our perceptions*: Shakil Choudhury, *Deep Diversity: Overcoming Us vs. Them* (Toronto: Between the Lines, 2015).

15   *Reconditioning*: Bruce Ecker, *Unlocking the Emotional Brain: Eliminating Symptoms at Their Roots Using Memory Reconsolidation* (New York: Routledge, 2012).

17   *They learned that the brain "at rest"*: Damien A. Fair, Alexander L. Cohen, Nico U. F. Dosenbach, Jessica A. Church, Francis M. Miezin, Deanna M. Barch, Marcus E. Raichle, Steven E. Peterson, and Bradley L. Schlaggar, "The Maturing Architecture of the Brain's Default Network," *Proceedings of the National Academy of Sciences* 105 (March 2008): 4028–32.

17   *"the plane of open possibilities"*: Dan Siegel, *The Mindful Therapist: A Clinician's Guide to Mindsight and Neural Integration* (New York: W. W. Norton, 2010), 8–17.

17   *the default network is where*: Matthew Lieberman, *Social: Why Our Brains Are Wired to Connect* (New York: Crown Publishers, 2013), 17–23.

18   *Dissociation is one of the brain's most powerful mechanisms*: Van der Kolk, *The Body Keeps the Score*, 66–68.

22   *the brain learns best through a practice of little and often*: Paul Gilbert, "The Practice of Learning and Change," Mindfulness and Compassion conference, Greater Good Science Center, University of California, Berkeley, September 2015.

22   *mindfulness and self-compassion practices*: Richard Davidson and Daniel Goleman, *Altered Traits: Science Reveals How Meditation Changes Your Mind, Brain, and Body* (New York: Avery, 2017), 105–7.

22   *But the brain also needs a perception*: Stephen Porges, "Neuroception: A Subconscious System for Detecting Threats and Safety," paper presented at conference "The Healing Power of Emotion: Integrating Relationships, Body and Mind," Lifespan Learning Institute, Los Angeles, CA, March 10, 2007.

23   *The roots of resilience*: Fosha, *The Transforming Power of Affect*.

24   *Close to half of us didn't*: Louis Cozolino, *The Neuroscience of Human Relationships: Attachment and the Developing Brain* (New York: W. W. Norton, 2006).

24   *the positive psychology pioneer Barbara Fredrickson*: Barbara Fredrickson, *Love 2.0: Finding Happiness and Health in Moments of Connection* (New York: Hudson Street Press, 2013).

25   *"change your brain to change your life for the better"*: See Daniel Amen, *Change Your Brain, Change Your Life* (New York: Harmony Books, 2015).

Chapter Two: Practices of Somatic Intelligence

27   *Your ANS constantly scans*: Bessel van der Kolk, *The Body Keeps the Score: Brain, Mind, and Body in the Healing of Trauma* (New York: Penguin, 2015), 79.

29   *a third branch of the ANS, the ventral vagus pathway*: Stephen Porges, "Neuroception: A Subconscious System for Detecting Threats and Safety, paper presented at conference on "The

Healing Power of Emotion: Integrating Relationships, Body and Mind," Lifespan Learning Institute, Los Angeles, CA, March 10, 2007.

30 *Porges's collaborator*: Deborah Dana, *A Beginner's Guide to Polyvagal Theory*, 2017, www .debdanalcsw.com/the-rhythm-of-regulation.php.

31 *Exercise 2-1: Mini Breath Meditation*: Adapted from Deb Dana, *The Polyvagal Theory in Therapy* (New York: W. W. Norton, 2018).

32 *Exercise 2-2: Affectionate Breathing*: Adapted from Christopher Germer and Kristin Neff, *Mindful Self-Compassion Teacher Guide* (San Diego, CA: Center for Mindful Self-Compassion, 2016).

33 *Exercise 2-3: Focusing on the Soles of the Feet*: Adapted from Christopher Germer and Kristin Neff, *Mindful Self-Compassion Teacher Guide* (San Diego, CA: Center for Mindful Self-Compassion, 2016).

35 *According to Dacher Keltner*: Dacher Keltner, *Born to Be Good: The Science of a Meaningful Life* (New York: W. W. Norton, 2009), 182.

37 *Exercise 2-7: Savor a Moment of Connection*: Inspired by Barbara Fredrickson, *Love 2.0: Finding Happiness and Health in Moments of Connection* (New York: Hudson Street Press, 2013).

38 *Exercise 2-8: Equanimity for Two*: Adapted from Frank Ostaseski, training in compassionate caregiving, Zen Hospice Project, San Francisco, CA, April 1998.

39 *You can experience this shift*: Daniel J. Siegel, "Awakening the Mind to the Wisdom of the Body," paper presented at conference "The Embodied Mind: Integration of the Body, Brain and Mind in Clinical Practice," Lifespan Learning Institute, Los Angeles, CA, March 4, 2006.

40 *Exercise 2-10: Savor a Moment of Relief*: Adapted from Dana, *The Polyvagal Theory in Therapy*.

40 *Exercise 2-11: Progressive Muscle Relaxation*: Adapted from Marsha Davis, Elizabeth Robbins Eshelman, and Matthew McKay, *The Relaxation and Stress Reduction Workbook* (Oakland, CA: New Harbinger Publications, 2008), 41–46.

42 *Exercise 2-13: Friendly Body Scan:* Adapted from Jon Kabat-Zinn and Saki Santorelli, mindfulness-based stress reduction training for mental health professionals, Mount Madonna, CA, June 2000.

44 *Exercise 2-14: Forest Bathing*: Inspired by Florence Williams, *Nature Fix: Why Nature Makes Us Healthier, Happier, and More Creative* (New York: W. W. Norton, 2017).

46 *Exercise 2-16: Pendulation*: Based on Peter Levine, clinical training in somatic experiencing trauma therapy, University of California, Berkeley, October 15–16, 2004.

47 *Fully 25 percent of your brain's real estate*: Daniel J. Siegel, "Awareness, Mirror Neurons, and Neural Plasticity in the Development of Well-Being," paper presented at conference "The Healing Power of Emotion: Integrating Relationships, Body and Mind," Lifespan Learning Institute, Los Angeles, CA, March 10, 2007.

49 *Exercise 2-19: Creating a Safe Place*: Adapted from Francine Shapiro, EMDR Institute training, South San Francisco, CA, July 14, 2000.

51 *Exercise 2-20: Soften, Soothe, Allow*: Adapted from Germer and Neff, *Mindful Self-Compassion Teacher Guide*.

53 *Exercise 2-21: Focusing*: Adapted from Ann Weiser Cornell, personal communication, October 5, 2017.

Chapter Three: Practices of Emotional Intelligence

58 *Emotions are signals to act*: Diana Fosha, *The Transforming Power of Affect: A Model for Accelerated Change* (New York: Basic Books, 2000); Daniel Goleman, *Emotional Intelligence: Why It Can Matter More than IQ* (New York: Bantam Books, 1995), 5–8.

58   *Managing the entire range of your emotional landscape*: Bonnie Badenoch, *Being a Brain Wise Therapist: A Practical Guide to Interpersonal Neurobiology* (New York: W. W. Norton, 2008), 30, 33–35.

59   *whether our emotional responses are based on present or past events*: Daniel J. Siegel, "Awareness, Mirror Neurons, and Neural Plasticity in the Development of Well-Being," paper presented at conference "The Healing Power of Emotion: Integrating Relationships, Body and Mind," Lifespan Learning Institute, Los Angeles, CA, March 10, 2007.

59   *In order to survive*: Rick Hanson, *Hardwiring Happiness: The New Brain Science of Contentment, Calm, and Confidence* (New York: Harmony Press, 2013), 17–31.

59   *We have Velcro for the negative*: Rick Hanson and Richard Mendius, *Buddha's Brain: The Practical Neuroscience of Happiness, Love, and Wisdom* (Oakland, CA: New Harbinger Publications, 2009).

60   *the upside of their dark side*: See Todd Kashdan, *The Upside of Your Dark Side: Why Being Your Whole Self — Not Just Your "Good" Self — Drives Success and Fulfillment* (New York: Hudson Street Press, 2014).

60   *intentionally cultivating positive emotions*: Barbara Fredrickson, *Positivity: Groundbreaking Research Reveals How to Embrace the Hidden Strength of Positive Emotions, Overcome Negativity, and Thrive* (New York: Crown Publishers, 2009).

60   *emotional contagion*: Daniel Goleman, *Social Intelligence: The New Science of Human Relationships* (New York: Bantam Books, 2006), 13–17.

60   *Mindful self-compassion*: Kristin Neff, *Self-Compassion: The Proven Power of Being Kind to Yourself* (New York: HarperCollins, 2015).

61   *Positivity*: Fredrickson, *Positivity*.

62   *Theory of mind*: Louis Cozolino, *The Neuroscience of Human Relationships: Attachment and the Developing Social Brain* (New York: W. W. Norton, 2006), 195–98.

63   *To be present is far from trivial*: Jon Kabat-Zinn, *Coming to Our Senses: Healing Ourselves and the World through Mindfulness* (New York: Hyperion, 2005), 82.

64   *Guy Armstrong*: Guy Armstrong, training in loving-kindness practice, Spirit Rock Meditation Center, Woodacre, CA, September 18, 2004.

64   *Anna Douglas*: Anna Douglas, training in mindfulness practice as we grow older, Spirit Rock Meditation Center, Woodacre, CA, May 21, 2007.

67   *Ninety-three percent of all emotional communication*: Albert Mehrabian, *Silent Messages: Implicit Communication of Emotions and Attitudes* (Belmont, CA: Wadsworth, 1972), 44–45.

72   *Exercise 3-8: Practicing Gratitude for the Web of Life*: Inspired by Robert Emmons, "The Science of a Meaningful Life: Gratitude Training," Greater Good Science Center, University of California, Berkeley, October 22, 2010.

73   *Exercise 3-9: Awe Practice*: Inspired by conference "The Art and Science of Awe," Greater Good Science Center, University of California, Berkeley, July 2016.

73   *The most beautiful thing*: Albert Einstein, *Living Philosophies* (New York: AMS Press, Inc., 1931).

74   *To see a World*: William Blake, "Auguries of Innocence," in *The Oxford Book of English Mystical Verse*, ed. D. H. S. Nicholson and A. H. E. Lee (Oxford: Clarendon Press, 1917), 57.

74   *Exercise 3-10: Taking In the Good*: Adapted from Rick Hanson, *Hardwiring Happiness: The New Brain Science of Contentment, Calm, and Confidence* (New York: Harmony Press, 2013), 61–63.

76   *Exercise 3-11: Meeting Your Compassionate Friend*: Adapted from Christopher Germer and

Kristin Neff, *Mindful Self-Compassion Teacher Guide* (San Diego, CA: Center for Mindful Self-Compassion, 2016).

77 *Researchers have found it's far and away easier*: Neff, *Self-Compassion*.

79 *If you discover [within yourself]*: Sri Auribindo, painting in the hall of California Institute of Integral Studies, San Francisco, CA.

79 *Whenever you're about to venture*: Bill Bowen, clinical training in somatic resourcing, John F. Kennedy University, Pleasant Hill, CA, June 13, 2008.

79 *"feel the fear and do it anyway"*: Susan Jeffers, *Feel the Fear…and Do It Anyway* (New York, Ballantine Books, 2007).

79 *a sign that you're about to grow*: Jack Kornfield, dharma talk, Spirit Rock Meditation Center, Woodacre, CA, January 2006.

79 *doing "one thing every day which scares you"*: Eleanor Roosevelt, *You Learn by Living: Eleven Keys for a More Fulfilling Life* (New York: Harper Perennial, 2011), 23–42.

80 *you can also generate a sense of self-confidence*: George Bonnano, cited in Phillip Moeller, "Happier People Deal Better with Hardships," *Huffington Post*, April 11, 2012, www.huffingtonpost .com/2012/04/11happiness-andhardships_n_1417944.html.

82 *Exercise 3-15: Giving Yourself a Self-Compassion Break*: Adapted from Germer and Neff, *Mindful Self-Compassion Teacher Guide*.

84 *Exercise 3-17: Cultivating Compassion with Equanimity*: Adapted from Germer and Neff, *Mindful Self-Compassion Teacher Guide*.

84 *the brain processes compassion*: Emiliana Simon-Thomas, Science of Happiness, course, Greater Good Science Center, University of California, Berkeley, 2014, https://ggsc.berkeley.edu /what_we_do/event/the_science_of_happiness.

84 *Have compassion for everyone you meet*: Miller Williams, "Compassion," *The Ways We Touch: Poems* (Champaign-Urbana: University of Illinois Press, 1997).

87 *Exercise 3-18: Rewiring a Negative Emotion through Movement*: Adapted from Natalie Rogers, training in expressive arts therapy, San Francisco, CA, April 15–17, 2004.

88 *Exercise 3-19: Power Posing*: Amy Cuddy, "Your Body Language May Shape Who You Are," TED Global, 2012, www.ted.com/talks/amy_cuddy_your_body_language_shapes_who _you_are.

Chapter Four: Practices of Relational Intelligence within Yourself

97 *The neural circuitry for this inner secure base*: Louis Cozolino, *The Neuroscience of Human Relationships: Attachment and the Developing Social Brain* (New York: W. W. Norton, 2006), 81–92.

97 *The roots of resilience*: Diana Fosha, *The Transforming Power of Affect: A Model for Accelerated Change* (New York: Basic Books, 2000).

98 *The turning point*: Max Lerner, *The Unfinished Country: A Book of American Symbols* (New York: Simon & Schuster, 1959).

98 *That larger, authentic experience of self*: Richard Schwartz, clinical training in internal family systems, Psychotherapy Networker Symposium, March 24, 2009.

99 *Experiencing shame occasionally*: Bonnie Badenoch, *Being a Brain Wise Therapist: A Practical Guide to Interpersonal Neurobiology* (New York: W. W. Norton, 2008), 105–10.

100 *Shame has been called the great disconnector*: Jane Conger, clinical training in shame, The Psychotherapy Institute, Berkeley, CA, March 2003.

100   *Just that action of paying attention*: Elisha Goldstein, personal communication, October 5, 2012.

104   *Exercise 4-4: Working with Symbols of Traits of Resilience*: Inspired by Barbara Fredrickson, *Positivity: Groundbreaking Research Reveals How to Embrace the Hidden Strength of Positive Emotions, Overcome Negativity, and Thrive* (New York: Crown Publishers, 2009), 215–22.

105   *If we don't experience being fully loved*: Richard Schwartz, clinical training in internal family systems, Psychotherapy Networker Symposium, March 24, 2009.

109   *Oh, the comfort*: Dinah Craik, *A Life for a Life* (1859; repr., London: Hurst and Blackett, 1985), 264.

114   *Exercise 4-10: Carrying Love and Appreciation in Your Wallet*: Inspired by Fredrickson, *Positivity*.

115   *Exercise 4-11: Loving and Accepting Yourself, Even Though…*: Adapted from John Freedom, clinical training in emotion freedom technique, San Rafael, CA, August 16, 2007.

118   *Exercise 4-14: Writing a Compassionate Letter to Retire the Inner Critic*: Adapted from Christopher Germer and Kristin Neff, *Mindful Self-Compassion Teacher Guide* (San Diego, CA: Center for Mindful Self-Compassion, 2016).

120   *Exercise 4-15: Cultivating the Wiser Self*: Adapted from fundamentals training course, Coaches Training Institute, San Rafael, CA, August 19, 2005.

122   *Exercise 4-16: Befriending the Many Parts of Yourself*: Based on Virginia Satir, training at Marina Counseling Center, San Francisco, CA, January 1992.

122   *This being human*: Jalaluddin Rumi, "The Guest House," *The Essential Rumi*, trans. Coleman Barks (San Francisco: HarperCollins, 1995), 109.

125   *Exercise 4-18: Imagining a Good Inner Parent*: Inspired by Bessel van der Kolk, *The Body Keeps the Score: Brain, Mind, and Body in the Healing of Trauma* (New York: Penguin, 2015), 299–306.

Chapter Five: Practices of Relational Intelligence with Others

133   *Human beings are social beings*: Matthew Lieberman, *Social: Why Our Brains Are Wired to Connect* (New York: Crown Publishers, 2013).

133   *We hurt people, and are hurt by people*: Jack Kornfield, dharma talk, Spirit Rock Meditation Center, Woodacre, CA, October 2012.

133   *We learn "rules" about interacting with others*: Louis Cozolino, *The Neuroscience of Human Relationships: Attachment and the Developing Social Brain* (New York: W. W. Norton, 2006), 139.

135   *Sometimes the models of relating to others*: Cozolino, *The Neuroscience of Human Relationships*, 140.

136   *Exercise 5-1: Deep Listening to Develop Resilience*: Adapted from Jon Kabat-Zinn, training on mindful parenting, Spirit Rock Meditation Center, Woodacre, CA, March 4, 2000.

136   *The most basic and powerful way*: Rachel Naomi Remen, *My Grandfather's Blessings: Stories of Strength, Refuge, and Belonging* (New York: Riverhead Books, 2000).

136   *When we shift our attention*: Ruth Cox, quoted in Mark Brady and Jennifer Austin Leigh, *The Little Book of Listening Skills: 52 Essential Practices for Profoundly Loving Yourself and Other People* (Grand Rapids, MI: Paideia Press, 2008).

137   *A "moment of meeting"*: Daniel Stern, *The Present Moment in Psychotherapy and Everyday Life* (New York: W. W. Norton, 2004), 173.

142   *Exercise 5-6: Communicating without Shame or Blame*: Adapted from Marshall Rosenberg, *Nonviolent Communication: A Language of Life* (Encinitas, CA: Puddle Dancer Press, 2003).

146   *Out of a great need*: *The Gift: Poems by Hafiz, the Great Sufi Master*, trans. Daniel Landinsky (New York: Penguin Putnam, 1999), 165.

147 *Exercise 5-9: Comfort with Closeness and Distance*: Adapted from Stan Tatkin, clinical training, California Association of Marriage and Family Therapists, Marin chapter, March 15, 2011.

148 *Exercise 5-10: Negotiating Change*: Adapted from Rosenberg, *Nonviolent Communication*.

152 *we spend about one-third of the time in actual* relating: Edward Tronick, "Rupture in Relationship," paper presented at conference "Toward a New Psychology of Interpersonal Relationships," Lifespan Learning Institute, Los Angeles, CA, March 11, 2012.

153 *"Out beyond the ideas"*: Jalaluddin Rumi, *The Essential Rumi*, translated by Coleman Barks (San Francisco: HarperSanFrancisco, 1995).

155 *Exercise 5-13: Us versus Them*: Adapted from Shakil Choudhury, *Deep Diversity: Overcoming Us vs. Them* (Toronto: Between the Lines, 2015).

155 *transactional analysis identified many different games*: Lynne Forrest, "An Overview of the Drama Triangle," June 26, 2008, www.lynneforrest.com/articles/2008/06/the-faces-of-victim.

160 *Exercise 5-16: Just Like Me*: Adapted from Mark Coleman, *Make Peace with Your Mind: How Mindfulness and Compassion Can Free You from Your Inner Critic* (Novato, CA: New World Library, 2016), 199.

161 *Exercise 5-17: Forgiveness*: Adapted from Jack Kornfield and Fred Luskin, "The Science and Practice of Forgiveness," seminar at Greater Good Science Center, University of California, Berkeley, May 15, 2010.

163 *Exercise 5-18: Honoring Shared Humanity*: Adapted from Jack Kornfield, training in the Brahma viharas, Spirit Rock Meditation Center, Woodacre, CA, July 2003.

163 *Then it was as if*: Thomas Merton, quoted in Jack Kornfield, *The Wise Heart: A Guide to the Universal Teachings of Buddhist Psychology* (New York: Bantam Books, 2008), 11.

Chapter Six: Practices of Reflective Intelligence

167 *Anchoring in that awareness*: Based on teachings of Sylvia Boorstein and James Baraz, Spirit Rock Meditation Center, Woodacre, CA, 1998–present.

168 *some of the steps of basic mindfulness*: Based on teachings of Sylvia Boorstein and James Baraz, Spirit Rock Meditation Center, Woodacre, CA, 1998–present.

169 *Be willing to have it so*: William James, in *The Harper Book of Quotations*, ed. Robert I. Fitzhenry (New York: HarperCollins, 1993), 17.

171 *Mindfulness is simply being aware*: James Baraz, *Awakening Joy for Kids*, quoted in Michelle Gale, *Mindful Parenting in a Messy World* (Carlsbad, CA: Motivational Press, 2017), 5.

175 *common thought processes that human beings use*: Kelley McGonigal, "The Neuroscience of Change," Neuroscience Summit Training webinar, Sounds True, Boulder, CO, March 2017.

182 *A central practice of mindfulness-based cognitive therapy*: Elisha Goldstein, personal communication, October 2012.

185 *In her book* Mindset: Carol Dweck, *Mindset* (New York: Ballantine Books, 2006).

188 *People are always telling themselves stories*: Stephen Joseph, quoted in Michaela Haas, *Bouncing Forward: Transforming Bad Breaks into Breakthroughs* (New York: Atria, 2015).

189 *Exercise 6-15: Creating a Coherent Narrative*: Adapted from Bessel van der Kolk, "Clinical Implications of Neuroscience Research in PTSD," paper presented at conference "Healing Moments in Trauma Treatment," Lifespan Learning Institute, Los Angeles, CA, March 13, 2011.

190   *"Autobiography in Five Short Chapters"*: Portia Nelson, *There's a Hole in My Sidewalk: The Romance of Self-Discovery* (New York: Atria Books, 2012), xi–xii.

195   *Praise and blame*: Jack Kornfield, *Buddha's Little Instruction Book* (New York: Bantam, 1994).

196   *intentions phrased with* May I: James Pennebaker and Joshua M. Smyth, *Opening Up by Writing It Down: How Expressive Writing Improves Health and Eases Emotional Pain* (New York: Guilford Press, 2016).

Chapter Seven: Full-On Resilience

202   *the emerging field of post-traumatic growth*: Jim Rendon, *Upside: The New Science of Post-traumatic Growth* (New York: Touchstone, 2015).

205   *We all accept that no one controls the weather*: Jon Kabat-Zinn, "The Art of Conscious Living," *VHL Family Forum*, September 1993, www.vhl.org/newsletter/vhl1993/93/cazinn.

213   *morning pages*: Julia Cameron, *The Artist's Way: A Spiritual Path to Higher Creativity* (New York: Tarcher and Perigee, 1992), 33–35.

214   *Wisdom tells me*: Sri Nisargadatta, *I Am That* (Durham, NC: Acorn Press, 2012).

215   *Stephen Levine*: Stephen Levine, *A Year to Live: How to Live This Year as If It Were Your Last* (New York: Bell Tower, 1997).

Chapter Eight: Caring for and Nourishing Your Amazing Brain

219   *The human brain is the most dazzlingly complex entity*: Rick Hanson and Richard Mendius, *Buddha's Brain: The Practical Neuroscience of Happiness, Love, and Wisdom* (Oakland, CA: New Harbinger Publications, 2009), 6–7.

220   *we need to move our bodies*: Wendy Suzuki, *Healthy Brain, Happy Life: A Personal Program to Activate Your Brain and Do Everything Better* (New York: HarperCollins, 2016).

221   *Exercise regenerates our telomeres*: Elizabeth Blackburn and Elissa Epel, *The Telomere Effect: A Revolutionary Approach to Living Younger, Healthier, Longer* (New York: Grand Central Publishing, 2017), 177–79.

221   *Exercise 8-1: Four-Minute Brain and Body Workout*: Adapted from Suzuki, *Healthy Brain, Happy Life*, 133–34.

224   *Exercise 8-3: Neuromovement*: Adapted from the "learning switch," one of the nine Anat Baniel Method NeuroMovement essentials for positive brain change. See Anat Baniel, *Move into Life: The Nine Essentials for Lifelong Vitality* (New York: Harmony Books, 2009), 65–69.

226   *Many of us routinely don't get enough sleep*: Kat Duff, *The Secret Life of Sleep* (New York: Atria Books, 2014).

226   *Restoring the equilibrium of the nervous system*: Matthew Walker, *Why We Sleep: Unlocking the Power of Sleep and Dreams* (New York: Scribner, 2017), 216–217.

227   *the brain is not like the engine of a car*: Robert Sapolsky, *Why Zebras Don't Get Ulcers* (New York: Holt Paperbacks, 2004), 226–38.

229   *the brain has a third form of sleep*: Emily Anthes, "Six Ways to Boost Your Brain Power," *Scientific American Mind*, February–March 2009, 56–61.

230   *foods that promote good brain health*: "The MIND Diet: A Detailed Guide for Beginners," HealthLine, July 30, 2017, www.healthline.com/nutrition/mind-diet.

232 *Exercise 8-10: Savor a Raisin Meditation*: Adapted from Jack Kornfield, class in meditation, Spirit Rock Meditation Center, Woodacre, CA, July 2000.

233 *The brain learns and rewires itself from experience*: Louis Cozolino, *The Healthy Aging Brain: Sustaining Attachment, Attaining Wisdom* (New York: W. W. Norton, 2008).

234 *The first two examples*: David A. Bennett, "Banking against Alzheimer's," *Scientific American Mind*, July–August 2016, 28–37.

234 *A colossal number of brain cells*: Quoted in Bennett, "Banking against Alzheimer's."

236 flow *is the sweet spot of mental activity*: Mihaly Csikszentmihalyi, *Flow: The Psychology of Optimal Experience* (New York: HarperCollins, 1991), 74.

237 *When I look*: "Mud Puddles and Dandelions," Christian Family Institute, http://www.christian familyinstitute.net/mud-puddles-dandelions, accessed October 15, 2017.

237 *Both curiosity and creativity*: Sharon Begley, "Play On! In a First, Brain Training Cuts Risk of Dementia 10 Years Later," STAT, July 25, 2016, www.statnews.com/2016/07/24/brain -training-cuts-dementia-risk.

238 *Many people think of laughter*: Ode magazine, "Ode to Laughter," August 2009.

238 *Those who play rarely become brittle*: Stuart Brown, *Play: How It Shapes the Brain, Opens the Imagination, and Invigorates the Soul* (New York: Avery, 2009).

241 *This is what our brains were wired for*: Matthew Lieberman, *Social: Why Our Brains Are Wired to Connect* (New York: Crown Publishers, 2013).

242 *To exist is to change*: Henri Bergson, *Creative Evolution: Humanity's Natural Creative Impulse* (New York: Henry Holt & Co., 1911).

242 *Exercise 8-18: Taking Stock of Healthy Social Connections*: Very loosely adapted from Mind Mapping, www.mindmapping.com, accessed November 1, 2017.

245 *American adults now spend*: "Fact Tank: News in the Numbers," Pew Research Center, June 28, 2017, www.pewresearch.org/fact-tank/2017/06/28/10-facts-about-smartphones.

245 *No matter how fond or proud you are*: Nicholas Carr, *The Shallows: What the Internet Is Doing to Our Brains* (New York: W. W. Norton, 2011), 132–33.

246 *We all have our preferences*: Sherry Turkle, *Alone Together: Why We Expect More from Technology and Less from Each Other* (New York: Basic Books, 2011).

246 *people have reduced tolerance for messy emotions*: Sherry Turkle, *Reclaiming Conversation: The Power of Talk in a Digital Age* (New York: Penguin, 2015).

247 *Unfortunately, the ability even to be aware*: Turkle, *Reclaiming Conversation*.

247 *Technology can be*: "Spielberg in the Twilight Zone," WIRED online, June 1, 2002, www.wired .com/2002/06/spielberg.

248 *Exercise 8-21: Digital Detox*: Adapted from Catherine Steiner-Adair, *The Big Disconnect: Protecting Childhood and Family Relationships in the Digital Age* (New York: Harper, 2013), 260–95.

248 *time spent talking at the dinner table*: Jonah Lehrer, *A Book about Love* (New York: Simon & Schuster, 2016).

250 *a three-day immersion in a wilderness setting*: Florence Williams, *Nature Fix: Why Nature Makes Us Healthier, Happier, and More Creative* (New York: W. W. Norton, 2017).

251 *It is not the strongest*: attributed to Charles Darwin by Leon Megginson, presentation at Southwestern Social Science Association convention, 1963.

Selected Bibliography

Alter, Adam. *Irresistible: The Rise of Addiction Technology and the Business of Keeping Us Hooked.* New York: Penguin, 2017.

Amen, Daniel. *Change Your Brain, Change Your Life.* New York: Harmony Books, 2015.

Badenoch, Bonnie. *Being a Brain Wise Therapist: A Practical Guide to Interpersonal Neurobiology.* New York: W. W. Norton, 2008.

Baniel, Anat. *Move into Life: The Nine Essentials for Lifelong Vitality.* New York: Harmony Books, 2009.

Begley, Sharon. *Train Your Mind, Change Your Brain: How a New Science Reveals Our Extraordinary Potential to Transform Ourselves.* New York: Ballantine Books, 2007.

Blackburn, Elizabeth, and Elissa Epel. *The Telomere Effect: A Revolutionary Approach to Living Younger, Healthier, Longer.* New York: Grand Central Publishing, 2017.

Brach, Tara. *Radical Acceptance: Embracing Your Life with the Heart of a Buddha.* New York: Bantam Dell, 2003.

Brach, Tara. *True Refuge: Finding Peace and Freedom in Your Own Awakened Heart.* New York: Bantam, 2012.

Brown, Brené. *The Gifts of Imperfection: Let Go of Who You Think You're Supposed to Be and Embrace Who You Are.* Center City, MN: Hazelden, 2010.

Brown, Stuart. *Play: How It Shapes the Brain, Opens the Imagination, and Invigorates the Soul.* New York: Avery, 2009.

Bush, Ashley Davis. *Simple Self-Care for Therapists: Restorative Practices to Weave through Your Workday.* New York: W. W. Norton, 2015.

Carr, Nicholas. *The Shallows: What the Internet Is Doing to Our Brains.* New York: W. W. Norton, 2011.

Choudhury, Shakil. *Deep Diversity: Overcoming Us vs. Them.* Toronto: Between the Lines, 2015.

Coleman, Mark. *Make Peace with Your Mind: How Mindfulness and Compassion Can Free You from Your Inner Critic.* Novato, CA: New World Library, 2016.

Cozolino, Louis. *The Neuroscience of Human Relationships: Attachment and the Developing Social Brain.* New York: W. W. Norton, 2006.

Cozolino, Louis. *The Healthy Aging Brain: Sustaining Attachment, Attaining Wisdom.* New York: W. W. Norton, 2008.

Csikszentmihalyi, Mihaly. *Flow: The Psychology of Optimal Experience.* New York: HarperCollins, 1991.

Cullen, Margaret, and Gonzalo Brito Pons. *The Mindfulness-Based Emotional Balance Workbook.* Oakland, CA: New Harbinger Publications, 2015.

Dana, Deb. *The Polyvagal Theory in Therapy.* New York: W. W. Norton, 2018.

Davenport, Leslie. *Healing and Transformation through Guided Imagery.* Berkeley, CA: Celestial Arts, 2009.

Desmond, Tim. *Self-Compassion in Psychotherapy: Mindfulness-Based Practices for Healing and Transformation.* New York: W. W. Norton, 2016.

Doidge, Norman. *The Brain That Changes Itself.* New York: Penguin Books, 2007.

Doidge, Norman. *The Brain's Way of Healing: Remarkable Discoveries and Recoveries from the Frontiers of Neuroplasticity.* New York: Viking Press, 2015.

Duff, Kat. *The Secret Life of Sleep.* New York: Atria, 2014.

Dunckley, Victoria. *Reset Your Child's Brain.* Novato, CA: New World Library, 2015.

Dweck, Carol. *Mindset: The New Psychology of Success.* New York: Ballantine, 2006.

Eagleman, David. *Incognito: The Secret Lives of the Brain.* New York: Vintage, 2011.

Ecker, Bruce. *Unlocking the Emotional Brain: Eliminating Symptoms at Their Roots Using Memory Reconsolidation.* New York: Routledge, 2012.

Ekman, Paul. *Emotions Revealed: Recognizing Faces and Feelings to Improve Communication and Emotional Life.* New York: Henry Holt and Company, 2003.

Flowers, Steve, and Bob Stahl. *Living with Your Heart Wide Open: How Mindfulness and Compassion Can Free You from Unworthiness, Inadequacy, and Shame.* Oakland, CA: New Harbinger Publications, 2011.

Fosha, Diana. *The Transforming Power of Affect: A Model for Accelerated Change.* New York: Basic Books, 2000.

Frederick, Ron. *Living Like You Mean It: Use the Wisdom and Power of Your Emotions to Get the Life You Really Want.* San Francisco: Jossey-Bass, 2009.

Fredrickson, Barbara. *Positivity: Groundbreaking Research Reveals How to Embrace the Hidden Strength of Positive Emotions, Overcome Negativity, and Thrive.* New York: Crown, 2009.

Fredrickson, Barbara. *Love 2.0: Finding Happiness and Health in Moments of Connection.* New York: Hudson Street Press, 2013.

Gelb, Michael. *Brain Power: Improve Your Mind as You Age.* Novato, CA: New World Library, 2012.

Germer, Christopher. *The Mindful Path to Self-Compassion.* New York: Guilford Press, 2009.

Gilbert, Paul. *The Compassionate Mind.* Oakland, CA: New Harbinger Publications, 2009.

Gilbert, Paul. *Mindful Compassion: How the Science of Compassion Can Help You Understand Your Emotions, Live in the Present, and Connect Deeply with Others.* Oakland, CA: New Harbinger Publications, 2014.

Goldstein, Elisha. *The Now Effect: How This Moment Can Change the Rest of Your Life.* New York: Atria, 2012.

Goldstein, Elisha. *Uncovering Happiness: Overcoming Depression with Mindfulness and Self-Compassion.* New York: Atria, 2015.

Goleman, Daniel. *Emotional Intelligence: Why It Can Matter More than IQ.* 10th anniversary ed. New York: Bantam, 2005.

Goleman, Daniel. *Social Intelligence: The New Science of Human Relationships*. New York: Bantam, 2006.

Goleman, Daniel, and Richard J. Davidson. *Altered Traits: Science Reveals How Meditation Changes Your Mind, Brain, and Body*. New York: Avery, 2017.

Graham, Linda. *Bouncing Back: Rewiring Your Brain for Maximum Resilience and Well-Being*. Novato, CA: New World Library, 2013.

Greenfield, Susan. *Mind Change: How Digital Technologies Are Leaving Their Marks on Our Brains*. New York: Random House, 2015.

Haas, Michaela. *Bouncing Forward: Transforming Bad Breaks into Breakthroughs*. New York: Atria, 2015.

Hanson, Rick. *Hardwiring Happiness: The New Brain Science of Contentment, Calm, and Confidence*. New York: Harmony, 2013.

Hanson, Rick, and Rick Mendius. *Buddha's Brain: The Practical Neuroscience of Happiness, Love, and Wisdom*. Oakland, CA: New Harbinger Publications, 2009.

Hayes, Steven, and Kirk D. Strosahl, eds. *A Practical Guide to Acceptance and Commitment Therapy*. New York: Springer, 2005.

Henderson, Lynne. *The Compassionate-Mind Guide to Building Social Confidence: Using Compassion-Focused Therapy to Overcome Shyness and Social Anxiety*. Oakland, CA: New Harbinger Publications, 2011.

Hone, Lucy. *Resilient Grieving: Finding Strength and Embracing Life after a Loss That Changes Everything*. New York: The Experiment, 2017.

Johnson, Sue. *Hold Me Tight: Seven Conversations for a Lifetime of Love*. New York: Little, Brown and Company, 2008.

Kabat-Zinn, Jon. *Coming to Our Senses: Healing Ourselves and the World through Mindfulness*. New York: Hyperion, 2005.

Kahneman, Daniel. *Thinking, Fast and Slow*. Farrar, Straus and Giroux, 2011.

Kardaras, Nicholas. *Glow-Kids: How Screen Addiction Is Hijacking Our Kids — and How to Break the Trance*. New York: St. Martin's Press, 2016.

Kashdan, Todd B. *The Upside of Your Dark Side: Why Being Your Whole Self — Not Just Your "Good" Self — Drives Success and Fulfillment*. New York: Hudson Street Press, 2014.

Kornfield, Jack. *The Art of Forgiveness, Lovingkindness, and Peace*. New York: Bantam, 2002.

Lehrer, Jonah. *Imagine: How Creativity Works*. New York: Houghton Mifflin, 2012.

Levine, Peter. *In an Unspoken Voice: How the Body Releases Trauma and Restores Goodness*. Berkeley, CA: North Atlantic Books, 2010.

Lieberman, Matthew. *Social: Why Our Brains Are Wired to Connect*. New York: Crown, 2013.

Lyubomirsky, Sonja. *The How of Happiness: A Scientific Approach to Getting the Life You Want*. New York: Penguin, 2007.

Makransky, John. *Awakening through Love: Unveiling Your Deepest Goodness*. Boston: Wisdom Publications, 2007.

McGonigal, Kelly. *The Upside of Stress: Why Stress Is Good for You and How to Get Good at It*. New York: Penguin Random House, 2016.

Neff, Kristin. *Self-Compassion: The Proven Power of Being Kind to Yourself*. New York: HarperCollins, 2015.

Ogden, Pat, and Janina Fisher. *Sensorimotor Psychotherapy: Interventions for Trauma and Attachment*. New York: W. W. Norton, 2015.

Ogden, Pat, Kekuni Minton, and Clare Pain. *Trauma and the Body: A Sensorimotor Approach to Psychotherapy*. New York: W. W. Norton, 2006.

Paquette, Jonah. *Real Happiness: Proven Paths for Contentment, Peace, and Well-Being*. Eau Claire, WI: PESI, 2015.

Pollan, Michael. *Food Rules: An Eater's Manual*. New York: Penguin, 2009.

Porges, Stephen. *The Pocket Guide to the Polyvagal Theory: The Transformative Power of Feeling Safe*. New York: W. W. Norton, 2017.

Rosenberg, Marshall. *Nonviolent Communication: A Language of Life*. Encinitas, CA: Puddle Dancer Press, 2003.

Sandberg, Sheryl, and Adam Grant. *Option B: Facing Adversity, Building Resilience, and Finding Joy*. New York: Alfred A. Knopf, 2017.

Schiraldi, Glenn. *The Resilience Workbook: Essential Skills to Recover from Stress, Trauma, and Adversity*. Oakland, CA: New Harbinger Publications, 2017.

Schlitz, Marilyn, Cassandra Vieten, and Tina Amorok. *Living Deeply: The Art and Science of Transformation in Everyday Life*. Oakland, CA: New Harbinger Publications, 2007.

Schwartz, Richard. *Internal Family Systems Therapy*. New York: Guilford Press, 1995.

Seligman, Martin. *Authentic Happiness: Using the New Positive Psychology to Realize Your Potential for Lasting Fulfillment*. New York: Free Press, 2002.

Siegel, Daniel. *The Mindful Brain: Reflection and Attunement in the Cultivation of Well-Being*. New York: W. W. Norton, 2007.

Siegel, Daniel. *Mindsight: The New Science of Personal Transformation*. New York: W. W. Norton, 2010.

Siegel, Ron. *The Mindfulness Solution: Everyday Practices for Everyday Problems*. New York: Guildford Press, 2010.

Steiner-Adair, Catherine. *The Big Disconnect: Protecting Childhood and Family Relationships in the Digital Age*. New York: Harper, 2013.

Stephen, Joseph. *What Doesn't Kill Us: The New Psychology of Post-traumatic Growth*. New York: Basic Books, 2011.

Stern, Daniel. *The Present Moment in Psychotherapy and Everyday Life*. New York: W. W. Norton, 2004.

Suzuki, Wendy. *Healthy Brain, Happy Life: A Personal Program to Activate Your Brain and Do Everything Better*. New York: HarperCollins, 2016.

Tedeschi, Richard, and Bret Moore. *The Post-traumatic Growth Workbook*. Oakland, CA: New Harbinger Publications, 2016.

Turkle, Sherry. *Alone Together: Why We Expect More from Technology and Less from Each Other*. New York: Basic Books, 2011.

Turkle, Sherry. *Reclaiming Conversation: The Power of Talk in a Digital Age*. New York: Penguin, 2015.

Van der Kolk, Bessel. *The Body Keeps the Score: Brain, Mind, and Body in the Healing of Trauma*. New York: Penguin, 2015.

Walker, Matthew. *Why We Sleep: Unlocking the Power of Sleep and Dreams*. New York: Scribner, 2017.

Willard, Chris. *Raising Resilience: The Wisdom and Science of Happy Families and Thriving Children*. Boulder, CO: Sounds True, 2017.

Index

About the Author

Linda Graham, MFT, is a licensed psychotherapist and mindful self-compassion teacher in the San Francisco Bay Area. She teaches "Resilience: Facing the Mess We're in with Compassion, Clarity, and Courage"; "Shift Happens: The Neuroscience of Resilience and Well-Being"; and "Bouncing Back: Coping with Difficulty, Disappointment, Even Disaster" in international trainings, consultations, workshops, and conferences. Her first book, *Bouncing Back: Rewiring Your Brain for Maximum Resilience and Well-Being*, won the 2013 Books for a Better Life award and the 2014 Better Books for a Better World award. She posts a monthly e-newsletter, *Healing and Awakening into Aliveness and Wholeness*, and weekly *Resources for Recovering Resilience*, archived at www.lindagraham-mft.net.

NEW WORLD LIBRARY is dedicated to publishing books and other media that inspire and challenge us to improve the quality of our lives and the world.

We are a socially and environmentally aware company. We recognize that we have an ethical responsibility to our customers, our staff members, and our planet.

We serve our customers by creating the finest publications possible on personal growth, creativity, spirituality, wellness, and other areas of emerging importance. We serve New World Library employees with generous benefits, significant profit sharing, and constant encouragement to pursue their most expansive dreams.

As a member of the Green Press Initiative, we print an increasing number of books with soy-based ink on 100 percent postconsumer-waste recycled paper. Also, we power our offices with solar energy and contribute to non-profit organizations working to make the world a better place for us all.

Our products are available in bookstores everywhere.

www.newworldlibrary.com

At NewWorldLibrary.com you can download our catalog,
subscribe to our e-newsletter, read our blog,
and link to authors' websites, videos, and podcasts.

Find us on Facebook, follow us on Twitter, and watch us on YouTube.

Send your questions and comments our way!
You make it possible for us to do what we love to do.

Phone: 415-884-2100 or 800-972-6657
Catalog requests: Ext. 10 | Orders: Ext. 10 | Fax: 415-884-2199
escort@newworldlibrary.com

NEW WORLD LIBRARY
publishing books that change lives   14 Pamaron Way, Novato, CA 94949